How to Write Your Literature Review

Online resources to accompany this title are available at: https://www. bloomsburyonlineresources.com/how-to-write-your-literature-review. If you experience any problems, please contact Bloomsbury at: onlineresources@ bloomsbury.com

www.thestudyspace.com – the leading study skills website

Bloomsbury Study Skills

Academic Success
Academic Writing Skills for International Students
The Business Student's Phrase Book
Cite Them Right (11th edn)
Critical Thinking and Persuasive Writing for Postgraduates
Critical Thinking for Nursing, Health and Social Care
Critical Thinking Skills (3rd edn)
Dissertations and Project Reports
Doing Projects and Reports in Engineering
The Employability Journal
Essentials of Essay Writing
The Exam Skills Handbook (2nd edn)
Get Sorted
The Graduate Career Guidebook (2nd edn)
Great Ways to Learn Anatomy and Physiology (2nd edn)
How to Use Your Reading in Your Essays (3rd edn)
How to Write Better Essays (4th edn)
How to Write Your Literature Review
How to Write Your Undergraduate Dissertation (3rd edn)
Improve Your Grammar (2nd edn)
The Bloomsbury Student Planner
Mindfulness for Students
Presentation Skills for Students (3rd edn)
The Principles of Writing in Psychology
Professional Writing (4th edn)
Reading at University
Reflective Writing for Nursing, Health and Social Work
Simplify Your Study
Skills for Business and Management
Skills for Success (3rd edn)
Stand Out from the Crowd
The Student Phrase Book (2nd edn)
The Student's Guide to Writing (3rd edn)
The Study Skills Handbook (5th edn)
Study Skills for International Postgraduates
Studying in English
Studying Law (4th edn)
The Study Success Journal
Success in Academic Writing (2nd edn)
Smart Thinking
Teaching Study Skills and Supporting Learning
The Undergraduate Research Handbook (2nd edn)
The Work-Based Learning Student Handbook (2nd edn)
Writing for Biomedical Sciences Students
Writing for Engineers (4th edn)
Writing for Nursing and Midwifery Students (3rd edn)
Write it Right (2nd edn)
Writing for Science Students
Writing Skills for Education Students
You2Uni: Decide, Prepare, Apply

Pocket Study Skills

14 Days to Exam Success (2nd edn)
Analyzing a Case Study
Brilliant Writing Tips for Students
Completing Your PhD
Doing Research (2nd edn)
Getting Critical (2nd edn)
How to Analyze Data
Managing Stress
Planning Your Dissertation (2nd edn)
Planning Your Essay (3rd edn)
Planning Your PhD
Posters and Presentations
Reading and Making Notes (2nd edn)
Referencing and Understanding Plagiarism (2nd edn)
Reflective Writing (2nd edn)
Report Writing (2nd edn)
Science Study Skills
Studying with Dyslexia (2nd edn)
Success in Groupwork
Successful Applications
Time Management
Using Feedback to Boost Your Grades
Where's Your Argument?
Where's Your Evidence?
Writing for University (2nd edn)

50 Ways

50 Ways to Boost Your Grades
50 Ways to Boost Your Employability
50 Ways to Excel at Writing
50 Ways to Manage Stress
50 Ways to Manage Time Effectively
50 Ways to Succeed as an International Student

Research Skills

Authoring a PhD
The Foundations of Research (3rd edn)
Getting to Grips with Doctoral Research
Getting Published
The Good Supervisor (2nd edn)
The Lean PhD
Maximizing the Impacts of Academic Research
PhD by Published Work
The PhD Viva
The PhD Writing Handbook
Planning Your Postgraduate Research
The Postgraduate's Guide to Research Ethics
The Postgraduate Research Handbook (2nd edn)
The Professional Doctorate
Structuring Your Research Thesis

For a complete listing of all our titles in this area please visit **https://www.bloomsbury.com/uk/academic/study-skills/**

How to Write Your Literature Review

Bryan Greetham

BLOOMSBURY ACADEMIC
LONDON • NEW YORK • OXFORD • NEW DELHI • SYDNEY

BLOOMSBURY ACADEMIC
Bloomsbury Publishing Plc
50 Bedford Square, London, WC1B 3DP, UK
1385 Broadway, New York, NY 10018, USA
29 Earlsfort Terrace, Dublin 2, Ireland

BLOOMSBURY, BLOOMSBURY ACADEMIC and the Diana logo
are trademarks of Bloomsbury Publishing Plc

First published 2021 by RED GLOBE PRESS
Reprinted by Bloomsbury Academic, 2022, 2023, 2024

A catalogue record for this book is available from the British Library.

A catalogue record for this book is available from the Library of Congress.

ISBN: PB: 978-1-3520-1104-3
ePDF: 978-1-3520-1105-0
ePub: 978-1-3520-1105-0

Printed and bound in Great Britain

To find out more about our authors and books visit
www.bloomsbury.com and sign up for our newsletters.

To all my students, whose passion for ideas and joy of discovery have made my teaching so fulfilling. And to Pat for your undiminished courage in accepting each new challenge.

It is a lesson which all history teaches wise men, to put trust in ideas, and not in circumstances.

Ralph Waldo Emerson

Conversation enriches the understanding, but solitude is the school of genius.

Edward Gibbon

Contents

Part 6   Writing Your Review

Part 7   Using Your Sources

Part 8   Editing

Acknowledgements

Writing a literature review is like finding yourself in a strange country with unfamiliar terrain stretching out ahead of you. Making your way across it, mapping it out, responding to the challenges it poses and exploring those areas that most intrigue you is always an exciting experience. But, if this is the first time you have made such a perilous journey, you will need the guidance of experienced supervisors as you take your first tentative steps. I owe a considerable debt to all those who helped me take these first few steps as a student.

By the same token, I am grateful to friends and colleagues with whom I have worked over the years. Their knowledge and expertise have at times been invaluable in guiding me through the literature on topics that were new to me. I owe a similar debt to my reviewers whose kind and encouraging advice has helped me improve the text. They brought their experience to bear on my work and made suggestions that have helped me see things that I would not otherwise have seen. For this I am very grateful.

To my editors at Red Globe Press I owe a special debt. To Suzannah Burywood for her friendship, advice and sound judgement over the years; to Helen Caunce for her quiet patience and professionalism; and to Rosemary Maher, who has coped with every problem with such tactful patience and understanding; to all of you I owe an enormous debt for investing such confidence in me.

And, finally, to Pat Rowe, my lifelong companion, who has faced each new challenge with such courage and good humour, I owe the biggest debt of all. When problems filled my mental space and a thoughtful silence descended, you have always known just what to do. Without you, this would have been so much more difficult.

Introduction

The most notable feature of literature reviews, in contrast with many other academic assignments, is that they present us with an exciting challenge to carve out of the literature an opportunity to do something truly original. Much of our education is spent recycling the ideas of our authorities without analysing and critically evaluating them in any depth to identify their weaknesses and omissions. Now, it is our opportunity to address these shortcomings and discover something new and insightful.

However, the problem for many of us as we set about a literature review is that we are told we must do things that are not only confusing, but also lack serious intellectual challenge. We are told we must produce a synopsis of the literature, summarising sources that provide the 'background' to our research. Not only does this take up too much of our time while filling our review with irrelevant material that is never referred to again, but it only draws on our lower cognitive abilities to describe one source after another in an attempt to impress examiners with how much we've read and understood.

This leaves many students so confused that they simply have no idea where to start. It makes it difficult for them to decide what's relevant, while encouraging them to summarise all the findings of each article they read, when they only need comment on those issues that throw light on what they plan to do.

Synopsis

1 Takes up too much space and time.
2 Fills our review with a mass of irrelevant material.
3 Uses just the lower cognitive abilities.
4 Makes it difficult to decide where to start.

In fact, whether it's a stand-alone review or it's for a dissertation or thesis, a literature review should present us with an opportunity to do really exciting work – to use and demonstrate our higher cognitive abilities:

- to critically evaluate the assumptions, methods and conclusions found in the literature we read;
- to analyse concepts and arguments;
- to synthesise ideas from different sources to reveal new insights and new ways of approaching a problem.

Why are literature reviews necessary?

Nevertheless, if yours is part of a dissertation or thesis as opposed to a stand-alone review, the purpose of which tends to be a lot clearer, it's still reasonable to ask why it is necessary to review the literature before you start your research. The answer is in two parts. First, a literature review is for you, to find a gap in our knowledge that will give you the opportunity to make a genuinely original contribution.

And, second, it is for your readers, so they can see the relevance of your work in the context of the research done by others. By showing how one piece of research builds on another you lay firm foundations, which will justify your particular approach and your use of certain research methods, while demonstrating that your research will advance our knowledge in the area by contributing something new.

A literature review is for …

1   you – to find a gap, an opportunity to make an original contribution;
2   your readers – to see the relevance of your work, to lay firm foundations that will justify your approach.

Readers will want to know why you are asking your research question and why you think it is significant. They will want to know if anyone else has done anything similar. Then they will want to know what is already known about your topic and how your research will add something to this understanding by challenging what is already thought to be the case: the established theories, concepts and beliefs.

And to do this, of course, we have to do more than just describe the relevant theories and concepts. More important, we have to lay the foundations for our research by analysing the concepts and theories, critically evaluating them and synthesising the ideas they represent to find genuinely original questions to research. In Part 3 of this book, you will learn what theories and concepts are and how to analyse, critically evaluate and synthesise them.

In short, whether yours is a stand-alone review or a review that lays the basis for a dissertation or thesis, your aim is to show what is known and highlight what is not known or is uncertain. To do this, you will need to do the following things:

1   Formulate the **research question** or **hypothesis** that you want to research.
2   Describe the **context** of your research – to show how the various research studies relate to each other and address issues that have a bearing on your own research project.
3   Present your **critical evaluation** of the findings of these studies.
4   **Outline and justify your choice** of the relevant theories, methodology and research tools and instruments that you want to use in your research.
5   Identify **new ways** in which to interpret previous research or **resolve conflicts** between previous studies.
6   Identify the **gap** or the **unanswered question** that your research will address or a **theory** against which you want to test a hypothesis.

7 If yours is a **stand-alone review**, the aim is to summarise and evaluate the current knowledge in a particular field and, in the process, assess how well you have developed the professional skills that you will need to analyse and synthesise studies in your field.

8 For those undertaking a **systematic review**, the aim is to compare, synthesise and assess the various studies that have measured the effect of a particular intervention, such as a new policy or a clinical trial, to reveal the range and reliability of the results of each of these studies.

Integrated literature reviews

Of course, in some research projects, particularly those that are textual and literature-based as in many humanities subjects, there is no discrete chapter dedicated to the literature review. References to the literature that underpins the research are made throughout your work without there being a specific, dedicated chapter. The literature itself is the subject of the study, so it is integrated within each chapter.

It is usual to analyse the text in the introduction so the reader has an interpretative structure, a key to the most important issues raised by the text. Then, as you write your critical discussion in each subsequent chapter, you can pick up each of these issues, so the reader knows what you are doing and that it is consistent with your original analysis.

Sir William Petty's *Political Arithmetick*   EXAMPLE

In this thesis, the literature review appears first in the introduction with an analysis of the *Political Arithmetick*, which highlights the key issues that are examined in the thesis. Then the review reappears at the start of each chapter as each one of these issues is taken up and discussed in the light of what other researchers have found.

The most common problems

Nevertheless, regardless of whether the review is a stand-alone review or lays the foundation for a dissertation or thesis, many students start working on it without being clear about its purpose, what it consists of and how to set about it. As we've seen, they're often told they must produce a synopsis of the relevant literature, so they include anything that seems to provide the 'background' to their work and easily get buried in the literature, lose focus and struggle to decide what's relevant. As a result, the review becomes much larger than it should, taking up far too much of the word count, if it is for a dissertation or thesis, leaving them without the time they need for the other elements of their project.

Much of this is reflected in tutors' assessments:

1 Perhaps the most common criticism is that reviews contain **too much material that is irrelevant to the project**. Without a clear idea of what they are looking for, students tend to read everything that is remotely related to their topic and waste time on articles that add little to their understanding of the issues they will have to confront.

2 As a result, **reviews lack depth**, amounting to little more than annotated lists of sources, summarising their content. They describe their sources and report their findings, rather than compare and discuss their agreements and disagreements, and critically evaluate their assumptions, the design of the research and the analysis of the results.

3 Above all, they **fail to synthesise** the literature. Our aim in doing a literature review is to find connections between ideas that will synthesise our sources to create a meaningful picture that reveals those parts that are unclear, those that reveal important gaps to be filled and those problems that need to be explored further. In the process we reveal what we intend to do: the hypothesis or research question we intend to test, the solutions we intend to find, the gap we intend to fill or a different approach to a problem we intend to pursue.

4 This results in two very common criticisms: that the **link** between the project and the literature is often weak and unclear; and the review **lacks a clear and effective organisational structure**.

To deal with this, you may be advised to 'build an argument'. However, this is not about 'an' argument, which suggests we have already made up our mind and we are merely looking around in the literature for the support that we need. Research is an inductive process not a deductive one. We don't start out with a point of view, from which we deduce conclusions and then set off into the literature in search of support.

Genuine research follows the evidence, not avoid it if it fails to support a precon-ceived point of view. It analyses and discusses the implications of sources that oppose as well as support your point of view. It is about creating a thesis from the literature and from this a hypothesis that you then test in your research and pursue in the literature.

Why this book

In this book, we will deal with all of these problems and more. Using detailed step-by-step methods and simple systems, it will take you through each stage of your work from generating your initial ideas and pinning the research question down, to search-ing traditional sources and the Internet, planning the review, writing it, citing refer-ences and editing. You will learn simple methods to organise your work and manage the material and ideas you work on. You will be shown how to organise your retrieval system to catch and develop all of the ideas that come to you whenever and wherever they arise.

Thinking skills

Beyond the more practical concerns of how you work through each stage and organise your work, the most serious challenges facing you lie in the thinking and writing that your literature review will entail. This book will show you how you can develop all the thinking skills, the cognitive abilities, you will need:

● how to critically evaluate the arguments you read;
● how to create consistent, persuasive arguments of your own;

- how to analyse the key concepts used to describe a problem;
- how to generate, record and process more of your own ideas;
- how to synthesise ideas into patterns using a simple method;
- how to identify and create the connections between patterns in the literature that will enable you to see the significance and deeper meaning of what you read;
- and, in turn, how to form the key structures into which your review will be organised.

Writing

Similarly, you will learn methods to tackle all of the problems you confront in planning and writing your review. You will be taken through each of the stages from developing the outline to planning, writing the review, referencing and editing. This book will teach you simple methods that will make the challenge of writing such a complex piece of work more manageable.

Writing about our own ideas as they develop in response to the material we read is the most powerful and effective tool in education and learning. It engages our imagination, our intellect and emotions, all of which are different ways of generating insights and developing our understanding. It places us at the heart of our ideas. It forces us to pin our ideas down, clarify our thinking, check the consistency of our arguments and then capture all of this in language that conveys it accurately.

Writing is the most difficult, yet most effective, form of thinking.

It's a way of finding out what we think about something. As we write, it tells us what we know, what we still need to pin down clearly, and what we don't know and need to find out. You might gather a mass of information, read widely, analyse the issues involved and give it all sustained deep thought, but not until you write to explain it to someone else will you realise just how clear you are about it and whether it all makes consistent sense.

But perhaps more significantly, it gives you and your supervisor a window into your mind as you work out problems and bring greater clarity to your thoughts. Unlike much of our education, your supervisor can see *how* you think, not just *what* you think. You can both see your false starts, your inconsistent conclusions, your misuse of evidence and the unexamined assumptions that lurk unnoticed in the concepts you might use unreflectively. The act of writing is the most effective means we have to work towards the centre of a problem.

In this book you will learn how to:

- construct sound arguments;
- use language consistently;
- deploy your evidence convincingly;
- convey your ideas simply and economically with a light effective style to produce a memorable, thought-provoking piece of work;
- and revise and edit your review, so that the quality of your work and the extent of your achievements really shine through.

In short, the distinctive feature of this book is that it will not just give you general advice, valuable though this is, but will spell this out in simple, practical strategies and systems that are necessary for you to produce your best work.

How to manage your work

As we set about our review, it's not unusual to feel stress that comes from two sources: the uncertainty involved in tackling such a large and complex project, and the fear that we might fail. Although it's natural to feel uncertain, this should not be because you suspect you lack the ability to do it well. This is a daunting project simply because it is new, something you haven't done before, not because it is beyond you.

As for the fear of failure, the important thing to remember is that this is a task not about *what* you know or *what* you think, but about *how* you think. Given this, it's no longer a simple question of pass or fail on the basis that you either know something or you don't, but about showing your teachers how well you can think. And as soon as you accept that this is not about the possibility of failing, but about showing people what you can do, you should feel less stress.

This is not about whether you could fail, but about how much you can achieve.

Managing your time

Another common reason we worry is time: we look ahead and worry about how we are ever to get it all done in time. The number of texts we must read and respond to seems daunting. The simple answer is to break it down into smaller stages, plan each of these carefully and deal with one thing at a time. After that, if we can avoid frightening ourselves by looking at the whole project, we can get on with the manageable challenges that each new stage presents and allow our confidence to grow.

This is exactly what we will do in this book. You will be shown how to break the task down into small manageable stages, plan each one and then work through them carefully. You will learn simple skills, techniques and methods you can adopt, along with useful systems that will help you organise yourself to take away most, if not all, of the worry about completing such a large project.

Planning your time

1 Break the task down into smaller, manageable stages.
2 Plan the time you need to complete each of these (use the Work Schedule on pages 139–40).
3 Avoid looking too far ahead.
4 Routine pattern of work – plan your weekly timetable (use the Weekly Timetable on page 138).

Timeline

To give you a clear idea of all the stages you will have to work through and how this book will help you meet each challenge as it arises, look at the timeline below. There you will see all of the stages and the chapters that deal with them. You may be worried about how you search for all the sources you need or about how you assemble your ideas and plan your review. Whatever the problem, the timeline will help you find the answer easily.

Timeline

Stages	Chapters
1. Generate ideas	4
2. Pin down your research question/hypothesis	5, 6, 7
3. Plan your work schedule – deadlines, stocktaking	13
4. Organise your retrieval system	14
5. Search the literature	6, 7, 15
6. Take notes from articles	15, 16
7. Critically evaluate sources	8, 9
8. Search for patterns of ideas in the literature	10, 11, 12
9. Write drafts of sections as the ideas come together	14
10. Plan the review	17, 18, 19
11. Write 1st draft	20-24
12. Revise structure – check logic, signposting, paragraphs	27
13. Revise content 1 – check citing, plagiarism	25, 26
14. Reference list/bibliography	25, 26
15. Revise content 2 – check sentences, word use, de-clutter	28
16. Final presentation – check loose ends, word count	28

Companion website

In most chapters, you will find material that will make your work easier: forms to help you organise your work, checklists you can have by your side to remind you of the things you need to work through and tables listing things you need to do. You can download all of these from the companion website (www.macmillanihe.com/greetham-literature-review), along with additional exercises that will help you develop your skills.

Summary

1 Our aim in a literature review is to carve out an opportunity to do something original.
2 In doing this, we lay the foundations that will justify our particular approach.
3 Rather than just summarise texts, a literature review involves your higher cognitive abilities to analyse, synthesise and critically evaluate ideas.
4 Writing places us at the heart of our ideas, forcing us to pin them down and express them clearly and consistently.
5 The only reason this is a daunting project is because it is new to you, not because it is beyond you.

What next?

In the next chapter, we will examine the distinction between reviews that form part of a thesis or dissertation and stand-alone reviews – systematic and non-systematic. We will explore the steps involved in writing non-systematic stand-alone reviews and their structure.

PART 1

Types of Literature Reviews

Chapter 1

Stand-alone Literature Reviews 1: Non-systematic

In this chapter, you will learn...

- the distinction between systematic and non-systematic reviews;
- the reasons for the wider use of stand-alone reviews;
- their structure and the steps we need to work through to produce one;
- the importance of screening with clear inclusion and exclusion criteria..

There are three types of literature review. The first forms part of a longer work of research for a dissertation or thesis. The other two are stand-alone reviews that students are asked to write as part of their training in the research methods of their profession: one a systematic review and the other a non-systematic review.

Stand-alone reviews

A stand-alone review aims to summarise and evaluate the current knowledge in a particular field. Unlike a review that forms part of a dissertation or thesis, it doesn't set about identifying the gaps in order to lay the foundations for researchers to collect and analyse their own primary evidence. Instead, it is useful for professionals in many fields who need to keep up to date with current knowledge, including new government policies and other initiatives, and new commercial, industrial and technological developments.

Systematic stand-alone reviews

As one form of this, the aim of most systematic reviews is to measure the effectiveness of trials and policy initiatives in a rigorous and scientific way. This involves comparing, synthesising and assessing the various studies that have measured the effect of a particular intervention, such as a new policy or a clinical trial, to reveal the range and reliability of these results. The benefit of this is that it can reveal whether these findings are consistent across different studies.

> ### New policies and drug trials   EXAMPLE
>
> A minister might introduce a new benefit, education officials might make changes to the national curriculum, or a new drug trial might be conducted. Revealing variations in the findings as to the effectiveness of these is often useful in identifying where changes are necessary to make the initiative more successful.

But the credibility of a systematic review depends upon its rigour, which in turn depends upon how scientific it can claim to be. In other words, like any scientific theory, a systematic review must be **transparent** and **reproducible** by anyone following the same method and reviewing the same studies. To achieve this it must be **systematic** in following a repeatable methodology, **explicit** in explaining the procedures that were worked through, and **comprehensive** in its scope in that it must include all relevant material.

Systematic stand-alone reviews – scientific

- Transparent
- Reproducible
- Systematic
- Explicit
- Comprehensive

Non-systematic stand-alone reviews

In contrast, non-systematic stand-alone reviews, as the name implies, are not so rigorous and scientific. Although they are not used by researchers to lay the foundations for their own research, they are nevertheless used to see what the literature says about a particular problem and where effective research might be undertaken. In this way they save scholars the time needed to read and synthesise a large body of material.

The wider use of stand-alone reviews in fields like criminal justice, health and social care, welfare, education and employment reflects the recognition of the importance of evidence-based practice to inform policy decisions and professional practice. Having the evidence on a specific issue brought together and synthesised into one review saves valuable time for practitioners.

> ### Autonomy and dependency: their influence on learning behaviour and study skills in the 16–19 age group   EXAMPLE
>
> This project would no doubt be valuable to all those who have the responsibility of helping students who experience study skills problems in schools, colleges and universities, and the stress that inevitably results. From subject teachers, study skills instructors and personal tutors to counsellors, psychologists and administrators, all would benefit professionally from this sort of review.

A literature review to explore integrated care for older people   EXAMPLE

This review would be helpful to all those who provide health and social care for older people. Historically, there have been divisions in the UK not just between health and social care, but between care and services, such as housing and transport. Therefore, most service providers would no doubt value a review of the literature on greater integration in the way they work to meet the needs of the elderly.[1]

However, for this to be effective scholars and practitioners must feel confident that they can repeat the process if they have any doubts. Therefore, all 'non-systematic' reviews, including those that lay the foundations for their own research, have to be systematic to some degree. They need to be as rigorous and comprehensive as possible, following a clear, transparent approach that they can make explicit to establish their credibility. And this, of course, means that they must be reproducible by any reviewer who follows the same methodology.

All non-systematic reviews must be systematic to some degree to establish their credibility.

Nevertheless, the work and complexity involved in a fully systematic review would be too much for the purpose of conducting a review for a research project, like a dissertation or thesis. Indeed, it would be too much to expect of every stand-alone review.

Non-systematic stand-alone reviews   EXAMPLE

It would not be particularly effective or useful to conduct a systematic review in an area where there might only be a limited number of studies published. Similarly, it would be ineffective if the research question was too general, which is likely to produce hundreds of different studies covering a wide area, or if it was too narrow, which is likely to produce too few studies to be of any help.

However, the key difference between systematic and non-systematic stand-alone reviews, which will determine when it is best to use one and not the other, lies in the question of subjectivity. With systematic reviews, it must be possible to extract material that is as free as possible from subjectivity. It relies as much as possible on quantitative evidence presented objectively using tables, graphs and diagrams free from any overt subjective judgement.

The problem here, of course, is that the review process is full of opportunities that allow for subjectivity, most of which are impossible to eradicate. No matter how they are presented, facts, observations and data are theory-laden: the theoretical assumptions we bring to our work determine what is relevant, what is important and what is not. Moreover, reviewing, like research, is intensely iterative: the more we read the more it shapes our judgements as to what is relevant to our review and what significance we see in it. To remove this sort of subjectivity, among other things reviewers would have to be able to justify objectively:

- their choice of subject;
- how this has changed in response to the literature they have read;
- their choice of what they included;
- what they have done with what they have included;
- and, of course, how this has influenced the case they make for further research.

To summarise, no matter what type of review they choose, reviewers must be able to describe as objectively as possible what they have looked for, what they found, what they did with what they found and what conclusions they arrived at on the basis of what they found. For some subjects this is possible with almost complete objectivity, but for most it is not.

Writing a non-systematic stand-alone review – the steps

In this book, you will see that each step in producing a literature review is dealt with in detail in each of the chapters. With very few exceptions, these chapters apply equally to all three types of review. Where there is more to add that is specific to each of the three types, it is dealt with in these three chapters in Part 1. However, with those steps, like the last three listed below (writing the review, editing and citing your sources), where there is nothing specific to add and where each step is described in chapters that apply equally to all three types, it would be repetitive to summarise them here.

To produce a non-systematic stand-alone review, we have to work through the following steps:

1 Formulate the research question
2 Screening – the inclusion and exclusion criteria
3 Searching the literature
4 Synthesising
5 Writing the review
6 Editing
7 Citing your sources.

1 Formulate the research question

Like all reviews, stand-alone reviews analyse and critically evaluate the literature in relation to a particular problem in search of gaps in the current research, so they can give a clear picture of where effective research could be undertaken. In addition, as we've seen, they are also a very useful means of gathering information to show how effective are government interventions and professional practice.

So, although students are set stand-alone reviews largely to help them develop the skills and abilities they might need in their professional lives and to show what the literature says about a particular problem, they still need a question to answer or a problem to solve, in order to give clarity, cohesion and direction to their work. Without this, they would have nothing by which they could judge what is relevant to their topic.

> ### Autonomy and dependency: their influence on learning behaviour and study skills in the 16–19 age group
> **EXAMPLE**
>
> In this review, we would not only need to know what is meant by the concepts 'autonomy' and 'dependency' and how we are to recognise their effects in concrete evidence of student behaviour, but we would need to know what questions we want to answer. Only then will we have a clear idea what we are looking for in the literature, so we can decide what's relevant.

> ### A literature review to explore integrated care for older people
> **EXAMPLE**
>
> In this review, the authors needed to know what is meant by 'integration' and the different forms it would take between service sectors (health and social care), between professions (nurses, social workers, doctors, physiotherapists), between settings (institutions and community, primary and secondary care), between types of organisations (statutory, private and voluntary sector) and between types of care (acute and long-term care).

Moreover, although we may have a clear idea of the topic, within it we must find a question that will give focus and direction to our thinking, one that will guide us as we structure and analyse our sources. If we allow the question to remain vague, we will run the risk of producing a literature review that lacks cohesion. Therefore, we have to start with a question that forces us to concentrate on something that is specific: a question we want answers to or a comparison that we've drawn between authors, theories or arguments.

2 Screening – the inclusion and exclusion criteria

However, the best research questions are hardly ever just found: they are worked on carefully and designed to give clear direction to our work. The time we spend on them is well worth it. Otherwise, we will find that much of what we have included will have to be dumped. In this lies the importance of translating the research question into inclusion and exclusion criteria.

These lay out the formal requirements that will have to be met for papers to be reviewed. They address the question of exactly what kinds of studies you're looking for to answer your research question and the sub-questions that you derive from it, which will translate it into concrete terms.

> ### Autonomy and dependency: their influence on learning behaviour and study skills in the 16–19 age group
> **EXAMPLE**
>
> In this review, we would need to identify those studies that translate these two concepts into recognisable concrete evidence of student behaviour. We might define the concept of autonomy in terms of a student who is self-regulating, self-monitoring and able to develop her abilities and self-knowledge. She has the confidence to arrive at her own convictions and explore and develop her own abilities in an innovative and exploratory way.

A literature review to explore integrated care for older people   EXAMPLE

In this review, the authors were guided by an expert panel that identified the key topics and issues of interest. In practical terms this meant that only those studies that involved the UK were included, except for sources covering a foreign context, which, nevertheless, could be applied to the UK; those that involved interventions or evaluated services and initiatives; and studies which contained substantive, detailed descriptions of services and initiatives. The review excluded all literature that was not academic with the exception of some professional literature where coverage of an issue was sparse.

Given these and other characteristics, we can set clear inclusion and exclusion criteria to determine which studies we will review. This can reduce the number of sources to be reviewed from a bewildering number in the thousands to a few hundred or less.

A literature review to explore integrated care for older people   EXAMPLE

In this review, a total of 4,222 items were identified, but only 148 were selected for review.

For more information on this, you might find it helpful to read 'Step 3. Searching and screening' in the next chapter (pages 14–16).

3 Searching the literature

Then the search strategy will dictate how we locate these studies. Ideally, this needs to be as rigorous and transparent as we can make it, so that others can see exactly what we have done and repeat it if necessary. It will also demonstrate that our search has been thorough and presents a fair and balanced picture of the current research.

4 Synthesising

This brings us to synthesising the studies we have found. Here we are doing two things. First, we are critically evaluating the methodological quality of the studies and the impact this has on the interpretation of the findings. The screening step should have eliminated those studies that have only an indirect bearing on the topic, but we still have to know how reliable are those that remain and how much we can depend upon their conclusions.

Second, we are synthesising the various studies to lay the foundations for our own conclusions. In Chapter 12 (Synthesis – Creating patterns and finding gaps), I have outlined a simple strategy you can use to synthesise the arguments and ideas you find in the literature.

A literature review to explore integrated care for older people   EXAMPLE

In this review, the authors identified common themes running through the studies they examined, which they then synthesised into five 'central themes':

- Macro strategies (societal level);
- Mezzo strategies (organizational level);
- Vertical and horizontal integration strategies;
- Changing working arrangements;
- Micro strategies (individual service user level).

These formed the structure of their review and provided the foundations from which they were able to draw their conclusions.

Try this …

As you analyse the various studies to identify their common themes and trends, you may find it helpful to lay out the connections between each one in a table or matrix describing their key features along one side and the studies along the other. This will give you a clear idea of their similarities and dissimilarities and the contrasts and conclusions you can draw.

Finally, at this point, if you feel that you need to adopt a more rigorous and transparent approach, look at the next chapter and the way systematic reviews deal with these last three steps (screening, searching and synthesising).

Synthesising   EXERCISE

In this exercise, take two studies that are relevant to your topic and find three similarities and dissimilarities between them that would provide the basis for discussion that compares and contrasts them.

Structure

As you can see, writing a stand-alone review is not a simple exercise in showing how much we know and the depth of our understanding. It is a critical evaluation of the literature in a field, in which we analyse key issues and concepts, identify trends and highlight the gaps in the research. Consequently, most stand-alone reviews tend to be structured more like an empirical dissertation or thesis with the following sections:

1 Introduction
2 Methodology
3 Findings
4 Discussion
5 Conclusion
6 References.

A literature review to explore integrated care for older people   EXAMPLE

This review was organised into six main sections with the conclusion and discussion sections merged into one:

1 Abstract;
2 Introduction;
3 Methodology – in this section the authors explained how they searched the literature and selected their sources from different types of material – not just published papers, but also 'grey' literature (see Chapter 6);
4 Results – here they discussed the five 'central themes' in the literature, outlining their key findings;
5 Conclusions – from these results they showed how the thinking about integrated care has developed and how knowledge of the different strategies outlined in the 'Central themes' has become more available;
6 References.

In Chapter 18 (Planning the Review), you will find a detailed step-by-step account of how to plan and structure the review.

 You can download a copy of the steps in this chapter from the companion website (www.macmillanihe.com/greetham-literature-review).

Summary

1 Systematic reviews are designed to be scientific, transparent and reproducible.
2 Non-systematic reviews reveal what the literature says about a problem and where effective research might be undertaken.
3 To command confidence they have to be systematic to some degree.
4 The key difference between the two lies in the extent to which they avoid subjectivity.

What next?

To understand the demands of non-systematic reviews, it helps to understand how different they are from systematic reviews. In the next chapter, we will examine systematic reviews and the steps involved in producing one.

Note

1 Adapted from Reed J, Cook G, Childs S, McCormack B, 'A literature review to explore integrated care for older people', *International Journal of Integrated Care,* (2005); 5(1):None. DOI: https://doi.org/10.5334/ijic.119.

Chapter 2

Stand-alone Literature Reviews 2: Systematic

In this chapter, you will learn...

- the seven steps involved in writing a systematic review;
- how to ensure your review is transparent, reproducible and comprehensive;
- how to design screening criteria for your search;
- how to use meta-analysis to do a quantitative synthesis of your sources;
- the three steps involved in doing a narrative synthesis.

In the last chapter, we saw that stand-alone reviews, unlike those that form part of dissertations and theses, are not used by researchers to lay the foundations to collect and analyse their own primary evidence. Rather, their purpose is to summarise and evaluate the current knowledge in a particular field. And within this, systematic reviews search for the best currently available answer to a specific focused question to support decision-making.

Most of them set out to measure the effectiveness of trials and policy initiatives in a rigorous and scientific way by assessing the various studies that have measured their effects in order to reveal the range and reliability of these results. To achieve this, it means that a systematic review must be:

Transparent and **reproducible** – its methodology must be detailed and clear to ensure that it can be replicated by others;

Systematic and **explicit** – not only must it have a repeatable methodology, but it must openly explain what has been done and why;

Comprehensive – it must include all relevant studies, which means it must make clear and justify its own criteria, determining what it will include and exclude.

Synthesising and evaluating studies in this way can reveal disagreements in the results, giving policymakers and managers the information they need to decide whether to introduce a policy, change it or abandon it altogether, or, in other cases, whether to make changes to an organisation and how best to do it.

How to do a systematic review – the seven steps

The question now is: how do we do one? Set out below you will see a detailed step-by-step method. However, some of the steps are covered in much greater detail in later chapters in this book, so I have only summarised these here.

The Steps

The communication of information about older people   **EXAMPLE**
between health and social care practitioners[1]

As you can see below, in this review the authors explain their review procedure, listing the core stages involved as they searched the literature, extracted what was relevant, assessed its quality and then synthesised it to provide the foundations from which they could draw their conclusions.

> We conducted a systematic review of the literature in the following stages:
> - Search strategy;
> - Inclusion criteria;
> - Assessment of relevance and validity of primary studies;
> - Data extraction;
> - Data synthesis.

1 The research question

As we will see in Chapters 4 and 5, this involves two things. First, we have to generate our own ideas and then use these to hone a research question and sub-questions that will drive and give clear focus to our review.

In a stand-alone systematic review, there is certain information that you will need to assemble before you can design your research question. You will need to know the population at which the intervention is targeted, the nature of that intervention, how you are going to measure the effects, compared with, say, doing nothing, and the timeframe that you are going to allow in which to measure these effects.

PICOT   **EXAMPLE**

In clinical research, the acronym PICOT is often used to answer these questions. It stands for:

> P – Patient population/sample of subjects – age, gender, ethnicity, people with a specific disorder
> I – Intervention – the indicator or variable in which you are interested, a medical intervention designed to restrict the spread of a disease or a government policy designed to limit the health risk of certain behaviour, like smoking
> C – Comparison with an alternative intervention or doing nothing
> O – Outcome – risk of catching the disease or the success of a policy
> T – Time frame – the time it takes for the intervention to take effect

For instance, you may want to know the risk of becoming obese among children who have obese adoptive parents compared with those whose adoptive parents are not obese. Using this to frame your question, you would fill in the following blanks:

In/Among _____ (P), how does _____ (I) compared with _____ (C) influence _____ (O) over _____ (T)?

Are children (P) who have obese adoptive parents (I) compared with children without obese adoptive parents (C) more at risk of becoming obese (O) between the ages of 5 and 18 (T)?

You may want to know how effective is the influenza vaccination among elderly patients compared with those who do not agree to receive it. Again, filling in the blanks you might frame the following question:

Among patients 65 and over (P), how does the use of the influenza vaccination (I) compared with those who do not receive it (C) influence the risk of developing influenza (O) during the flu season (T).

2 Planning your search

However, unlike a review that forms part of a dissertation or thesis, the research question in a systematic review is not directed at a particular problem you want to solve by collecting and analysing your own primary evidence. It aims instead to analyse and assess the evidence taken from the literature to provide a clear view of where effective research could be undertaken or to generate information on the effectiveness of interventions, like changes in policy or drug trials. So, we have to be clear who we are writing the review for and what would be most useful to them.

The best way of tackling this, which will make your judgements transparent, is to design a clear protocol, in which you describe how you're going to go about it: the steps you'll take and the procedure you'll follow. This is particularly important if you're collaborating with others on the review. Everyone needs to agree to the protocol and any changes that may have to be made.

The problem is that this is an intensely iterative process, so your protocol may have to undergo several changes.

Even then, once you have agreed to it, problems will arise as you uncover your sources. They may be limited or more than you expected. It's not unusual to find hundreds of relevant papers to review. In these circumstances, the focus of the review may have to change. The point is this is an intensely iterative process, which may mean several changes to your protocol. Even so, you still need a clear protocol before you start, agreed to by your collaborators.

To make all of this as transparent, explicit and reproducible as possible, you will need to record your search carefully, along with every change you make to your protocol. Before you start you will find it helpful to spell out at least the six things listed below:

1   The steps you will need to follow.
2   Whether the review will be broad or narrow.
3   The locations to be searched for literature.
4   The major keywords that will dictate the material to be retrieved.
5   The screening criteria that each paper needs to pass to be considered.
6   A checklist to record the screening qualifications of each paper.

3 Searching and screening

As you can see, the underlying imperative is to keep accurate records of each step you take, in this case how you searched the literature and how effective this was in ensuring that the review is comprehensive. To whittle down the hundreds, even thousands, of papers you might review in depth, the first step is to design screening criteria. This should make clear the studies you considered for the review and those you rejected, giving reasons why you excluded these and why you think this will not compromise the comprehensive range of your review.

This is not about the quality of the papers, but simply a practical question of deciding, in view of the purpose of the review, which papers are worth reading further. Obviously the review should be broad enough to cover a sufficient number, but also small enough to be manageable. As an assessment exercise, systematic reviews are set to evaluate your abilities to appraise and synthesise empirical evidence. But you also have to make sure you satisfy the two main reasons for doing one:

1 to ensure that every step of your review is reproducible;
2 and to guarantee the quality of your review by making sure it is comprehensive.

To ensure your review is comprehensive and trustworthy, you will need a screen that is clear and doesn't exclude anything significant. To design your screen, work through the following screening list and make a record of what you decide:

1 **Journals** – you might limit your search just to certain trusted ones;
2 **Date of publication**;
3 **Named authors** – you might limit it to certain authors whose work is well-known in this area;
4 **Location** – where the research was undertaken a hospital, health department, factories, banks, and so on;
5 **Funding** – consider whether it was funded by a commercial concern, which might affect its impartiality;
6 **Research question** – you might only consider those that address a research question relevant to yours;
7 **Type of methodology**;
8 **Population and sampling methodology** – consider what size of sample was chosen and how the subjects were selected;
9 **Intervention** – you will have to consider what sort of intervention was involved and how the data was analysed.

The communication of information about older people between health and social care practitioners
EXAMPLE

In this example, the selection criteria limited the review to literature relating to similar healthcare systems published between January 1994 and June 2000. The review was limited to empirical studies from peer-reviewed sources, theoretical papers from non-peer-reviewed sources, research papers from non-peer-reviewed sources and professional documents. All literature relating to mental health problems were excluded, while those selected had to include a majority of older people. This produced a database of 373 potentially relevant studies and, of these, 53 were accepted for further analysis.

A systematic review and meta-analysis of the overall   EXAMPLE
effects of school-based obesity prevention interventions and
effect differences by intervention components[2]

In this review, the inclusion criteria restricted the review to literature reporting on:

1 randomised controlled trials;
2 school children aged 5 to 18;
3 studies that assessed body mass index scores;
4 anthropometric data collected by physical examination;
5 interventions lasting at least three months;
6 which aimed at preventing overweight, not just treating it;
7 comparison groups involved in normal school activities;
8 available in full-text English versions;
9 that provided data for meta-analysis.

It excluded studies that only used questionnaires to collect evidence and studies specifically designed for the treatment of obesity-related diseases.
This left 50 trials, reported in 56 publications.

Once you have your screen, you can begin your search. In Chapters 6 and 7, we will examine this in detail.

4 Deciding what sources to use

After this, you have to decide which of your sources to use. This involves two steps:

1 Extracting the data;
2 Assessing the quality.

4.1 Extracting the data

Like the application of the screening list to each source, extracting the relevant data from each one does not involve assessing its quality; this comes later in this step. In effect, what you are doing here is systematically taking out relevant information from each paper, which you will then use in the next step (step 5) as you synthesise your raw material.

However, this often seems to be presented as a simple bureaucratic exercise, as you extract data according to a preconceived protocol. But, of course, it cannot be just that: there is no substitute for the insights that creative thinkers can generate, when they see significant connections in the material that open up new ways of interpreting the ideas, which is likely to result in changes to the protocol. This is an act of creative synthesis and no bureaucratic method can act as a substitute for it. As we saw above, this is an intensely iterative process, which necessarily entails reactive changes to the protocols to take account of these creative insights.

At this point, it's worth noting that there are six cognitive domains – the six ability ranges that academic work seeks to assess:

1 Recall
2 Comprehension
3 Application
4 Analysis
5 Synthesis
6 Evaluation.

At this level of education, it is not the lower, simplest level that is being assessed (recall, comprehension and application), which would be the case if you were merely ticking the boxes in a bureaucratic exercise of applying your screening list. On the contrary, it is the higher, more complex abilities to analyse concepts and arguments, synthesise ideas to find new ways of approaching problems, and critically evaluating arguments. No simple bureaucratic system of extraction can act as a substitute for this.

4.2 Assessing the quality

Once you have extracted the information, this is combined with your evaluation of the quality of each article, which is then synthesised with other studies in the next step (step 5). Assessing the quality of sources is also often referred to, confusingly, as 'screening'. Effectively you make a judgement as to the quality of each paper, scoring them on the criteria you have chosen to use and the likely quality of their results. As with screening, the criteria for this need to be made clear and explicit.

The practical screening in step 3 excluded papers from the review, either on the grounds that they were not relevant or just to reduce the number of papers to a manageable number. It didn't consider the quality of papers. Here we are aiming to do two things:

1 exclude papers that are judged to be poor methodologically;
2 and to prioritise those left according to their quality.

The communication of information about older   EXAMPLE
people between health and social care practitioners

In this review, after all papers were assessed independently by members of the research team and disagreements resolved, the methodology of each study was graded according to the reliability of its results. A data extraction form was devised, covering 10 areas: abstract and title; introduction and aims; method and data; sampling; data analysis; ethics and bias; results; transferability or generalisability; implications; and usefulness. Each area was rated on a 4-point scale – 1 (very poor) to 4 (good) – and a score calculated for each paper (10 for very poor to 40 good), which indicated its methodological rigor.

Of course, there is no definitive answer as to what represents quality in a study, and standards for different methodological tests vary from field to field. The only solution is to be aware of the criteria you are using and make these explicit so that other researchers can check the review. Nevertheless, checklists that are designed to assess the quality of studies have their limitations. Inevitably, they incorporate the biases and subjective responses of those who design them. All you can do is be conscious of this, which, of course, on its own doesn't guarantee it will be avoided.

As you can see, this will struggle to meet the demands of a systematic review to be explicit, reproducible and comprehensive. It is difficult to incorporate the subjective responses of reviewers into an objective list or a set of yes/no questions. Just ticking a checklist to assess the quality of a paper seems to sacrifice depth and the significance of a researcher's subtle arguments for a bureaucratic procedure. And, even then, those who compile the list of things to check are themselves incorporating their own biases in the very instruments and checklists they are devising.

Understandably, checklists like this generate widely shared criticisms that:

- They lack the depth needed for some specialist topics;
- Some items on the list are difficult to interpret;
- A single overall quality score can be arbitrary: it can give serious defects the same weight as minor concerns.

Beyond the contentious area of how you evaluate the quality of a reviewer's judgements and subjective responses, the only solid ground on which you can evaluate a paper is the quality of the justifications it puts forward for its conclusions:

1 the consistency of its arguments;
2 its use of evidence – whether it is relevant, reliable and sufficient, whether arguments are made on the basis of mere assertion or supposition;
3 and whether it conveys arguments using language clearly and consistently.

In Chapters 8 and 9, we examine in detail how you can develop your skills to critically evaluate in this way the sources you use.

5 Planning your review – synthesis

In this step, the aim is to create a plan for your review by combining facts from studies and making connections between them using techniques designed for qualitative and quantitative studies. This is synthesis, although it is often confusingly referred to as its opposite, 'analysis'. In effect, our aim is to answer our research question by combining a large number of studies to make comprehensive sense of them. The way this is done varies depending upon whether the studies are composed largely of quantitative or qualitative evidence.

Quantitative synthesis – meta-analysis

Where this involves quantitative evidence, it is achieved by comparing the studies against a common standard, the results of which can then be aggregated or processed statistically. This is meta-analysis, in which each individual study is analysed quantitatively and then synthesised with the others to produce an aggregate result.

The aim is to assess the 'outcome measure' or the degree of the effect of a particular intervention, such as a new policy or a clinical trial, to reveal the range and reliability of these results. By looking at different studies it is possible to compare and aggregate the effect found in them to see the range of the effect over a number of them. This gives a clearer, more reliable picture of the effect of a drug that is being trialled, a clinical intervention or a policy initiative.

Usefulness of research synthesis

A good research synthesis can give us a trustworthy answer to our research question, thereby indicating to policymakers, managers and practitioners how much confidence to place in the results. It can tell us how a particular intervention affects certain groups, the possible harm it might cause, the best way to organise its delivery and whether it represents value for money.

However, for this to be effective studies need to be homogeneous, and this can present serious problems. The lack of homogeneity may be:

- **Statistical** – the statistics used in different studies may be measuring different things;
- **Methodological** – different studies simply use different methods, for which there is no common standard of measurement;
- **Conceptual** – not only might different concepts be used to describe key elements of the research methodology, but studies might employ different interventions, use different populations of subjects and sampling techniques and measure different outcomes.

In some fields, homogeneity raises more serious problems than in others. In fields like health studies, where meta-analysis is used more often, replicating trials of drugs and treatment is much easier to achieve.

Social sciences

Compare that with the social sciences, where randomised controlled trials and other replicable studies are often difficult to conduct both practically and ethically. Even if we could resolve the many ethical problems involved in experimenting on individuals and social groups, to repeat the experiment it is more difficult to find a suitable, fresh supply of subjects who are sufficiently similar in relevant respects to the first. What's more, once we have introduced changes in a social system to see the results, they may be irreversible, making it impossible to repeat the test, because the initial conditions of the second test will be different from those of the first.

However, there's no doubt about the usefulness of a meta-analysis: unless you have a clear picture of where things stand at the moment, there is not a lot of use adding one more study to the confusing picture. But it seems there is no reliable consensus about the best evidence to include, and some question whether the reviewer's bias can easily seep into the selection process. To measure the extent to which this might have occurred a 'risk of bias' assessment is often conducted. This assesses various forms of bias, including selection bias, reporting bias, performance bias, detection bias and attrition bias.

Problems

1 Lack of homogeneity.
2 No reliable consensus about the best evidence to include.
3 Reviewer's bias can easily seep into the selection process.

To test their overall robustness, meta-analyses are often assessed by conducting a sensitivity analysis. In this the aggregated outcome or effect that the meta-analysis has produced is tested by conducting the meta-analysis again, this time with one of the criteria altered to measure the extent to which the outcome changes as a result.

Qualitative synthesis – narrative synthesis

In contrast, a narrative synthesis is used in many cases when a particular intervention has not been well understood. You may want an overall picture of the current knowledge about an issue, which could then be used to guide policymakers. In such cases, the aim is to synthesise the various theories as to how or why the intervention does or does not work in certain circumstances. Sometimes known as 'scoping', it lays out the landscape and the theories within it that relate to a particular intervention.

Narrative syntheses   EXAMPLE

'A Systematic Review and Narrative Synthesis of Interventions for Parental Human Immunodeficiency Virus Disclosure' – Conserve, D.F, Teti M, Shin G, Iwelunmor J, Handler L and Maman S., *Frontiers in Public Health*, 2017.
'Screening and Interventions for Childhood Overweight' – Whitlock, E.P, Williams, S.B, Gold, R, Smith, P and Shipman, S., *Agency for Healthcare Research and Quality* (US), 2005.

The steps

To do a narrative synthesis, we must work through three steps:

1 Analysis
2 Mapping
3 Synthesis

1 Analysis

The first step is to analyse the text of each study, focusing on the words used. This is sometimes described as identifying the 'story' of each one, although this can be misleading: this is not a 'story' in the strict sense, but an analysis of the themes, the key concepts and ideas in the text. It is sometimes referred to as 'meta-synthesis' or 'qualitative meta-analysis', which is essentially a thematic analysis of each study under review. It might also include 'vote counting', where each type of effect of a certain type of intervention is counted.

2 Mapping

The second step is to use this information to create a map of each study – a structure of the relationship between these characteristics. Vote counting will merely produce a cardinal scale indicating how many times each characteristic appears. Much more significant is an ordinal scale, which indicates that some characteristics are more significant than others, that there exists a hierarchical structure in the relationships between them. The best way of representing this is to create a visual map of the ideas using pattern notes, like concept maps, mind maps and flowcharts. You will find a more detailed examination of each of these in Chapter 16.

3 Synthesis

Then, in the third stage, this information from all the studies is synthesised by mapping the relations between them, according to their particular methodologies or common design features. It might be based on the reviewer's interpretation of the study, on the commonalities in the explanations that researchers give or on common stylistic characteristics.

Differences   EXAMPLE

The aim might be to discover why various studies show different effects and different degrees of effect from a given intervention, or why there are different factors that limit or enhance an intervention. Of course, the level of homogeneity among the studies would be one obvious explanation for this. The less homogeneous the studies are the less reliable are the conclusions of the review, unless some explanation can be found for it.

Unfortunately, there is no consensus about what is the best evidence to take from each study and use in each of these steps (analysis, mapping and synthesis). To compound the problem, narrative syntheses are often criticised for failing to maintain transparency in the way they interpret data and come to their conclusions, which ultimately threatens their value and the extent to which their conclusions can be relied upon.

But, perhaps inevitably, systematic reviews will always be shaped by subjective interpretation. In their defence, those that are more transparent do at least give an explicit description of their methodological procedure to allow future researchers to replicate or amend the process.

Conceptual framework for personal recovery in   EXAMPLE
mental health: systematic review and narrative synthesis[3]

In this review, the authors produced a preliminary synthesis through thematic analysis of primary data and vote counting of themes. The type of data that was extracted and tabulated from each paper included type of paper, methodological approach, participation and inclusion criteria, study location and summary of main study findings. In this way, the main themes and sub-themes across the data were identified and vote counting used to establish the frequency with which the themes appeared in all the papers. From this, they were able to produce a preliminary conceptual framework.

With this tabulated information, they were then able to explore the relationships within and between studies. The aim was to identify any additional themes as well as areas of different emphasis. Finally, they asked an advisory panel with academic, clinical and personal expertise to comment on the positioning of concepts within different hierarchical levels of the conceptual framework and identify important areas of recovery which they thought had been omitted.

6 Writing the first draft

7 Editing

These last two steps are covered in detail later in this book: Chapters 20, 21, 22, 23 and 24, for the writing of the first draft, and Chapters 27 and 28, for editing.

Structure

Like non-systematic stand-alone reviews, the structure of systematic reviews resembles those of empirical theses and dissertations:

1 Introduction
2 Methodology
3 Findings
4 Discussion
5 Conclusion
6 References

The communication of information about older people between health and social care practitioners   EXAMPLE

Although this review is structured using slightly different terms, you can see that it follows broadly the same structure:

1 Background
2 Review procedure
    2.1   Search strategy
    2.2   Inclusion criteria
    2.3   Assessment of relevance and validity of primary studies
    2.4   Data extraction
    2.5   Data synthesis
3 Findings
4 Results
5 Discussion
6 Conclusions
7 Acknowledgements
8 References

In line with the core commitment entailed in any systematic review, as you write your review you will need to give a clear, detailed explanation of the process you've adopted so that other reviewers can reproduce the same results independently. Beyond that, ask yourself whether the literature you have reviewed supports an existing theory or establishes a new model, opening up fresh avenues for future research. In particular, highlight any novel findings and unexpected results.

You can download a copy of the steps and the other checklists in this chapter from the companion website (www.macmillanihe.com/greetham-literature-review).

Summary

1 A systematic review aims to be transparent, reproducible, systematic, explicit and comprehensive.
2 There are seven steps in producing one.
3 To reduce the number of papers to review, you need to design screening criteria.
4 In meta-analysis, each study is analysed quantitatively and then synthesised with others to produce an aggregate result.
5 Narrative synthesis aims to create a thematic analysis of each study by analysing the themes, key concepts and ideas in the text.

What next?

In contrast to stand-alone reviews, literature reviews written for dissertations and theses aim to find a gap in our understanding and lay the foundations for our own research. We will examine this in the next chapter.

Notes

1   Payne S, Kerr C, Hawker S, Hardey M, Powell J, 'The communication of information about older people between health and social care practitioners', *Age and Ageing*, vol. 31 (2002), pp. 107–17.
2   Liu, Z., Xu, H., Wen, L. et al., 'A systematic review and meta-analysis of the overall effects of school-based obesity prevention interventions and effect differences by intervention components', *International Journal of Behavioral Nutrition and Physical Activity*, vol. 16, 95 (2019), https://doi.org/10.1186/s12966-019-0848-8.
3   Leamy M, Bird V, Le Boutillier C, Williams J and Slade M, 'Conceptual framework for personal recovery in mental health: systematic review and narrative synthesis', *The British Journal of Psychiatry*, vol. 199 (2011), pp. 445–452, DOI: 10.1192/bjp.bp.110.083733.

Chapter 3

Literature Reviews for Dissertations and Theses

In this chapter, you will learn…

- the different ways you can find gaps in the literature for your research;
- the simple ways in which your work can be original;
- the seven steps to producing a literature review for your dissertation or thesis;
- the four things to avoid as you search the literature;
- the importance of getting the structure right.

All reviews have to be systematic to some degree, including those that form part of a dissertation or thesis, which lay the foundations for their own research. Although the full rigour of a systematic review would be too much for a dissertation or thesis, a review still needs to be as rigorous and comprehensive as possible, following a clear, transparent approach that you can make explicit to establish its credibility. You need to be able to describe accurately what you looked for, what you found, what you did with what you found and the conclusions you reached on this basis.

Integrated reviews

However, with some types of dissertations and theses, this is clearly not possible. In those that are text-based and theoretical, there might not be a single chapter dealing with the literature. This is common in the humanities and in theoretical research in the social sciences, where the subject matter *is* the literature itself in the form of novels, plays, philosophical texts and theoretical and historical works.

Indeed, in these disciplines a literature review as a separate chapter can be quite an alien concept. As you'll be referring to this literature in the body of your thesis or dissertation, there seems no need to do a lengthy review. Nevertheless, a comprehensive review of the literature throughout your work is still vital to demonstrate that you have been thorough in laying the foundations of your research.

Gaps

In this way, we find the gaps in our knowledge that our research will fill or ways in which we can advance our knowledge by extending research to new ideas and practices. Of course, for a PhD thesis the significance of the gaps will be greater and the degree to which it advances our understanding more significant than that of a masters or undergraduate dissertation. Nevertheless, all research starts from the recognition of a gap in our understanding:

- something that has been overlooked;
- an issue that has been neglected;
- an interpretation that others have not thought of;
- or a research method that has not been used in quite this way and in this context before.

Finding a gap in our knowledge calls for a careful and thoughtful selection of only the most important documents that are relevant to our research. As research is intended to make an original contribution to our understanding, the one thing we must do is demonstrate that we are not just repeating what has gone before.

Originality

This has an obvious bearing on the question of originality, which concerns many of those writing dissertations. However, this need not be as daunting as many fear. Although a dissertation might not have the originality of a PhD thesis, both still have to show that they have broken new ground: that they will advance, even in a small way, our knowledge and understanding of certain ideas, issues and methodology. But there are many quite simple ways in which research can be original for both PhDs and dissertations:

- in terms of the subject you choose;
- in the way you approach it;
- the client group or material you focus on;
- and the particular data you collect.

You don't have to show that what you plan to do has never been done before: you can replicate knowledge by testing old results with new participants or new research sites; and you can add to our knowledge the voices of individuals whose perspectives have never been heard or whose views have been minimised in our society.

> **King, Diana, 'Translating Revolution in Twentieth-Century China and France', 2017, Columbia University**   EXAMPLE
>
> As part of her explanation of how she found the idea for her PhD thesis, this student explains, 'the tendency of much current scholarship to focus exclusively on the texts of prominent French or Chinese intellectuals overlooks the vital role played by translation, and by non-elite thinkers, writers, students and migrant workers in the cross-fertilization of revolutionary discourses and practices.'

Generating your own ideas

What's more, you don't have to start with just a blank sheet, worrying how you're ever going to summon up an original idea. In Chapter 4, you will learn a simple method of generating your own ideas, which will reveal all the possible gaps you can look for in the literature.

Then, as you'll see in Chapter 5, with an idea you have generated the gaps will appear as you map out the territory, asking yourself if the writer has possibly overlooked anything. You may find your topic can fit neatly into a gap, or can be adapted to fit. Someone may have investigated a phenomenon, which is sufficiently similar for you to carry out a comparative study. Note the characteristics of the problem or the features of the situation he or she chose to measure. Use the same yourself. Or perhaps the writer has used a research strategy that you could use on a case study of your own?

- You might apply an existing theory to a new area, or test other people's findings and ideas for yourself using different subjects.

Intellectual history   EXAMPLE

You might know of a number of studies that have compared the work of the nineteenth century English philosopher John Stuart Mill and the Scottish essayist Thomas Carlyle, but you have been unable to find any studies that have compared their respective theories of history.

- Your research might build on existing studies to follow up new leads or to refine or qualify the findings of earlier studies.

Rationing healthcare   EXAMPLE

You read the studies that have been done on the challenge and effects of rationing healthcare during a time of austerity, so you might decide to explore this, concentrating on how this has affected dialysis patients.

- The instruments you design might yield new, surprising evidence.

Questionnaires and interviews   EXAMPLE

You might design a questionnaire that asks questions not posed before or examines a group not previously examined. You might conduct interviews using a series of well-crafted questions that reveal new, fascinating insights into a problem.

- You might devise exercises for subjects to complete, which produce evidence of behaviour from a perspective not seen before.

Study skills   EXAMPLE

You might decide to test the belief that the study skills problems experienced by most students at universities are due largely to the neglect of these skills in schools. So you design tests and a questionnaire from which you discover that there appears to be not one cause but a number.

In the following examples, you can see that many students have found ways of approaching a subject that has been studied before, but not from this particular perspective:

Dissertation and theses titles   EXAMPLE

Dissertations:

Caring for special needs children: A mother's view (University of Surrey);
Themes and images in the female gothic novel: Ann Radcliffe, Jane Austen and Charlotte Bronte (University of Sussex);
'We'll show those city bastards how to fight': a social geography of domestic football hooliganism (University of Cambridge);
Shakespearian influences in the work of the Pre-Raphaelite Brotherhood (Oxford Brookes University);
Prohibition of smoking tobacco products in public places including the workplace (University of Johannesburg).

Theses:

Complexity & hegemony: technical politics in an age of uncertainty (University of East London);
Evaluating the impact of financial incentives on inequalities in smoking cessation in primary care (Imperial College London);
Assessment of Biodiversity Impacts in Swedish Forestry – Attitudes and Experiences in the Product Chain (Chalmers University of Technology).

Writing a literature review for a dissertation or thesis – the steps

As in the previous two chapters, set out below is a step-by-step method. Each of these we will examine in more detail in the following chapters.

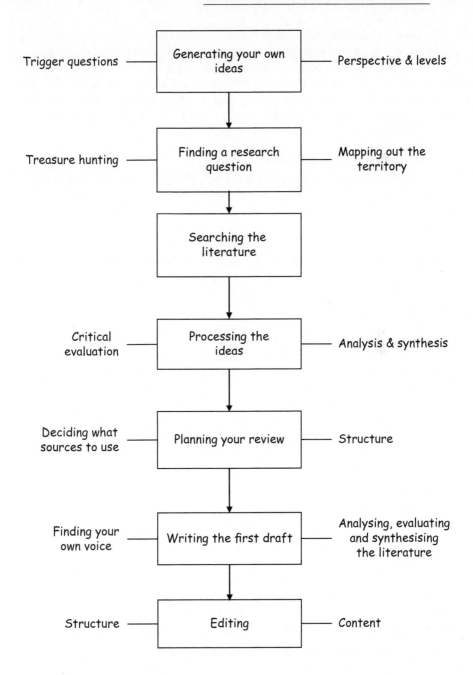

Trigger questions ——— **Generating your own ideas** ——— Perspective & levels

Treasure hunting ——— **Finding a research question** ——— Mapping out the territory

Searching the literature

Critical evaluation ——— **Processing the ideas** ——— Analysis & synthesis

Deciding what sources to use ——— **Planning your review** ——— Structure

Finding your own voice ——— **Writing the first draft** ——— Analysing, evaluating and synthesising the literature

Structure ——— **Editing** ——— Content

1 Generating your own ideas

A literature review is useful only if there is a real question to answer. In other words, we don't start out with an opinion that we seek to validate. The question must come first before our conclusions: it must be provisional, a thesis that could go both ways that we genuinely test in our research.

In Chapter 4, you will learn how to pin this question down by first generating your own ideas and then honing these into an effective research question for a literature review. Using a simple set of trigger questions you will learn how to assemble the ideas and information you need to form your research question. Then you will learn how to think outside our own limited perspectives and on different levels by asking questions you might otherwise dismiss as irrelevant and unthinkable. As you'll see, the result is often surprisingly insightful and innovative research questions.

2 Finding a research question

Despite the title of this step, the best research questions are hardly ever just found; rather, they are worked on carefully and designed to give clear direction to our work. The clearer they are the more relevant and usable will be the material we collect. However, at this stage, as we search the material for the right question, it is all too easy to get drawn into the literature and spend too much time reading things too deeply; spending too much time in areas that are likely to be irrelevant. So, we have to keep our search within the bounds of two practical objectives:

- to search for treasure;
- and to map out the territory.

As we treasure hunt, we are identifying things that may be useful, anything that looks like it might be worth reading in more depth later. We are scanning the material for ideas, information and the methods the researcher might have used, which we, too, could adapt and use.

Our second objective is to map out the territory, all the current issues being debated, to get as full a measure as possible of the context in which our research is set: the subject, the research methods employed and how researchers analyse, synthesise and evaluate evidence and ideas to develop their arguments. We have three questions at the front of our minds:

1 What has been done before?
2 What information is available?
3 What gaps are there in the research?

After this, you will be clearer than at any previous time exactly what your project is about and the question you want to pursue.

3 Searching the literature

However, although we are now clearer about how to conduct our search, there are things we need to avoid if we're to use our time well:

1 Don't confuse the search with the review;
2 Be clear about what you're looking for;
3 Don't get bogged down;
4 Don't get diverted into irrelevant areas.

We all know how easily each of these problems can soak up our valuable time. In Chapters 6 and 7, you will learn how to avoid this, while you use only the most relevant literature from sources that you have checked for reliability.

4 Processing the ideas

The increased ease of access to a wider range of material makes it even more important that we process the ideas to reveal their implications, their weaknesses and where they all fit in with our research project. In other words, we need to

1 analyse the concepts and arguments to reveal their implications;
2 critically evaluate the consistency of the arguments, the use of evidence and the language used to develop the ideas;
3 and synthesise the ideas to create new ways of approaching the problem.

A literature review is not just a summary of our sources; it must also present a detailed justification of our own research by identifying the limitations, deficiencies and gaps in the literature. Consequently, the most significant part of a review lies in showing how our research will fill these gaps and bring different studies together to form a new understanding of the problem. In Chapters 8, 9, 10, 11 and 12, you will learn ways in which you can develop the skills you need to do this effectively.

5 Planning your review

However, the dilemma all students face is how to describe and demonstrate their broad understanding of the background of their research and the debates that dominate their subject, while only using sources that bear directly on the specific issues raised by their research. The sort of scene-setting implied by the first problem often leads them into areas that are irrelevant to their research. This makes two decisions that are already difficult much more so:

1 how to decide what's relevant;
2 how to organise the mass of material.

At the heart of these lies the importance of processing our ideas thoroughly, knowing what is likely to be our own contribution. The review should build up naturally to the specific questions at the heart of your project as you move from the general to the specific texts and from the theory to the practice. It should build naturally to those texts that directly touch on the issues that interest you, providing the platform on which your research will be built and finishing with a direct lead that establishes clear contact with your work.

> Your review should build naturally to the specific questions at the heart of your project.

In Chapters 17, 18 and 19, you will learn how to plan a review that not only builds in this way but ties in with other chapters to create a coherent dissertation or thesis, in which everything is related and performs a clear, well-conceived role.

6 Writing the first draft

One of the most difficult tasks in producing a literature review is to write it clearly and concisely in a style that is simple to understand and interesting to read. Not only do we have to show that we understand our sources and the implications they have for our project, but we have to meet the complex, often conflicting, demands on our cognitive abilities to analyse concepts and arguments, critically evaluate our sources and synthesise our ideas.

The two conflicting demands are:

1 to show we understand our sources and their implications;
2 and to analyse concepts and arguments, critically evaluate our sources and synthesise our ideas.

The key to tackling this problem is to begin your first draft early. In Chapters 20, 21, 22, 23 and 24, you will learn that in all forms of writing, it's better to start when your ideas are most familiar and vivid. Equally important, you need to allow yourself to write freely as you develop and synthesise your ideas. As a result, the more your own voice will come through, bringing a lightness of touch to your expression, a naturalness to your writing, nearer to the spoken word, which will help you present your ideas and develop your arguments clearly, simply and economically.

7 Editing

The first draft of your literature review is for you: you are writing as you think, clarifying and developing your ideas. But the second and subsequent drafts are for your reader: you work to make sure your ideas come through so clearly that someone who knows nothing about your project can understand it and feel the impact of your ideas as you do.

To do this successfully, we shift our focus from the writer to the editor: from the creative activity of converting our ideas into language to a more self-conscious focus on the way we have used words, phrases and structures. There are two stages of revision here:

1 **Structure** – this concentrates on the thinking that went into it:

   - whether it is organised logically;
   - whether the connections between our ideas are consistently developed;
   - whether we have signposted these connections so our readers can see them clearly.

2 **Content** – this concentrates on the clarity with which we express our ideas:

   - Do our words and sentences convey our ideas succinctly and clearly?
   - Do they develop our arguments in the direction we want them to go?
   - Is the meaning of sentences obscured by meaningless words and phrases?

In Chapters 27 and 28 you will learn how to produce prose that reads like talk in print, with light effortless prose that glides across the page with a pace and rhythm that holds your reader's attention.

Getting the structure right

As you can see, there is a significant difference between the purposes of stand-alone reviews and those that prepare the ground for dissertations and theses. The intentions of stand-alone reviews are to give an overview of the present situation or, in the case of systematic reviews, to come to a conclusion about the effectiveness of a particular intervention, as revealed through currently available studies.

In contrast, reviews for dissertations and theses point beyond the review itself: they prepare the ground for research of your own. Their intention is not to summarise the findings to reveal the effectiveness of previous studies, but to explore where further research needs to be focused, where gaps need to be filled. As it is preparation for work beyond itself, it has to be more carefully structured to deliver you to the point where you can go on to address the subject of your own research.

 You can download a copy of the steps in this chapter from the companion website (www.macmillanihe.com/greetham-literature-review).

Summary

1 Literature reviews for dissertations and theses also need to be as rigorous, comprehensive and transparent as possible.
2 The need for originality doesn't mean that you have to show that what you mean to do has never been done before.
3 There are simple ways of generating ideas that lead to insightful and innovative research questions.
4 The question a literature review raises must be provisional, a thesis we set out to test in our research.
5 Your review should build naturally to the specific questions at the heart of your project.

What next?

In this chapter, we have discovered that finding gaps and original problems to research need not be such a daunting challenge. In the next chapter we will learn to generate our own ideas that we can then use to design our research questions.

PART 2

Searching Your Sources

Chapter 4

How to Generate Your Own Ideas

In this chapter, you will learn…

- how to liberate yourself from orthodox patterns of thinking to unlock a wealth of ideas;
- how to compile and use routinely a list of trigger questions;
- how to take advantage of a powerful ideas generator, using levels and perspectives;
- that the most creative minds solve problems by asking questions nobody else asks;
- how to develop a thinking style that is open, divergent and unconstrained.

All original thinking begins by asking difficult, unusual questions that appear to be quite off the scale. These are the 'What if', hypothetical questions for which there is no obvious answer. Out of these often develop that spark of an original insight, which appears vivid and interesting to you and will appear vivid and interesting to your reader too. Rather than go into the literature empty-handed in search of gaps, generate your ideas first. Although your sources are important to your research, don't let them dictate to you, swamping you with *their* ideas.

The problem is the problem

For many of us, the most confusing and difficult aspect of research is finding the right problem. It must be original and interesting: something that will not only strike readers as worth researching but be *interesting* enough to maintain your motivation over the long term. It must be *broad* enough to connect with the background theory and the ideas you find in the literature and *narrow* enough to deal with in depth in the time and words available.

- **Interesting** enough to maintain your motivation;
- **Broad** enough to connect with the background theory;
- **Narrow** enough to research in depth in the time and words available.

The secret to finding one is to suspend your judgement and allow yourself to think what might seem naïve and ludicrous ideas. Otherwise, you will slam the door on them before they are fully developed. As the philosopher A.N. Whitehead said, '[A]lmost all new ideas have a certain aspect of foolishness when they are first produced.'[1] In fact, often the most creative ideas seem the most foolish.

The questioning approach – trigger questions

Unfortunately, when anybody tells you to generate your own ideas, they mostly end up just giving you vague, unhelpful advice. They might tell you to, 'Think for yourself', like telling you to be clever, or suggest you 'Ask yourself questions', which doesn't tell you exactly what you should do. You might be advised just to lower or remove altogether your inhibitions, as if there is a huge torrent of ideas just waiting to cascade before you, if only you could overcome your fears about appearing to be foolish by saying things that seem naïve.

And yet, there is a simple, organised, systematic way in which we can all do this. Indeed, most of us do it already without realising it, as we study our subject or go about our profession. The first thing we do is work through a list of trigger questions we routinely ask ourselves to assemble ideas. Most creative thinkers are constantly refining and adapting them, adding new ones they might hear elsewhere. Those whom we describe as 'geniuses', who solve problems by seeing something no-one else can see, come to their solutions in exactly this way. They ask questions nobody else asks. They approach the problem from a different direction with different classifications.

Genius: someone who asks questions nobody else asks.

Try this …

List the 10 most useful questions that you could use routinely in your own subject or profession to generate novel ideas of your own that will help you solve a problem.

Then, as you use it every day, be alert to every new question and classification you think might be useful or you hear others use, and add them to your list. Collect them like an avid stamp collector collects new or rare stamps. They are the generators of your most inventive ideas, those that nobody else is likely to have.

Compiling a checklist

So, what sort of questions should you expect to find on your trigger list? Although the following are not specific to any particular subject or profession, you will probably find some of your questions take a similar form.

1 What do we mean by X?
2 Why did that happen?
3 What is the connection between A and B?
4 How do we know that?
5 What evidence have we got for that claim? Is it reliable?
6 If that's the case, what follows?
7 How is it that A is the case when B is or is not the case? Is there an inconsistency?

8 What other examples are there for this sort of thing happening? Are there grounds here for a general rule?

9 What is the history, the background, to this?

10 Is it something quite unique, or has it developed out of something else?

Each subject we study has a routine list of the most relevant questions to ask. If you are studying history, a well-designed course would teach you not just the facts of history, but how to think like a historian. So the sort of routine questions you would learn to ask might include:

1 What was the cause of the event?

2 What was his motive?

3 Is there sufficient evidence to justify that explanation?

4 What were the effects?
  4.1 How large?
  4.2 How significant?
  4.3 Who was most affected: individuals, groups, social classes?
  4.4 What type of effects: economic, social, political, intellectual?

5 Who was involved: social classes, individuals, groups (religious, professional, military)?

The Scientific Revolution of the Seventeenth Century   EXAMPLE

If you were interested in 'The Scientific Revolution of the Seventeenth Century', you would have to ask yourself, 'What is it that interests me about it?' To answer this you would then work through each of the routine questions above, asking yourself what the causes were, what the motives were and so on. You might discover that it is the motives of those who were involved that most interest you, so you look for commonalities and you find that a very high proportion were Puritans. Now you have something that seems very interesting.

If you were a police detective investigating a suspicious death, you might organise for yourself a simple alphabetical list of routine questions to work through to gather vital evidence each time you begin an investigation. Each question would remind you to gather evidence on a particular feature of the person who has been found dead:

1 Age

2 Build

3 Clothes

4 Distinguishing marks

5 Ethnic origin

6 Face

7 Glasses

8 Hair

9 Items he or she had with them[2]

The point is that for every subject and profession there is a routine set of trigger questions that we use to generate and marshal our ideas – things we routinely look for. As you work with your own trigger list, it helps to keep in mind four useful rules:

Trigger list – four rules

1   Generate as many questions as possible.
2   Make them as clear and specific as you can.
3   Collect new, interesting questions and add them to your list.
4   Pursue them as far as they will go.

The power of questions

This simple step can generate a wealth of novel ideas that provide the key to solving the most difficult problem. The one significant handicap to our thinking is that often we have too many ideas of one kind: too many about one aspect of the problem or one way of approaching it. Trigger questions give us a way of kick-starting a flow of different ideas. Through a series of questions, we can negotiate a vast territory of possible answers to a problem and find what we're looking for.

Identikit   EXAMPLE

Prior to the computer age, police sketch artists would use the 'Identikit' system to help witnesses put together a likeness of a suspect. The face would be divided up into, say, 10 building blocks: the hairline, forehead, eyes, nose and so on down to the chin. Each would be represented on transparent strips with a variety of options to choose from. Let's say there were 10 hairlines, 10 foreheads, 10 eyes and so on, amounting to a total of 100 transparent slips. Using this it would be possible to create 10 billion different faces, out of which the witness could produce a very close likeness of the suspect quickly. So here you have a problem with 10 billion possible solutions, yet using this simple system, composed of a routine set of questions, it is possible to arrive at a solution in no time at all.

Using a set of routine questions, you can find that one in 10 billion possible solutions.

The superstore   EXAMPLE

A large chain of superstores submits an application to build a new superstore on land outside a small town. This will serve an area untapped by the company or any other chain of superstores, so they are pressing hard for it to go ahead. But you wonder what might be the impact on the community.

This could be the subject of an interesting research project or a stand-alone review, if you were an official advising the local planning authority. But how do we take it further? To explore all the topics that might possibly interest us, we have to generate freely as many ideas as we can, without, at this stage, stopping to critically evaluate them.

Trigger questions   **EXERCISE**

First compile a list of questions that you can then work through systematically, exploring all the ideas and issues they raise.

Answer:

Although your list will be different from mine, no doubt it contains similar questions:

1 What has been the experience of similar towns?
2 What are the likely benefits?
3 What will be the impact on shops, cafes and restaurants in the main shopping area in the town?
4 How will local people be affected?
5 How will it affect the flow and density of traffic?
6 How will the decision be reached?
7 Who is consulted?
8 What influence will local people have on the decision?
9 What factors will be taken into account?
10 What does the local community think?

Once you have devised your list, you would answer each of them in turn as fully as you can, taking brief notes, preferably using a mind map or pattern notes (Chapter 16) of your own design, whichever helps you record your ideas as fast as you generate them. Of course, as you do this other questions will occur to you, which you could also pursue.

If an idea comes to you out of sequence concerning another issue, note it. The mind works much faster than you can write, so the secret is to keep up with it and not allow your note-taking to put a brake on it. You want to catch every idea and insight your mind throws up, every connection it makes with other ideas. Don't tell yourself that you will list the idea or connection later, when you have a moment. The rich insights that the mind throws up rarely come again, so don't waste them.

The rich insights that the mind throws up rarely come again, so don't waste them.

Perspectives and levels

You can already see the wealth of ideas you can generate, but there is more. As we've said, original thinkers invent new questions to open up new perspectives others have not seen. Likewise, we need a method that gets us to think outside our own limited perspective in order to ask questions we might otherwise dismiss as irrelevant and unthinkable.

In certain subjects, of course, such as history, moral philosophy, social work, nursing, indeed all the caring professions, you learn to do this: you place yourself in someone else's position and vicariously experience their feelings, anxieties, hopes and so on. But no matter what you're studying, you, too, can do this routinely. After you've answered all your trigger questions, do two things:

1   Examine your topic from the perspective of all those involved: all those who affect or are affected by it.

2   As you do this, think about each one on the different levels listed below:

Levels	
Physical	1. Material needs
	2. Transport
	3. Climate, etc.
Individual	1. Biological
	2. Psychological
	3. Moral
	4. Intellectual
Social	1. Cultural
	2. Political
	3. Economic

The Industrial Revolution   EXAMPLE

Say you're interested in the Industrial Revolution. First, place yourself imaginatively into the situation faced by those historical agents who were affected and could affect events: farmers, merchants, industrialists, politicians, labourers and so on. Then consider their situation and responses to events not just on the level of individuals with their particular self-interests, but in terms of how they affect and are affected by society (the cultural, political and economic effects) and the physical conditions of life (material needs – food and shelter – transport, climate and so on).

A powerful ideas generator

Of course, not all of these levels will be relevant for each perspective and for each problem, but a routine that gets us to explore them before we reject an idea makes it less likely that we will miss important ideas and insights. Here we have a very powerful ideas generator at our fingertips. For each of your 10 trigger questions, you have different perspectives. Then for each of these you have three different levels, each of which is subdivided further. So, from a comparatively simple set of questions, you can generate not just hundreds but thousands of ideas.

The Industrial Revolution   EXAMPLE

In this case, the moment you begin to think from the perspective of farmers on the physical level of material needs you might find that what really interests you is how improvements in transport affected market gardeners in your own local area. Here you have a fascinating and original topic to research.

Superstore   EXERCISE

Now that you have compiled a list of questions to work through systematically, take just one of them and explore it from the perspectives of those who will affect and be affected by the building of the new superstore, exploring each perspective on these three different levels.

Question: How will local people be affected?

Perspectives

Obviously, the first thing we need to do is list all those involved. Then we need to place ourselves in their position and see the construction of the superstore from their perspectives: how are they likely to feel about it; what changes are they likely to see in their lives; will they benefit or will they be disadvantaged? Although your list is likely to be different from mine, it will no doubt include many of the following:

1 Local residents
2 The owners of local shops, cafes and restaurants
3 Local people looking for work
4 The management, shareholders and staff of the superstore
5 Local council officials
6 Elected representatives on the local council
7 National and local pressure groups
8 The local representative in Parliament
9 Central government ministers
10 Departmental officials in central government

Levels

On their own, each of these is quite likely to produce a wealth of interesting ideas to pursue as you search the literature for a stand-alone review or to lay the foundations for your own research in a dissertation or thesis. But for this exercise, just take one to explore on the three levels:

The owners of local shops, cafes and restaurants

1 Physical

1.1. They will regret the loss of the unique character of the town centre as shops, cafes and restaurants that have been serving the public for many years are forced to close as a result of fewer numbers shopping there, while the high street and public areas begin to show signs of neglect with empty, boarded-up shops and graffiti.

1.2.   Along with other local people, they will fear that local roads will become more congested and dangerous with higher levels of noise and air pollution as the superstore attracts shoppers from a wide area and heavy lorries make frequent deliveries.

1.3.   Many local people will also worry that the superstore will spoil the local countryside with a huge development, large parking areas and new feeder roads built just outside the town.

2 Individual

2.1.   Many of the owners of shops, cafes and restaurants will fear that they will have to close as people do more of their shopping at the superstore, where prices will be much lower.

2.2.   Given the long hours that most owners have to work, it will no longer be so convenient for them to do their own family shopping. With high street shops closing, they cannot just buy what they need when they have a moment. Instead, they will have to get into their cars after work to go shopping at the superstore.

2.3.   On the other hand, like other local people, they will benefit from lower prices at the superstore.

3 Social

3.1.   They will all no doubt be saddened by the loss of the sense of community in the high street, where everyone meets their neighbours as they shop, have lunch and enjoy coffee together.

3.2.   Along with other local people, they might feel that decisions are being made over which they have very little influence, reflecting more the views of local government officials, central government and the interests of the management and shareholders of the superstore.

3.3.   On the other hand, the local council's income is likely to benefit from the high local taxes that will be paid by the superstore. As a result, local people might expect new investment that will improve local community facilities, like schools, medical facilities, libraries and community centres.

Possible research projects

From this single perspective, you can probably already see very interesting ideas of your own that could form the subject of a stand-alone review or provide the basis of a research project.

The planning decision   EXAMPLE

You might want to write a stand-alone review to see what the local planning authority should take into account in coming to their decision. To do this, you could search the literature for studies that have been undertaken into the effects of superstores on local people, particularly the owners of local businesses, cafes and restaurants: factors like the impact on town centres, increased traffic flow and congestion, levels of noise and air pollution, and the level of new investment in local facilities as a result of the council's increased income from taxes.

Commercial interests of local businesses   EXAMPLE

As a topic for your own research, you may want to know what measures have been taken in similar cases by local authorities and central government to compensate the owners of businesses, cafes and restaurants in the centre of towns affected in this way, and what measures have been taken to protect the integrity, heritage and uniqueness of town centres and public spaces.

Representing local opinion   EXAMPLE

You may want to know what means of representation local people and the owners of shops, cafes and restaurants have when these decisions are made. What influence was exerted by councillors, local members of parliament and pressure groups on their behalf? In how many cases did the decision go the way of the company, despite local opinion? Was there an appeals procedure and in how many cases was it successful?

As you can see, in this systematic way it is possible to generate a whole range of interesting ideas that you would not otherwise have realised were there, which could be developed into fascinating projects. And within each one you can see that there are three or four interesting sub-questions that will direct your search of the literature and, if your review is for a dissertation or thesis, drive your research.

Sustainability and biodiversity   EXERCISE

Take the following problem and generate your ideas as to what can be done about it. First compile a list of ten trigger questions, then list the perspectives of all those that affect and are affected by it and, finally, as we have done in the example above, take one of the trigger questions and generate your ideas from one of the perspectives on each of the three levels.

The world population has doubled over the last 50 years and now stands at eight billion people. This places unprecedented strain on renewable and sustainable resources. We are harvesting trees faster than they can regrow, depleting fish stocks faster than they can restock, taking nutrients from the soil faster than they can be replenished and emitting CO_2 into the atmosphere faster than nature can absorb it. The planet's life support system – its soil, clean drinking water and clean air – are under threat, while the decline of biodiversity through intensive use of pesticides and habitat loss has had a devastating cost on pollinating insects and oxygen-producing plants, threatening to erode our ability to provide food, water and security for billions of people.

For much of the time, our thinking is trapped in orthodox patterns and expectations. To generate new ideas we need a different style of thinking, one that is open, divergent and unconstrained. Using trigger questions, perspectives and levels, we can learn to think divergently and generate more of our own ideas.

You can download copies of the tables in this chapter, along with additional exercises, from the companion website (www.macmillanihe.com/greetham-literature-review).

Summary

1 Every new idea has the appearance of being silly foolish.
2 A genius is someone who asks questions nobody else asks.
3 Using a set of routine questions we can find that one in 10 billion possible solutions.
4 Don't waste the rich insights the mind throws up, they rarely come again.
5 In trigger questions, perspectives and levels there is a powerful ideas generator.

What next?

Having worked through these steps and generated your ideas you should now have three or four possible topics and within each one a number of sub-questions you want to answer; issues you want to explore. In the next chapter, we will explore the literature to see what we can find that will sharpen up our project.

Notes

1 A.N. Whitehead, *Science and the Modern World* (Cambridge: Cambridge University Press, 1926), p. 60.
2 Boris Starling. *Visibility* (London: Harper, 2007), p. 14.

Chapter 5

Finding a Research Question

In this chapter, you will learn…

- the importance of a clear research question to your search;
- that we need to be clear about the ontological and epistemological assumptions that underpin the question;
- how to translate abstract concepts into terms that indicate the concrete evidence we need;
- how to choose a title that seals the clarity of our thinking;
- how to search for treasure and map out the territory.

Now that you have a clear idea of the topic of your literature search, the next step is to find a question within it that will give focus and direction to your reading and thinking; that will guide you as you collect, structure and analyse your ideas. The clearer you are the more relevant and usable will be the material you collect. If you allow the question to remain vague, you will run the risk of producing a review that lacks focus and cohesion. So make sure your question forces you to concentrate on something specific: a question you want answers to or a comparison that you've drawn between authors, theories or arguments.

Finding an argument

However, this doesn't mean you start out with an opinion, a question to which you think you already have the answer. If this were the case, we would all learn very little from your work. The problem is that students are often told they must have an argument, which seems to suggest that you must already have made up your mind before you then start searching for the evidence to support it.

The problem and the question it raises must come first. It must lay out a thesis, what's more familiarly known in the humanities as a 'general proposition', out of which we develop a hypothesis or a research question that we can test. This is provisional: the results could go either way. Your thesis should raise a question that can be tested and is falsifiable at least in principle.

Topic ——→Thesis/ ————————→Hypothesis/ ————→Test
　　　　　　General proposition　　Research question

The research question

Your research question or hypothesis drives your search: it defines your purpose. You may be evaluating a text; testing a theory or a model; evaluating a proposal, a policy or a technique; comparing and tracing similarities between texts, artists, writers and movements in thought; or finding the solution to a problem. Whichever it is, your research question will bring into play the literature you're searching for and, if your review is for a thesis or dissertation, the types of research methods you will use. So it is important to spend time thinking carefully about the issues that underlie and shape your question.

1 Ontological assumptions

As we frame our question, there are two things we need to be clear about. The first is what we think exists, what in our view are the important elements of the situation or problem we want to research. These are the ontological assumptions at the heart of our research. If you were undertaking a historical or social science project, they would amount to those assumptions you make about the nature of the social and political reality you're investigating: how it's made up and how its parts interact.

Superstore – representing local opinion   EXAMPLE

In this project, we would have to map out all of those influences that have a bearing on the planning process and how they are likely to interact: local opinion; the owners of shops, cafes and restaurants; councillors; local members of parliament; pressure groups, both local and national, those in favour and those against; and then, of course, there is the management and shareholders of the corporation that will own and run the superstore, the firms involved in the construction and the haulage companies that will supply the new superstore.

The problem is that we all have contrasting ways of understanding the reality of what we are researching, whether it's about how societies are made up or how we interpret the meaning of language, literature or social customs. Each way is shaped by our experiences of the world, which we bring to the research process. If we take this for granted, we may find ourselves making assumptions we would rather not have made.

Ontological assumptions

1 What is the nature of the reality we're investigating?
2 How is it made up?
3 How do its parts interact?

You might see society as the product of continual conflict between social classes or as a loose collection of isolated individuals. Either way will define what you think are the important aspects of the situation and, in turn, influence your research question and the literature you choose to review.

- Our experience influences our understanding of the research problem and the literature we choose to review.
- Take nothing for granted – examine your assumptions carefully.

2 Epistemological assumptions

The second thing we need to pin down is our epistemological assumptions about what we believe should count as knowledge in this context: the sort of evidence that would count as an answer to our question and how we are to come by it.

Epistemological assumptions

1 The sort of evidence that would count as an answer.
2 How we are to find it.

As you frame your question, ask yourself, 'What sort of problem is this and what sort of evidence will I need to gather to answer it?' The answer may lie in the contrasting interpretations of documents or literary texts; in the different levels of an organisation out of which policy emerges; or on the interaction of individuals, which might call for an empathetic approach to understand the choices they have made.

Superstore – representing local opinion   EXAMPLE

In this project, it is natural to assume that the problem is largely an organisational and institutional one, concerned with the procedures that must be worked through before a decision is reached. But it may also depend upon empathetic evidence of how those involved interact to come to a decision. Local councillors and members of parliament will fear for their re-election if they fail to empathise and take into account the fears of the local community and the owners of shops, cafes and restaurants. Similarly, how closely do the commercial interests and pressure groups interact with councillors and officials?

As you can see, these epistemological questions will determine how you frame your research question, which will, in turn, determine the literature you review and the methods you employ. It is not the literature or the methods that shape the sort of questions we can ask, but the reverse.

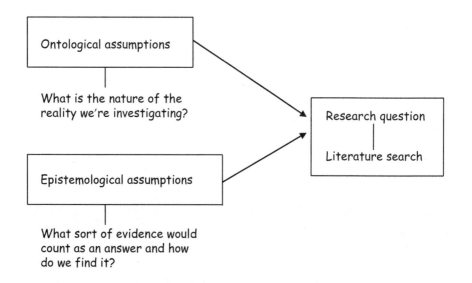

Outline the ontological and epistemological assumptions that underpin your research question.

Knowing what to look for in the literature

This largely explains what we want to find in the literature. But there is one other problem we need to resolve: how to translate the abstract concepts in our thesis into terms that indicate the concrete evidence we need to look for in the studies we review. Whether ours is a stand-alone review or is for a dissertation or thesis, this is the sort of concrete evidence that will ultimately confirm or falsify our thesis.

For example, our thesis or general proposition might be:

> The French Revolution was not a bourgeois revolution, but a revolt within the traditional ruling class.

From this, we can draw the research proposal or hypothesis, which, as the name implies, is the conditional form of the thesis, expressed in its characteristic 'If, then' form: 'If A, then B, C and D'. This is our 'What if' proposition:

> 'What if the French Revolution was not a bourgeois revolution?'

As you can see, from the hypothesis we can draw consequences ('... then B, C and D'), which we can test and find evidence for, which will, in turn, determine the sort of literature we want to review.

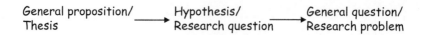

General proposition/   Hypothesis/   General question/
Thesis   Research question   Research problem

In practical terms, the hypothesis translates into a general question, which breaks down into sub-questions. Using these, we can apply the abstract concepts in the thesis or general proposition to the concrete evidence that we need in order to show whether the claim we've made is true or not. In turn, it shows us how to recognise the sort of literature we need to review. In Chapters 10 and 11, you will learn a simple method of analysing these concepts.

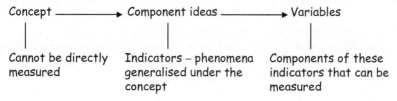

Concept ⟶ Component ideas ⟶ Variables

| | | |
Cannot be directly measured | Indicators – phenomena generalised under the concept | Components of these indicators that can be measured

So, from our thesis or general proposition above, we can derive the following general and sub-questions:

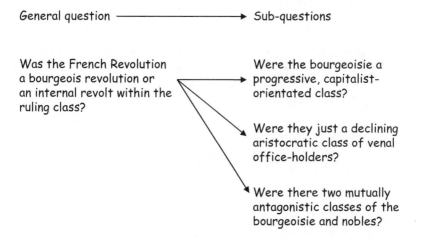

General question ⟶ Sub-questions

Was the French Revolution a bourgeois revolution or an internal revolt within the ruling class?

Were the bourgeoisie a progressive, capitalist-orientated class?

Were they just a declining aristocratic class of venal office-holders?

Were there two mutually antagonistic classes of the bourgeoisie and nobles?

Armed with these, we can go on to decide what variables we're going to use to assess whether the bourgeoisie were 'progressive' and 'capitalist-orientated' or a 'declining aristocratic class of venal office holders', which will, in turn, determine the sort of literature we want to review.

Variables   EXAMPLE

If they were a capitalist class, we might expect to see growing demand for economic reforms that would bring about a capitalist economy, reforms like free trade, laissez-faire policies and the removal of government restrictions on free enterprise. To confirm the opposite, that they were an aristocratic class, we could look for evidence of a growing demand for access to aristocratic sources of income.

An iterative process

Nevertheless, there is one qualification to this: research can appear a more complex process, in which questions more often than not change as a result of your search. It is an iterative process in which the more you learn the more you are able to reshape your question to answer aspects of the problem you hadn't seen when you first devised it. There is a constant interplay between the material and your interpretation of it. What started off as a simple proposition of what you thought you might find becomes more developed and nuanced as your understanding deepens and develops.

This means that you have to be conscious of the changing nature of your question and clarify it to give clear direction to your work. Analyse your assumptions to ensure that there are no inherent contradictions and pin down clear sub-questions. In this form it will chart a clearer course through the literature. Otherwise, you are likely to find that much of what you have included in your review will have to be dumped.

Searching the literature

The title

Now that you've thought your way through these issues, it's time to give your project a title. This will seal the clarity of your thinking, so that each time you read it you will be reminded of this. But it needs to be direct and succinct. The most common problem is choosing a title that is too broad.

The ban on smoking in public	**EXAMPLE**
A title like this is likely to produce thousands of documents, even if you were to limit it to scholarly articles.	

Although your title is quite likely to change as you begin to read your sources, think about how you could reasonably limit the breadth of your search. In this case, you could restrict it to pubs and restaurants and, perhaps, to a particular geographical area, a town or city. As you think of a title, keep the following things in mind. A good question should:

1 Be clear;
2 Be narrow;
3 Assume the possibility of different outcomes;
4 Be testable, at least in principle;
5 Contain no ambiguous terms;
6 Take no assumptions for granted.

Now we can turn to the literature. But first, we have to be clear about what we're trying to do; otherwise, we could get too involved in what we're reading. Without clearly defined aims to guide you through the material, you can spend too much time reading things too deeply at this stage. So, keep at the front of your mind two key objectives.

Treasure hunting

Obviously, our first concern is to see what's in the literature that might be useful: we're treasure hunting. Whether your review is laying the foundations for your own research in a dissertation or thesis or is a stand-alone review, you're looking for all those studies that appear to meet:

- the ontological conditions: does the study deal with the elements of the problem that you consider to be the most important;
- the epistemological conditions: in its analysis, does it measure those factors that are essential to answer your research question;
- the evidential conditions: does it have the concrete evidence you need to look for that will translate the abstract concepts in your research question?

In effect, you're looking for anything that you think may be useful – articles, conference papers, books, chapters, websites and theses, anything that you think might be worth reading later. You're not reading it word for word at this stage; that can be done later. You're just scanning it (Chapter 15) as you look for material that might be worth reading in more depth later. Systematically explore the literature, listing titles and where they can be found.

You're scanning the material for ideas and information that might be relevant to your review. How was the study designed? What methods did it use? Can you use these methods yourself in your own study? How was the population sampled and the results analysed? How did the researcher present her findings, set out her arguments and draw her conclusions?

Look for

1 Ideas
2 Information
3 Methods – gathering and analysing evidence
4 Presentation of findings
5 Development of arguments
6 How conclusions are drawn

Unfortunately, this is not always an easy thing to do. You're trying to cover a wide area, but with a sense of proportion as you try to keep at the front of your mind the relative importance of what you're reading to your topic as a whole. Without realising it, you can easily be drawn into reading in depth material which may only be peripheral to the issues raised by your topic. To safeguard against this, constantly remind yourself that all you're aiming to do is just assess how useful each item could be.

Remind yourself...

... you're only assessing how useful each item could be.

Mapping out the territory

As well as seeing what you can find that might be useful, your second concern is to map out the territory: to get as clear an impression as you can of the overall context in which your topic is set. The best place to start is with recent volumes of journals, which will have new articles, up-to-date references and reviews of the most recent books that might be relevant to your topic. In particular, use electronic journals, which you can more easily search for material that is most relevant to your study. But at the same time, don't ignore the classic texts in your subject that you might find useful to lay out the central theories that underpin your study.

Eventually, there will come a point when you realise that you have a good grasp of the territory and you can begin reading in more depth. When this occurs, compile a list of your sources and decide how important each one is. Then, start reading the three or four most crucial texts first. This is the best way to get to the heart of something, even though in the end these texts may not be as important as you first thought.

Mapping

1 The context – current issues;
2 Up-to-date references;
3 Classic texts;
4 List of sources;
5 Start reading crucial texts.

However, the one problem we all have to deal with as we read around our subject in this way is that we begin to see all sorts of connections with ideas and related issues that open up new ways of developing our ideas. Obviously, you don't want to lose these ideas, but at the same time you need to have some sort of control over a situation that can quickly become complex and confusing. So, as you read:

1 start mapping out the territory visually in general terms using pattern notes (Chapter 16);
2 then, once you have finished with a source, make brief notes on an index card or in a computer file recording why you think it was useful and how you could use it again. You don't have to write a great deal, just two or three sentences.

There should be at the front of your mind three questions that you want answers to:

1 What has been done before?
2 What information is available?
3 What gaps are there in the research?

1. What has been done before?

Read literature reviews in your area to get an idea of the themes that dominate your topic and ways in which reviews are organised. Are there topics that are neglected? What are the dominant trends? Is there a heated debate in the area? What methodologies are used? Are there common concepts used to identify, define and explain a phenomenon? What are the core ontological and epistemological assumptions that underpin the work of researchers in this area? You're trying to map out the extent and range of the research.

Inevitably, as you work through your list of sources, you will find yourself putting the pieces together, synthesising it all into one complete map. You will see connections between one piece of research and another, and chains will begin to link a number of sources as you navigate your way through them. Map out the key concepts and themes that reappear in different studies. As you do this, try to see how your research will follow on from it. What can you add to it?

2. What information is available?

After you have been able to form a clear idea about how your topic could contribute to this, you will have to assess whether there's enough material available or, indeed, whether there's too much. If yours is a small, largely unexamined topic, it will not be difficult to cover it fairly comprehensively, but it will be more difficult to come up with relevant, useful sources. On the other hand, if you find there is already an extensive literature on the topic, it will be easier to find sufficient sources, but you will have more to review.

You will have the same problem as you try to develop a good grasp of the material. Where there is only a small body of literature that covers the topic, which might not go into great depth, it will be easier to understand, but you might find it more difficult to find ideas that are useful and interesting. On the other hand, in an area that has been well-developed, you will probably have no difficulty in finding plenty of ideas, but there will be more to review and it may be more difficult to find just the right niche.

3. What gaps are there in the research?

As you map out the territory, if you read the literature critically and inquisitively, you will be asking yourself, 'Has the writer missed something? Has she overlooked part of the problem?' This will reveal gaps in what we know that need to be filled.

Stand-alone reviews

In a stand-alone review, although you are not identifying gaps that will lay the foundations for your own research, your aim, nevertheless, is to see what the literature says about a particular problem and where effective research might be undertaken. This involves analysing and critically evaluating the literature as you search for gaps in the current research, so that you can give a clear picture of where further research is needed.

Reviews for dissertations and theses

In a review that is part of a dissertation or thesis, your aim is to find a gap into which your topic will fit neatly or can be adapted to fit. You may find that a researcher has investigated a phenomenon sufficiently similar to yours so that you can carry out a comparative study. If you note the characteristics of the problem or the features of the situation she chose to measure, you can do the same yourself. Alternatively, you might find that a researcher has used a strategy that you could use on a case study of your own. Obviously, the most convincing way of justifying your approach is to cite work that has already been done and to identify the gaps your work is filling.

Make sure ...

... as you map the territory, read inquisitively: has the writer overlooked anything?

Nevertheless, one word of caution: try to avoid wasting time getting locked into an overdeveloped theoretical position, which may ultimately prove irrelevant. You can easily get drawn into this. After all, this is what academic authors seem to do: they develop and set out their theories and then test them, only to find they were right all along.

However, this is the way the story of discovery is often told after the event. As the Nobel laureate Sir Peter Medawar says, it is how we like to appear before the public when the curtain goes up. It is not how new theories and ideas are discovered. This is an intensely iterative process. A provisional theory is put forward and tested, then re-worked in line with the results and tested again. This process continues until there is a tight fit between theory and results.

 You can download copies of the tables in this chapter from the companion website (www.macmillanihe.com/greetham-literature-review).

Summary

1 The research question drives your search: it defines your purpose.
2 Ontological assumptions define our view of the elements that constitute the research problem.
3 Epistemological assumptions reflect our belief as to the sort of evidence that should count as an answer.
4 Using sub-questions, we can apply abstract concepts to the concrete evidence we need.
5 This is an iterative process, so we need to avoid getting locked into an overdeveloped theoretical position.

What next?

Now that we have a clearer idea of our research question, we can begin our search for the literature that we will review. In the next chapter, you will learn the best way of doing this and the things to avoid.

Chapter 6

How to Search

In this chapter, you will learn...

> - the importance of a retrieval system to catch ideas whenever they appear;
> - how to make the most of the snowball effect and the evolutionary way in which our ideas develop;
> - the most useful sources to work through;
> - how to avoid the most common mistakes;
> - how to record your searches.

When you start your search, the enormity of the task ahead can seem quite overwhelming. However, most of the challenges this presents can be overcome with careful organisation. In this and the next chapter, you will learn the best way to organise your work and the simple steps you need to take to search conventional sources and the Internet. Then, in Chapter 14 you will learn how to organise your retrieval system to catch all those ideas that suddenly appear whenever and wherever this occurs.

Retrieval system

Despite all our careful and systematic organisation, we can easily overlook those things that occur unplanned: ideas that seem to come out of nothing and in situations we least expect it. The more you're prepared to see, the more you will see. For this reason, we need to spend some time organising our retrieval system so that we register and note our ideas.

> The more you're prepared to see, the more you will see.

1 Impromptu moments

You may be talking to a friend at university or to a delegate at a conference. They may have little experience of your subject or with the problem you're researching, but they may suggest a way of approaching it that to them may be ordinary and predictable, but to you is novel and insightful. Similarly, good ideas or connections between them can come while you're doing unplanned things, like browsing along library shelves.

You might find sources that approach your project from a different direction or tackle it in a different way.

2 While you're searching

All of these ideas are likely to be invaluable, so we need to organise our work to make the best use of them. The same applies to those insightful sessions in the library when we come across unexpected ideas in an article that open up new ways of developing our thinking. Instead of filing them under things to do and putting it off until later, follow it up immediately. Although you're only skimming at this stage, take brief notes as you go. One idea will pick up and connect with another and quickly snowball into something significant as they make more connections with ideas you might otherwise have disregarded.

The snowball effect

Our thinking during research for the most part develops in an evolutionary way. As we read, our focus begins to change: we come across repeated references to ideas, arguments and authors, which we follow up with new keyword searches. This is often described as the 'snowball effect'.

Snowball effect   DEFINITION

> A process in which an insignificant idea or reference builds upon itself into something larger and more significant.

Many electronic databases and journals help you do this not only by following up references to previous work, but by tracking forward. If you come across a useful article, you can find others published afterwards that refer to it. In this way your research becomes more focused on those ideas you've found to be central to your work.

Reference searching   DEFINITION

> You can search forward either by reference to a particular author and his or her works or by citation to gather information about who cited a particular reference and where. You can do this through Google Scholar or ISI Citation Index to find those papers that have cited those you have found most useful. You can also search backward for those articles and books that have made a significant impact in your field.

And it's worth remembering that your searches will continue throughout the project as you come across a new idea, which you will have to search for to see if it's original or if others have come up with similar ideas. You may want to check to see if others have experienced the same problem that you're having or have found the same effects with a particular research method. So, as we'll see, it's vital to keep a record of all the searches and each of the steps you've taken in them.

Sources

The following is a fairly comprehensive list of the kind of sources you will find useful. It gives you a checklist of sources that you can work through.

1 Books

1.1 Textbooks – these are important to lay the groundwork of the core assumptions, theories and concepts in your topic.
1.2 Specialised books – these include chapters or articles on a particular topic. Included in this are papers from conferences and reports of conference proceedings.
1.3 Reference books – dictionaries, encyclopaedias, directories, many of which are now in electronic form.

2 Journal articles

This is a valuable source of the most recent and up-to-date ideas in peer-reviewed articles. Most of them you can find in electronic form or by using Google Scholar or through interlibrary loans.

3 Published literature reviews

Not only do these evaluate literature in the field, but they also give you a long list of useful references. Of course, stand-alone reviews are useful here, but if you find a particularly useful textbook, it is always worth checking the range of sources they refer to in the reference list.

4 Grey literature

This includes a wide range of different types of sources not published commercially and not peer-reviewed, which were difficult to get hold of through books and bibliographies before the Internet.

- Reports by companies or government organisations – white papers, working papers and investigations into particular developments or events.
- Theses and dissertations now collected in electronic form, which you can locate through the British Library's Electronic Thesis Online Service (EThOS) and through Open Access Theses and Dissertations (OATD).
- Conference proceedings – including collections of abstracts and selected papers.
- Popular media – national and local newspapers and professional trade journals.
- Monographs and reports on work-in-progress.
- Specialist literature and sources of primary data, including maps, music, diaries, journals, original manuscripts, patents and legal documents: sources like the General

Household Survey; the thousands of audio recordings, diaries and journals of those who fought in the First World War held at the Imperial War Museum; and the population records compiled from parish registers.

5 Websites

In the next chapter, we will cover this in more detail, but for now it's worth noting the usefulness of the sites of professional organisations, governments and charities. These regularly publish press releases, policy documents, reports and other resources. In addition they also use social media, like Twitter and Facebook, along with blogs, podcasts, YouTube videos and other up-to-date information on current debates and issues.

6 Hand searching journals

However, you can never rely on searching websites and electronic literature to be completely comprehensive. There will always be articles that search terms fail to locate. So, sitting down with a collection of the most recent journals and scanning the contents pages and individual articles can be surprisingly useful. You're likely to find new ideas about how to approach your project, different comparisons you could draw and ways of analysing your material, different research methods and questions, even a different focus for your project.

Efficient searching

The problem we all struggle with is how to make the best use of our time as we set about our search. To avoid the worst mistakes, it helps to keep four things in mind:

1 Don't confuse the search with the review.
2 Be clear about what you're looking for.
3 Don't get bogged down.
4 Don't get diverted into irrelevant areas.

1 Don't confuse the search with the review

Although the first of these sounds obvious, as you work on what you're reading it's all too easy to find yourself producing a thorough review covering every source you read. This will soak up at least half the time you have available to complete the whole project.

2 Be clear about what you're looking for

The second point has almost the same propensity, as anyone who has ever searched the Internet will know. So be clear about what you're searching for and the keywords you'll use for it, particularly on the Internet. Translate your topic into core search terms and sit down with a blank piece of paper listing all the ways you can think of to express the same ideas. Then, think of the best ways of combining them.

To organise your thinking as you read, it helps to compile a list of questions you ask each article, like:

1   How does this fit in with what I have already read?
2   Is it central or peripheral?
3   If it is central, what are its key points?
4   What conclusions does it reach?
5   What significance does this have for my project?

3 Don't get bogged down

The same is true of this point. It's easy to get bogged down in too much searching initially, doing a great deal of work you later realise is unnecessary and unusable. You may then find you've left yourself short of time to devote to the other stages. You can always go back and read another source or two later on, which you can then add to your review, but you can never recover the time you have unwisely spent getting bogged down in too much detail too early.

> Avoid getting bogged down in too much searching initially.

4 Don't get diverted into irrelevant areas

In the same way, we can find ourselves gathering references that are not strictly relevant, but which we don't want to waste, so we include them whether they're relevant or not, even though they will detract from the clarity of our work. To avoid this, we need to set clear boundaries.

> **Social care**   EXAMPLE
>
> A study involving the efficiency of a council's social care service might involve reading literature on nursing, medicine, gerontology and other healthcare-related specialities, along with literature on psychology, sociology, patients' experiences of social care and social care policy. In all of this, you need to be able to set boundaries and decide where you can safely explain that you will refer briefly to a subject, but not go into great detail.

Overall, the simplest advice is not to be too ambitious and try to keep your work fairly focused and limited. There will be a centrifugal force at the heart of your project, urging you to go out further, to pursue ideas to see where they lead just in case they open up new and stunning insights. Although you must allow for this, try to keep it within reason.

The steps

To make this a more manageable task, work through the following four simple steps:

1   Search the library catalogues.
2   Check there's enough up-to-date material.

3 Search the Internet.

4 Check the reliability of your sources.

1 Search the library catalogues

Your first search will probably produce a great number of hits, so change your key-words to restrict your search parameters by setting narrower inclusion and exclusion criteria. If, however, you don't get many, either your keywords are too narrow and you need to use alternative synonyms, or you're aiming to undertake really ground-breaking research. Although this is to be applauded, you may struggle to find enough material to critically evaluate, analyse and synthesise into a viable project. Nevertheless, before you consider abandoning your project, work through the following steps:

1.1 As I've said above, try synonyms, similar words that stand for the same thing, like 'renewable resources', 'sustainability' and 'ecological balance'.

1.2 Try changing the spelling of keywords, particularly those like 'anaesthesia', for which there are different American and British spellings.

1.3 If you're still not getting many hits, find an article that deals with a similar topic and look at the terms used to describe it and use them yourself.

1.4 If that doesn't help, look at review articles that summarise the literature on your topic.

1.5 If there are no helpful review articles, start with the most recent issues of journals and look for studies about your topic, then find references at the end of the articles for more sources to examine.

1.6 Then look at conference papers, which often report the latest research developments.

1.7 And, if all that fails, contact authors of relevant studies and ask them if they know of studies that might be helpful to you. Most authors are very willing to help.

2 Check there's enough up-to-date material

Once you've got a list of titles, browse through them, checking that there's enough relevant, up-to-date material available. And look around the catalogue location number on the library shelves. There you will find books on your topic and, next to them, filed under adjacent numbers, others that deal with the same topic from a slightly different perspective.

Then, throughout your research, get into the habit of regularly browsing along the shelves again. Allow for the evolution of your ideas. New ideas and connections between them will become more important, so browsing in this way may highlight texts you've previously ignored. The same applies to journals: go back to the most relevant for your project and regularly check the articles in new editions.

Allow for the evolution of your ideas and check the shelves regularly.

Web updates

You can do the same sort of thing electronically by incorporating RSS (Really Simple Syndication) feeds and email alerts into your search to ensure you get the latest notifications of new updates on websites, journals, databases and from publishers about new publications. Similarly, you can use newsfeed readers, like Google reader, that will constantly check news sites, databases, blogs and journals and send you new content. The danger, of course, is that you might be overloaded with information, so you need to choose from these sources wisely.

Libraries and librarians

If you have problems, ask your librarians for help. They can usually give you guidance on the range of services they offer and even book a place for you on a training course to improve your searching skills. Subject-specific librarians can direct you to the most relevant databases and help you identify the keywords that will give you access to what you want. But prepare yourself with a list of specific questions to ask them. And give yourself plenty of time to get documents and books that may have to be ordered well in advance. University library web pages are also a source of valuable advice on how to access a wealth of resources, including catalogues and links all over the world.

- Look around catalogue location numbers.
- Regularly browse along the same shelves throughout your research.
- Check regularly for articles in new editions of the most relevant journals.
- Register for RSS feeds and email alerts for updates on websites and new publications.
- Ask for help from your librarians.
- Check university library web pages.

Keeping records

After you've consulted each source, record onto an index card or in a computer file the details you'll need later for citing, and note why the source was useful, so you always know how the information might help you and how it relates to the project. Try to make sure you handle each source only once, so you only have to use the card each time you want to enter the information into your review. The following is the sort of information it would be useful to record:

1 Citing details:

    1.1 For a book: author, title, place of publication, publisher, and date.

    1.2 For an article: author, title of the article, name of journal, volume and issue number, date and page numbers.

    1.3 For a website: author, title of the article, blog, etc., web address, domain name and when you last accessed it.

2 Type of publication (book, journal article, book review, conference paper, etc.).

3 Comments (reason for consulting it, sections, quotations you might use).

4 How you might use it.

Alternatively, you could enter the same details into a reference management software package, like RefWorks, EndNote or Zotero, an open source, free equivalent, which you can use to create a reference list. These allow you to import references and manually enter data. You can then access the information from any computer.

Recording your searches

You will also find it valuable to record the details of each search, so that you can repeat them regularly on the same sources to see if new material has been published that might be useful for your review. In addition to the details of the reference, record the date of your search, the keywords you used, along with the 'Boolean operators' (see Chapter 7, p. 71), and any other information that might be helpful. Use the flowchart below or one like it of your own design to record the details each time you search.

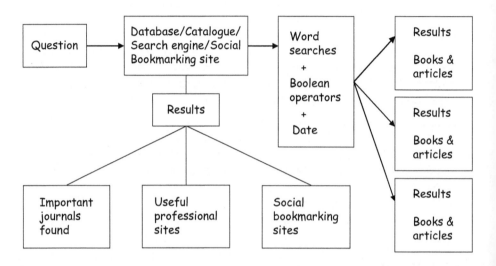

 You can download a copy of the flowchart and the checklists in this chapter from the companion website (www.macmillanihe.com/greetham-literature-review).

Summary

1 Organise your work to catch your most valuable insights whenever they occur.
2 Make sure you make the most of the evolutionary way in which your thinking develops.
3 To use your time efficiently, avoid the four worst mistakes in searching.
4 As your thinking develops, it's worthwhile regularly browsing along the library shelves and among the journals.
5 It's important to record the details of each source and each search.

What next?

Recording the details of your searches in this way will save you a lot of time and avoid numerous headaches. In the next chapter, we will examine the routine steps we need to take to search the Internet and check the reliability of our sources.

Chapter 7

Searching the Internet

In this chapter, you will learn...

- how to devise an organised and effective search strategy;
- how to use specialised databases and open access sources;
- how to access the advice of experts, organisations and societies interested in your project;
- how to find the right search parameters and Boolean operators to produce a wealth of relevant material;
- how to assess the reliability of your sources.

Although most of us have the skills to search the Internet, to avoid repetition and wasted time we need to devise an effective and organised strategy. A useful principle here is to work from the general to the specific.

1 General search engines

General search engines, like **Google** and **Yahoo**, are probably the most obvious places to start. But they both collect and present information in slightly different ways, so it is best to use both. Use a distinctive word or phrase that you think is most likely to locate relevant material and ideas, and put double quotation marks ("...") around it. If this produces too much material, use more than one word or phrase in quotation marks to narrow down the results. It also helps to use Boolean algebra search terms and logical operators (see page 71), such as AND, OR and NOT, to narrow down your search.

Google tools

There are three other Google tools that you will find useful. On **Google Scholar**, you can find not only journal articles, books, papers and reports, but also citations of books and a wide range of grey literature from academic sources.

Students in the humanities and social sciences will also find **Google Books** particularly useful. On here, you're able to read the full text of books out of copyright, which you can also search for specific sentences, terms and quotations. How much is accessible of books still in copyright will depend on the agreement they have reached with the publisher.

Once you've been able to narrow down the articles and books that are central to your search, look up the authors in **Google Scholar Citations**, a database of authors, where you can find out whether these authors have other publications on the same subject.

2 Specialised databases

In contrast, these are more narrowly targeted. They are collections of journal articles, conference papers and other material on particular subjects, which you can use to search for ideas. Some have a direct link to the full text of the journal article, although most only provide the full bibliographical reference and an abstract. Among these databases you'll find indexes to journals, official publications and reports. These include indexes such as:

- the Philosopher's Index;
- the Business Periodicals Index;
- the General Science Index;
- Index to Theses – UK theses;
- EThOS – British Library's Electronic Thesis Online Service.

If you search the most recent volumes of journals, you'll find new articles and reviews of recent books, which you might not otherwise have found. The abstracts of journal articles will help you identify those that you think will be the most relevant, which you can then read later in full. If you know the specialised database that covers the subject you are researching, it will save you time and yield a lot of reliable, up-to-date information. If you log on through your library web page, you'll no doubt find there is a wide range of databases available.

3 Open access sources

As the name implies, these give you free, unrestricted access to academic work. They include archive sites that store the full version of articles, chapters and papers, open access journals, leading blogs and alerting systems that will inform you when another researcher that you're interested in deposits new material. With their number increasing all the time, their coverage is wide. There are now also Twitter and Facebook streams linked to blogs or based on open access databases, and social networking sites, like ResearchGate, where scientists and researchers can share papers, find collaborators and ask questions.

Open access sources	EXAMPLES

Directory of Open Access Journals (DOAJ) – an online directory that gives full access to the text of articles listed

PubMed – a database of references and abstracts on health and medical science

Online Public Access Catalogues (OPACs), such as COPAC – this gives you bibliographical details and locations of all the publications held in a particular library

ProQuest – a multidisciplinary, full-text database

Scopus – an abstract and citation database of journals in medical science, social science and natural science

EBSCO – this covers the full range of academic subjects

4 University libraries

At this point, if you need further help, it's worth consulting your university library. Most have lists devoted to particular subject areas, listing the most useful search engines, sites, databases and Internet gateways and portals. One of the most useful is COPAC (Consortium of Online Public Access Catalogues), which covers a growing list of research libraries in the UK and Ireland, so that you can conduct a wide search. Others include:

- Library of Congress catalogue for the US;
- British Library Integrated Catalogue – here you can get full access to texts and papers and even set up RSS feeds and email alerts for up-to-date information on all sources that are added;
- BUBL Link – provides access to Internet resources linking universities around the world;
- Publishers' catalogues, like Macmillan and Sage.

5 Expert advice

Once you have exhausted these sources, think about doing simple common-sense things. You could contact experts in your field to ask them to assess your list of sources to see if you have omitted anything. You'll find this particularly useful if you suspect that you may have missed things that may not be publicly available.

There are likely to be organisations and societies that are interested in the topic of your search. There may be professional organisations or pressure groups whose members are affected by the issue you are researching.

The effects of the government's smoking ban on pubs and restaurants in the UK   EXAMPLE

If you were researching this topic, you would find pressure groups on both sides of the issue, some promoting the interests of pubs and restaurants, like 'Save Our Pubs and Clubs' and 'Bighospitality', others promoting the right to smoke, like 'Forest', and, on the other side, those promoting the health and the freedom of non-smokers, like 'Ash', 'Asthma', the 'British Heart Foundation', the 'BMA' and the 'Royal College of Physicians'.

From here, an obvious step is to check whether your topic might be the subject of a dedicated website. Your search might involve a particular writer, scientist or philosopher, a figure from history or a particular event in history. Is there a society devoted to it? Perhaps it has a forum where you could ask for help or links to people who run blogs?

Writers, scientists and philosophers   EXAMPLE

You will find societies with websites devoted to writers, like the Brontë sisters, Jane Austin and Charles Dickens, scientists, like Darwin and Einstein, and philosophers, like Jean-Paul Sartre, Bertrand Russell and Ludwig Wittgenstein.

Historical figures and events   EXAMPLE

Similar websites exist on major historical figures, like Churchill, Hitler, Stalin and Roosevelt, and events, like the Holocaust, the D-Day landing and the Watergate Affair. They all have societies dedicated to them, some more than one.

Many of these websites have blogs and forums on which you can post questions. They will also have useful links that you can follow. It's not unusual to find here the most unexpected and useful sources. If you find a page that looks particularly useful, you could email the author and ask questions. He or she may be able to point you to useful blogs or forums, where you will find contributors who have a lot of interesting ideas to contribute to your project.

Searching the Internet

1   General search engines
2   Specialised databases
3   Open access sources
4   University libraries
5   Expert advice

Search parameters

In the last chapter, we explored the simple, commonsense things to do as you search. There we emphasised the point that the quality of our results depends upon how well we break down our question into keywords and phrases that will generate relevant material when we use them in search engines. The more thought we invest in making sure that our search parameters are precise and as carefully targeted as we can make them, the more manageable will be the results.

Most libraries have Internet guides that will improve your skills in finding just the right parameters. But, as we discovered in the last chapter, there are simple things you can do to ensure that your search produces relevant material:

- Choose words that are distinctive in your research.
- If there are any technical terms in the question, use these – general terms are likely to produce too many pages, most of which will be irrelevant.
- If there are no technical terms, break the general words down into more specific narrower topics.
- If the words in your search question produce irrelevant or too few pages, think of synonyms that you can substitute for them.
- Check to see if there might be different ways of spelling your keywords.

Boolean operators

To make your searches more specific so they include only those sources you want, use Boolean logical operators – AND, OR and NOT:

- Combining two words using AND will produce articles that mention both words, but exclude those that only mention one.
- Using OR will widen your search, producing articles that mention both. This is useful when you have two search words with similar meanings.
- In contrast, using NOT will produce articles that contain the first word, but not the second.

There is also the useful wildcard symbol (*) that you can use to replace a letter in a word where there may be different spellings of the word or you want to search for different variations of it.

Wildcard symbol   **EXAMPLES**

P*diatric – will produce articles with both spellings: 'paediatric' and 'pediatric'
Generat* – this will produce articles with different forms of the word, not just 'generate', but 'generating', 'generation', etc.

How reliable are your sources?

So far, our concern has been with the relevance of our sources; now our attention must turn to their reliability. This is not so much of an issue when you're using a university library, where the books, journals and other material you consult have already been evaluated by a lecturer or librarian. But with Internet sources we need to work through the following seven questions.

1 What are the author's credentials? Is he or she well-respected in the field?

If you recognise the author from your studies – a book or a journal you have used before – then you have less of a problem. But if not,

- Is the author referred to by someone else you trust?
- Is the author mentioned on a website you know you can rely on?
- Does the document or the home page of the website on which it appears have biographical information, or is it linked to other documents that have? This should include the institution to which the author is affiliated and his or her position.
- Failing that, is there an email address you can use to ask these questions?
- Look the author up in Google, Yahoo and other search engines.

2 How accurate is the document?

- Does the author make clear the research methods used to gather and interpret the information?
- Check that the research methods used are the most effective for the topic.

- If you're writing a stand-alone review, or if the topic is part of the natural or social sciences, you will also want to know if it can be duplicated, so that you can verify the results.
- Does the document list the sources that it relies on? Are there links to them?
- If the document uses individuals or unpublished sources, does it name these?

3 How up-to-date is the document?

Although with some documents knowing the author's credentials and the accuracy of the document will have answered many of our doubts, for others it's equally important that we know how recently they have been updated. So check the following:

- Can you find a date on the document, or does it say when it was last updated?
- If not, check whether there are dates referred to in the text that may indicate how up-to-date it is.
- Is there a copyright notice at the end of the document? This is likely to include a date.
- If it has a bibliography, are the sources of its data listed and dated?

4 Who publishes it?

The problem with sources that we find on the Internet is that there is no third party that we can rely on that has checked their reliability. As we said earlier, when we borrow books or journals from a university library, we can be reassured that they have been evaluated by a lecturer or librarian. In addition, we know the publisher, who will have checked it carefully to ensure that it meets its standards of accuracy and reliability, most probably by peer-reviewing it. But on the Internet this is not so easy, so we have to ask certain questions about the site that hosts the document:

- On the page where the document appears, does it show the host or does it give a link to the home page?
- Does it show you how you can access the site administrator or is there a link to a page where you can get this sort of information?
- If there isn't, cut back the characters at the end of the URL until you reach the slash (/). Leave this in and press enter. This will give you information about the author and the site. If you continue to cut back the characters until you reach the first slash, this will give you the domain name: the page's server or publisher.
- See if you can tell whether the web page is part of the author's own personal website, rather than an official website? If it is an official site, is this an organisation that is recognised in your field? Can it be relied on to do this sort of research professionally?
- Can you tell whether the author is an employee of an organisation? If so, the article is probably the product of her professional work within the organisation, which gives you more reason to rely on it.

5 Can you detect bias?

Once you know the host, you can begin to ask the obvious questions about their impartiality.

- Can you tell whether this is an organisation with a political or commercial interest to promote?

- If there is nothing obvious on the page, click on 'About us', 'Our philosophy', 'Biography', 'Sponsors' and other pages that may say something about the host.
- Failing that, look at other articles on the site. These may give you a reliable indication of the sort of organisation this is and the views they are likely to promote.

6 Are there reliable signs of the quality of the document?

Having checked the author, the document and the publisher, you can now turn to the content of the document to see if there are reassuring signs that the arguments are well-supported by evidence, based on sound knowledge and are not one-sided.

- Is it well documented? Does it have a bibliography? Does it cite its sources? Does it have good links?
- Does it demonstrate a sound knowledge of the subject: its literature, theories and schools of thought?
- Is it one-sided in its treatment of the subject? Does it discuss the weaknesses as well as the strengths of the case it is presenting? Are the links to other sources biased?

7 What do others say about the page and the site?

There is a simple way of getting this sort of information:

- Copy the URL of the page into the search box on the site **alexa.com**, then click 'Get details'. Among other things this will show you the traffic on the site, information on who owns the domain name, other sites visited by those who visit this site and the sites that are linked to it.

How reliable are your sources?

1 What are the author's credentials? Is he or she well-respected in the field?
2 How accurate is the document?
3 How up-to-date is the document?
4 Who publishes it?
5 Can you detect bias?
6 Are there reliable signs of the quality of the document?
7 What do others say about the page and the site?

Reliability   EXERCISE

Take one of your sources and work through these seven steps checking its reliability.

 You can download copies of the tables in this chapter from the companion website (www.macmillanihe.com/greetham-literature-review).

Summary

1 To avoid wasted time and repetition, work from the general to the specific sources.
2 Use the specialised databases that cover your subject to save you time and yield a lot of reliable up-to-date information.
3 To check that you've not omitted anything, contact experts, organisations and societies interested in your topic.
4 The more precise your search parameters the more manageable will be the results.
5 To check the reliability of your sources, work through the seven questions.

What next?

Once you have worked through each of the stages described in this chapter, you will realise the value of having an organised method. Now, in Part 3, we can begin to process the ideas that you have found in your sources.

PART 3

Processing Ideas

Chapter 8

Critically Evaluating Your Sources 1: The Arguments

In this chapter, you will learn...

- the importance of learning how to process the ideas in depth;
- the difference between surface-level and deep-level processing;
- the common criticisms levelled at students' literature reviews;
- how to detect the undeclared assumptions in an author's arguments;
- how to check whether an author has created valid arguments.

Now that you have identified the sources that you will use in your review, it is time to process them more deeply. Part 3 is all about getting you to think more deeply about your sources. This demands patience and a willingness to read articles slowly, deliberating over the arguments. It is not the speed with which you process them but the depth that matters. Ultimately, the quality of the work we produce depends upon the quality of our internal processing of the ideas.

Surface-level processing

When we resort to just surface-level processing, we read our sources passively, without actively analysing and structuring what we read, and without critically evaluating the arguments, evidence and ideas the author presents. We tend to use just the lower cognitive abilities (see Chapter 2) to recall, comprehend and describe what we read.

Surface-level processing

1 Reading passively.
2 Without analysing and structuring what we read.
3 Without critically evaluating it.
4 Using just our lower cognitive abilities to recall, comprehend and describe.

Deep-level processing

In contrast, deep-level processing involves the use of our higher cognitive abilities to analyse, synthesise and critically evaluate the ideas and arguments authors present. In effect, as we read we discuss the author's ideas: analysing their implications, subjecting them to our own evaluation and, as our own ideas begin to take shape, we synthesise them into a form that reflects our own way of seeing and understanding the problem. From this, we begin to develop original ideas and insights.

Deep-level processing

1 Discussing the author's ideas as we read.
2 Analysing their implications.
3 Critically evaluating them.
4 Synthesising them into a form that reflects our own way of seeing and understanding the problem.

Common problems

Perhaps the most common criticism levelled at students' literature reviews is that they amount to little more than mere descriptions of sources without discussion of their weaknesses and strengths and how they compare. Arguments are described rather than analysed and evaluated. The findings of studies are accepted without critically evaluating their assumptions and the design of the study, and without analysing their results.

Reviewing the literature involves identifying limitations, deficiencies and gaps in the existing knowledge or practice that need to be addressed. If yours is a stand-alone review, your aim is not just to summarise the literature, but, more importantly, to evaluate current knowledge and identify where effective research might be undertaken. Similarly, if your review lays the foundations for your own research, the most significant part of your review lies in showing how your research will fill these gaps and bring different pieces of research together to form a new understanding of the problem. In this way, you develop a detailed justification of your own research strategy.

Autonomy and dependency: their influence on learning behaviour and study skills in the 16–19 age group   EXAMPLE

In this study, the researcher may have decided to examine the influence of teaching style to see if this promotes greater or less autonomy. So he interviews teachers and examines their lesson plans, in which there are long sessions devoted to discussion, which is likely to promote their autonomy.

But you suspect there is a methodological weakness in this strategy, which will throw doubt on the findings. To improve upon it in your own study, you decide you must test the evidence gained in this way by actually observing a lesson. When you do this, you suspect that you might find that much of the teacher's activity involves talking to his students and much of theirs involves quietly listening and noting, not discussion and developing the cognitive abilities that will help them become more autonomous. While the teacher might plan a lesson believing that at certain times students are doing one thing, in fact they are really doing something quite different. The perception fails to match the facts.

Critically evaluating the literature

As we discovered in the last chapter, the increased ease of access to a wider range of material makes it even more important that we critically evaluate what we read, particularly if we use this to lay the foundations of our own research. Our choice of material needs to be based on its reliability and relevance to our own project.

In this and the next chapter, you will be shown how to evaluate material not just on the basis of its accuracy, but on whether its arguments are valid, whether its evidence is atypical and incomplete, describing just one particular point of view, and whether the language it uses hides misleading, underlying assumptions. Authors may show bias in their selection of evidence. They may draw from it unreliable inferences, leaving room for different interpretations and valuations. These three types of mistake cover virtually all of the points of criticism you need to identify as you read the literature, so develop the habit of checking for them routinely.

- **Arguments** – are they valid?
- **Evidence** – is it atypical and incomplete – does the author draw unreliable inferences from it?
- **Language** – does it hide misleading, underlying assumptions?

Analysing and synthesising ideas

Once we have critically evaluated the literature, we need to analyse its implications and synthesise ideas to create a new way of looking at the problem. If yours is a stand-alone review, you want to reveal what the literature says about it and where effective research might be undertaken, whereas if your review is for a dissertation or thesis, you want to lay the foundations for your own research. Either way, as we analyse our material it will reveal new directions to go in as well as dead ends and false leads.

All of this calls for regular re-examination of our original proposition and the research question and sub-questions this gave rise to. There is a constant interplay between the material and our interpretation of it. What started off as a simple proposition of what you thought you might find becomes more developed and nuanced as your understanding deepens and develops. In Chapters 10, 11 and 12, you will learn how you can analyse the implications of concepts and arguments, and synthesise ideas from different sources to create a new way of looking at problems.

Arguments – are they valid?

In this chapter, you will learn how you can assess an author's arguments to see whether he has made any logical error that invalidates them. Without exception, we all make logical errors. We fail to apply elementary tests of logic to determine whether one idea does in fact lead to another. The first step in evaluating an argument is to check that all the components, the assumptions that the author makes, have been made clear. Then we can check that the connections between them are valid, that the conclusions the author draws from them follow from the reasons given.

1 Components – are there hidden assumptions in the argument?
2 Connections – do the conclusions follow from the reasons the author gives?

1 Components

We all take things for granted. It's not unusual for an author to be quite unaware that she has made an undeclared assumption or simply believe it's not worth making it clear because we know and agree with it. Of course, the arguments may still be valid, but we won't know that until we have revealed the assumptions.

Church attendance   EXAMPLE

You might read a claim like the following in the literature: 'The significant increase in church attendance in recent years shows that we are becoming a much more religious nation.'

As you can see, there is a hidden assumption here: that the only reason people attend is to celebrate their religion. In fact, there may be many reasons.

Hidden assumptions   EXERCISE

Read the following argument and ask yourself whether the author has made an undeclared assumption.

The new computer system will either deskill workers or make more of them unemployed. So there is a compelling reason why the bank should reverse its decision to introduce the technology to create a completely automated banking system.

Answer:

Without declaring it, the author has made the assumption that the effect on employees outweighs the other advantages that would result from the technology.

2 Connections

Now that we are confident all the assumptions have been revealed, we want to know whether the argument is valid: whether the conclusion does follow from the reasons given.

Check the qualifiers

The first thing we must do is check the qualifiers. Qualifiers are the words we use to indicate the strength of our claims, words like 'some', 'all', 'few', 'every' and 'never'. If an author claims that 'most' people agree about something, he cannot then conclude that 'all' people agree about it. In many cases, the mistake is made more difficult to spot because authors hide their qualifiers.

Drought and floods   EXAMPLE

A researcher might argue that instances of severe drought and floods are caused by global warming. He might then go on to claim that because the evidence shows a significant increase in atmospheric temperatures the recent floods in Bangladesh are caused by global warming. But he might have meant in his original claim that this is only true in 'some' cases, where in fact he has used this claim to mean it is true in all cases and, therefore, it must be true in the case of the floods in Bangladesh.

Distributing terms in an argument

Hidden qualifiers not only result in **exaggerated** conclusions, they also encourage authors to draw conclusions that are simply **not supported** by their arguments. If the hidden qualifier is 'some', rather than 'all', the terms of the argument are not 'distributed' in a way that would allow us to draw a conclusion. An author might assume they are distributed when they're not. To distribute a term means to refer to everything denoted by the term ('all' droughts and floods, not 'some'). If an author argues that:

'Young people want more concerted action against the sale of single-use plastics',

and then concludes:

'because Jayne is a young person she wants more concerted action against the sale of single-use plastics',

he has assumed that the hidden qualifier is a universal, like 'all', when it may in fact only be a partial qualifier, like 'some'. As only 'some' young people want this, Jayne might be one of those who don't want it or are not bothered. The best way of checking this is to get into the habit of asking the simple question, 'Is this a universal claim?'

Converting claims

When we convert our claims, we interchange the *subject* of the sentence with the *complement*. So if I say:

'No-one without a degree (subject) is a doctor (complement)',

I can also say:

'No doctor is without a degree.'

We assume that as long as we can argue 'All Xs are Ys' we can also argue 'All Ys are Xs'. But this doesn't work in all cases. The subject and the complement of certain propositions can be interchanged, but only if there is total exclusion between the two classes of things. If I say that no-one without a degree is a doctor, I can also say that no doctor is without a degree.

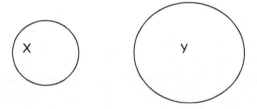

The same is true when there is partial inclusion. If you can argue that 'Some politicians are lawyers', you can also argue that 'Some lawyers are politicians.'

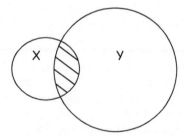

But where there's total inclusion, we cannot reverse it. We can't argue that given all statisticians are mathematicians, then all mathematicians are statisticians. This would be a case of illicit conversion.

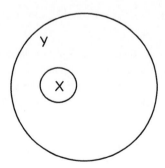

So, there are two principles to remember:

1 Total exclusion is a convertible relation, whereas total inclusion is not.
2 Partial inclusion is convertible too.

Affirming and denying

Finally, there is perhaps the most difficult of all mistakes to detect. This occurs when two ideas are connected in a hypothetical or conditional proposition, which has the distinctive 'If ... then' structure, as in:

> If an athlete is found to have taken performance-enhancing drugs, then he will be disqualified.

As you can see, this has two parts: the 'if' clause, known as the *antecedent*, and the 'then' clause, known as the *consequent*. In this case, it would be consistent to argue that:

> Stephen has been found to have taken performance-enhancing drugs; therefore, he will be disqualified.

In other words, it is consistent to **affirm the antecedent.** And, as you might expect, the opposite is also valid: it is consistent to **deny the consequent**. So we can argue,

> Stephen has not been disqualified; therefore, he has not been taking performance-enhancing drugs.

This gives us two quite simple rules: an argument is only valid if you *affirm the antecedent* or *deny the consequent*. As you read the literature, you can remind yourself of these by referring to the following simple table.

	Antecedent	Consequent
Valid	Affirm	Deny
Invalid	Deny	Affirm

Fallacies

In turn, this indicates the fallacies that we should prime ourselves to detect as we read the literature.

Invalid forms:

1 to deny the antecedent;
2 to affirm the consequent.

1. Denying the antecedent

To deny the antecedent means that our argument would take the following invalid form:

1 If an athlete is found to have taken performance-enhancing drugs, then he will be disqualified.
2 Stephen has not been found to have taken performance-enhancing drugs.
3 Therefore he will not be disqualified.

Clearly this is invalid. Stephen may not have been found to have taken performance-enhancing drugs, but this doesn't mean he will not be disqualified for cheating in other ways.

2. Affirming the consequent

This fallacy produces equally inconclusive and invalid results:

1 If an athlete is found to have taken performance-enhancing drugs, then he will be disqualified.
2 Stephen has been disqualified.
3 Therefore he has been found to have taken performance-enhancing drugs.

Again, Stephen could have been disqualified for many reasons; taking performance-enhancing drugs is just one of them.

Necessary and sufficient conditions

One of the reasons many of us make these mistakes is that in the proposition 'If X, then Y' we confuse the claim that X is a sufficient condition for Y with the claim that it is the *only* sufficient and necessary condition. If something is 'sufficient' and 'necessary' for the occurrence of something else, no other alternative reasons need be sought. If we were wrongly to assume this, we would in effect confuse the hypothetical 'If X, then Y' with the proposition 'If, and only if, X, then Y.'

In our example, we would in effect be arguing that 'If, and only if, an athlete is found to have taken performance-enhancing drugs, then he will be disqualified.' This means that no other reason will count as justification for his disqualification. So, if he is disqualified, it can only be because he has taken banned drugs.

Einstein   **EXERCISE**

Read the following argument, presented by a professional scientist to support Einstein's theory of general relativity. It seems perfectly plausible, but what's wrong with it?

If Einstein's theory is true, then light rays passing close to the sun are deflected. Careful experiment reveals that light rays passing close to the sun *are* deflected. Therefore Einstein's theory is true.

Answer:

If you set out the argument as we have in the example above, it looks like this:

1 If Einstein's theory is true, then light rays passing close to the sun are deflected.
2 Careful experiment reveals that light rays passing close to the sun *are* deflected.
3 Therefore Einstein's theory is true.

The fallacy committed is that the consequent has been affirmed. However, like Stephen's disqualification, the deflection of light rays may have been due to any number of reasons, not just Einstein's theories of special and general relativity. Of course, the argument could be made valid, but only if it was the sufficient and necessary condition for the deflection – that it was the *only* reason for it. However, for this to be the case we would have to argue instead, 'If, and only if, Einstein's theory is true, then light rays passing close to the sun are deflected.'

 You can download copies of the tables in this chapter and additional exercises from the companion website (www.macmillanihe.com/greetham-literature-review).

Summary

1 It is not the speed at which you process articles that matters, but the depth.
2 Reviewing the literature involves assessing whether arguments are valid, evidence is atypical and incomplete, and the language used hides misleading assumptions.
3 Once we have critically evaluated the literature, we need to analyse its implications and synthesise ideas into a new way of looking at the problem.
4 The first step in evaluating the literature is to check that the author has made clear all the components of the argument.
5 Then we need to check that the argument is valid: that the conclusion does in fact follow from the reasons given.

What next?

It's not difficult to remember most of these problems if we can organise a simple method to remind ourselves. At the end of the next chapter, you will find a complete checklist that you can copy and keep by your side as you process the literature. In the next chapter, we move on to look at the problems we need to keep in mind as we evaluate authors' use of evidence and language.

Chapter 9

Critically Evaluating Your Sources 2: The Evidence and Language

In this chapter, you will learn…

- how to identify when an author has not used enough reliable evidence;
- the most common mistakes in representing evidence in statistical form;
- the different ways in which authors draw unreliable and irrelevant inferences from evidence;
- how to check that the language authors use is clear and consistent.

In the last chapter, we examined the first of the three types of mistake that authors can make when they develop their arguments. Now, in this chapter, we move onto the other two: the evidence they use to support their arguments and the language they use to develop them.

Evidence

The last chapter was concerned with the validity of the arguments, whether the conclusions that are drawn are supported by the reasons given. In the first part of this chapter we are concerned with their truth:

1 Does the author have enough reliable evidence?
2 Does he represent the evidence accurately?
3 Does he draw reliable inferences from it?
4 Does he draw relevant inferences from it?

1 Does the author have enough reliable evidence?

Untypical examples and insufficient or weighted evidence

Regardless of who they are, most authors can, at times, find themselves generalising on the basis of untypical examples, or on insufficient or weighted evidence. It results from three fairly common errors, which we can identify by routinely asking three simple questions:

1 Is the generalisation based on a sufficient number of instances?
2 Do these instances represent a fair sample?

    2.1   Are they typical?

    2.2   Are there special conditions prevailing?

    2.3   Are there any exceptions?

  3 Does the probability of such a generalisation being true make it reasonable to believe it?

2 Does the author represent the evidence accurately?

Even then, when we have been able to answer each of these questions satisfactorily and found that there is enough reliable evidence, some authors still exaggerate or underestimate the evidence. Identifying this is not difficult, particularly when they use questionable qualifiers, as we discovered in the last chapter, or words, like 'typical', 'normal', or even 'average', when they don't specify the type of average: mean, median or mode. Resolving the imprecision of these words should be easy, particularly if they use statistics instead, but this can be just as misleading.

So, when an author presents his evidence, it helps to get into the habit of asking three simple questions:

  1 Are there **hidden factors** that need to be considered?

Breakfast cereal   EXAMPLE

In a recent advertising campaign, the makers of a popular breakfast cereal made the claim that 'Research shows that when they eat a cereal like ours kids are 9 per cent more alert.' To assess the reliability of this claim we need to know at least two things: the number of children involved in the study and any hidden assumption. In particular, we need to know whether this just means that if children eat a breakfast *at all*, of any sort, then they will not be falling asleep at their desks. Having eaten something their energy levels will be maintained so they can concentrate and perform better.

---

  2 Is there a **lack of uniformity** between different sets of statistics that are being compared?

  3 Are **absolute figures** being used in an argument to establish a comparison?

Departmental statements   EXAMPLE

When governments are criticised for failing to tackle a social problem, like homelessness, departments usually issue standard statements, like 'This year the government is spending an extra £100,000 on the problem.' But this is meaningless unless we know the size of the problem, the total budget and the extent to which it has failed to keep pace with inflation over previous years.

---

3 Does the author draw reliable inferences from it?

Once you have been able to satisfy yourself that there is enough reliable evidence and that it has been accurately represented, you can turn your attention to checking whether the author has drawn reliable inferences from it.

Analogies

The most natural way of drawing an inference from evidence is to find an analogy: a familiar thing that resembles in most respects what we are trying to explain, which we assume will continue to resemble it in some further respect, and this gives us our inference.

Sir Isaac Newton   EXAMPLE

Sir Isaac Newton used the analogy of billiard balls to explain the behaviour of light as molecules or particles. As billiard balls bounce off the cushions of billiard tables at different angles, so molecules were thought to refract at different angles as they hit the sides of a prism.

However, beware of authors who commit the **fallacy of analogy** by either ignoring the differences between the analogy and what they are explaining or by pushing similarities beyond what is reasonable.

Nuclear power   EXERCISE

Recently, an American politician defending nuclear power argued, 'We don't abandon highway systems because bridges and overpasses collapse during earthquakes.' This analogy is unreliable. Why?

Answer:

The weakness in this analogy lies in the depth and breadth of harm that a malfunctioning nuclear power plant can cause compared with the collapse of a bridge or an overpass. If a nuclear power plant goes into meltdown or releases nuclear radiation in whatever form, this can not only cause a large number of deaths, but result in long term illnesses, like cancer, and even genetic harm that can be passed on to future generations. In contrast, the collapse of a bridge or overpass results in fewer fatalities and casualties. You might also argue that in most cases with bridges and overpasses there is no alternative, whereas there are alternative methods of generating electricity.

The other thing to remember is that although analogies are remarkably effective in clarifying ideas, they can only *suggest* an inference, they cannot *establish* one. We can only safely argue from the possession of one set of characteristics to another if we can establish a causal connection between them and not just a vivid similarity.

Causal connection   EXAMPLE

A newspaper account of a speaker at a conference reported, 'He told the Conference last week that football hooliganism was exacerbated by press coverage. This was rather like blaming the Meteorological Office for bad weather.'

As you can see, the key difference is that the weather cannot be influenced by the Meteorological Office as football hooligans can by reading press reports of them and their behaviour.

So, when authors use an analogy to draw inferences, check three things:

1 The **connection** between the analogy and the inference:
   1.1 When does the connection break down? They all tend to at some point.
   1.2 Is there a causal connection: does the evidence show that one thing really does cause another?
2 The **numbers** involved:
   2.1 The number of examples between which the analogy holds – the more we have, the more confident we can be.
   2.2 The number and variety of the characteristics shared by the analogy and what it is being used to explain.
3 The **relation** between the analogy and the inference drawn from it:
   3.1 Is it the right strength or does it exaggerate the extent of the similarity?
   3.2 How significant are the similarities and differences between the analogy and what is being explained?

Oversimplifying

1 Stereotypes

All authors use stereotypes; some are justified, but many are not. So get used to questioning whether these are reliable generalisations about those who are the subject of these stereotypes. They are often just short cuts to avoid the difficult task of assessing the evidence thoughtfully.

Are these reliable generalisations or are they just short cuts?

Student protests over education cuts   **EXAMPLE**

In an article on student protests over education cuts, the writer uses stereotypes for certain groups involved. He describes a group as 'anarchists and professional agitators' and later describes the police, using another stereotype: 'the face of the Met was ugly, provocative and hostile'. It's reasonable to ask, 'How can he be sure of the beliefs of those he describes as 'anarchists and professional agitators' from their behaviour, and were all police officers 'ugly, provocative and hostile'?'

2 The straw man

To strengthen their arguments, some authors oversimplify their description of a situation or a proposition, either deliberately or accidentally, so that they can dismiss it as false.

Violent movies   EXAMPLE

Responding to the findings of forensic psychologists that violence seen on movies can make aggressive people more prone to violent crimes, one filmmaker responded,

> Does that mean that we mustn't have any villains in any film ever again?
> We must only have nice people doing nice things, because these already perverted and violent people, who should be in prison anyway, will identify with the villain? So we should only have films about flower-arranging?

3 Special pleading

Like the straw man, this, too, oversimplifies an argument, only this time by omitting those things that might weaken an author's argument, while emphasising those points that support it. Alternatively, an author might use an argument in one context, but refuse to use it in another where it would lead to an opposite conclusion.

If you suspect an author of either of these, test her claims:

1 Compare what she says with what she has said at other times.
2 Try to evaluate her **motivation** for making the argument. She might be paid to promote these opinions.
3 **Be specific** – for those arguments that omit relevant points and gloss over the omission using general, unspecific language, get into the habit of asking the author to be specific – the 'who', 'what', 'why' and 'how' questions:
   3.1 **Who** did the research? Who financed it?
   3.2 **What** does she mean by X? What numbers were involved in the study?
   3.3 **Why** should this be the only explanation? Why was the study undertaken?
   3.4 **How** was the research conducted?

Breakfast cereal   EXAMPLE

In the case of the advertisement for the breakfast cereal that we referred to earlier, we need to know:

1 **Who** did the research?
2 **What** numbers were involved?
3 **Why** should the same effect not be found with a breakfast of any type?
4 **How** was the children's alertness measured?

4 The fallacy of false dilemma

In this very common strategy, the argument is oversimplified in such a way that favours the conclusion the author wants you to draw. He encourages you to accept that the problem has an either/or solution; that there are just two solutions, when in fact there may be several. It forces you to accept a solution out of fear for the less desirable alternative. Many of the most obvious examples can be identified by the use of the word 'only'. So, whenever you see the word used in an argument, ask yourself whether these are indeed the 'only' alternatives.

Drug arrests   EXAMPLE

Recent research shows that in Britain black people are six times more likely to be arrested than white people for drug offences and 11 times more likely to be imprisoned. Responding to these findings, one academic argued that 'only decriminalisation of drug use would neuter such apparently discriminatory policies'.

This suggests that the only alternatives are either to accept the present unsatisfactory situation or to decriminalise drugs. But are these really the 'only' alternatives? Would better training or improved procedures help? The point is when writers use the word 'only', in almost all cases they are using a disjunctive to strengthen their argument.

Oversimplifying

1 Stereotypes
2 The straw man
3 Special pleading
4 The fallacy of false dilemma

Invalid causal inferences

You will often find that authors infer one thing causes another, when there is good evidence to suggest that it might not. There are three ways in which this commonly occurs:

1 the *post hoc* fallacy;
2 cause/correlation;
3 multiple and underlying causes.

1 The *post hoc* fallacy

More accurately, this is the *post hoc ergo propter hoc* ('After this, therefore because of this') fallacy. It is the mistake of assuming that just because an event follows another, it must be caused by it. When we see two things regularly occur together, one after the other, we're inclined to associate them as cause and effect.

Prayer   EXAMPLE

Someone might pray for something and then find that it happens. So they argue that it must have happened because they prayed for it.

2 Cause/correlation

A similar mistake occurs when we confuse a cause with a correlation.

> **Volcanic eruptions**   **EXAMPLE**
>
> During the period 1830–2013, relatively large changes in the speed at which the Earth rotated were immediately followed by an increase in the number of large volcanic eruptions. But is this just a mere correlation of two unconnected events or a causal relation?

3 Multiple and underlying causes

Situations are often more complex than we imagine. For most events, there are almost certainly many interrelated causes and not just one: the causes of the outbreak of the Second World War or the reasons for the increase in antisocial behaviour. A single cause is confirmed only if it *alone* can produce the effect. By contrast, in some circumstances, where there appear to be multiple factors operating, there may in fact be a single underlying cause explaining them all. So ask yourself:

3.1   Could this alone cause the effect?

3.2   Is there one underlying cause that explains all these effects?

4 Does the author draw relevant inferences from the evidence?

Eager to defend their point of view, some authors shift attention away from weaknesses in their argument by proving another that is irrelevant. As you read, check for the following:

1 Attacking the person (the *ad hominem* argument)

The weaknesses in the argument are sidestepped by discrediting the person who drew attention to them.

2 Popularity (the *ad populum* argument)

Some bolster their argument by appealing to popular opinion on the assumption that whatever the crowd thinks must be right. So, beware of those who make these appeals by starting a sentence with phrases, like 'As we all know' or 'It's common knowledge that'.

3 Authority

This diverts attention away from criticism by appealing to an authority. So get into the habit of asking these simple questions:

3.1   Does the authority know what she's talking about?

3.2   Are her views based on careful study or extensive experience?

3.3   Does her position offer her greater authority than others?

3.4   Has she shown herself to be a better observer and a shrewder judge than the rest of us?

3.5   What are her motives? Is she promoting her own self-interest?

4 Fear

Rather than show you that his argument can be trusted, an author might try to raise your fears about the consequences of accepting his opponent's argument.

5 Compromise

Alternatively, an author might get you to accept an argument on the basis that it is the most 'reasonable' compromise between two undesirable extremes. Almost any argument can be presented as a compromise between two others, so this alone doesn't mean there is good reason to accept it. And, of course, the truth is just as likely to lie on one of the extremes as in the middle.

Language

Writing is the most difficult, yet most effective, form of thinking. The effort of giving our ideas form in words and sentences crystallizes them, giving them clarity and consistency. But not all academic writers meet this standard, so get used to asking,

1   Is the author's meaning clear?
2   Does she use words consistently?

1 Is the author's meaning clear?

Jargon

There is no better way of revealing the confusion in our thinking than by writing down our ideas. The most effective way of concealing it is to resort to jargon. This is the language of specialists who have convinced themselves that their ideas cannot be expressed in any other way.

> The most effective way of concealing confusion in our thinking is to resort to jargon.

When authors use jargon, their aim is to import ideas into their writing without having to argue for them. Rather than reflect upon them, we are encouraged to move on, driven by our concern that we should know what all this means. But don't be fooled into thinking this is your fault. Train yourself to be a jargon buster. Where you don't understand something, demand to know what this means precisely. As you read, convert the jargon into concrete words that ground the ideas in everyday reality. Nothing short of that will do. If this is not possible, then it is meaningless.

Try this ...

Try your own jargon-busting skills by translating the following into everyday language. I cannot give you a reliable answer, because there's simply too much room for doubt.

> While our efforts cannot be characterized as having had a profoundly strategic horizon, the methodology utilized to identify strategy statements was not sufficiently program orientated for implementation.

Loaded language

Many of the words we use and read are 'loaded'. This is not like jargon, such that we don't understand the meaning of them; rather, not all the meaning is being disclosed to us. Loaded language contains an emotional content or a value judgement, which manipulates our thinking without us being conscious of it. In this way an author can encourage us to accept her argument without us looking at it too closely.

Words like 'democracy' and 'freedom' have positive associations, while those like 'hardliner' and 'extremist' are negative. So, without having to argue her case too strenuously, an author can just describe her points using words like these and be confident that we will accept her conclusions. Therefore, get into the habit of asking whether a word is loaded and, where you suspect that it is, translate it into neutral terms so you can see whether the argument is then so convincing.

> Translate them into neutral terms. Is the argument still convincing?

Begging the question

The other way authors manipulate our thinking is by begging the question, which occurs when they accept as an assumption what they are arguing for as a conclusion: in other words, they smuggle into their assumptions the conclusion they are about to deduce.

> ### A politician   EXAMPLE
>
> A politician might argue, 'You must admit that too much help for single parents is a bad thing,' or, 'You can't deny that giving students too much freedom in the classroom is not a good thing.'

And you cannot avoid agreeing, not because giving help to single parents or freedom to students is in principle a bad thing, but simply because of the phrase 'too much', which means 'a quantity so great that it is a bad thing'. We are presented with a mere tautology, nothing more significant than 'X is X', which is trivially true. Too much of anything is a bad thing, so the real point at issue is what do we mean by too much freedom or too much help?

2 Does the author use words consistently?

However, clarity on its own is not enough: once an author has made clear what he means by a word, he must stick to it. Often the most difficult errors to identify are the result of authors using words inconsistently.

The fallacy of equivocation

The most common form of this is known as the **fallacy of equivocation**, where an author uses a word to mean one thing in one part of the argument and something else in another part. So the argument still looks valid, but the meaning has changed.

> ### Australian commercial   EXAMPLE
>
> An Australian advertisement promoting concern for the environment has the presenter surrounded by people planting trees. He is clutching a handful of soil, which he allows to fall gradually through his fingers, while he tells us that those who fought for this (holding up the soil), their land, in the two world wars would be deeply disappointed by our generation, if we fail to protect it.

The aim of those who wrote the commercial was to exploit our inattention in not seeing that there is a difference between the 'Land' that was fought for, and the 'land' as in soil. By 'Land' we mean our culture, values and heritage, indeed our whole way of life, which might be threatened by an invader. This is quite different from the soil in which we plant crops. Clearly the persuasiveness of the argument rests on the equivocation of the concept 'land', which means different things at different stages in the argument.

Advertising campaign   EXERCISE

Read the following argument and see if you can identify what's wrong with it. As citizens, we all have a patriotic duty to protect our country from attack from other countries. At this very moment we are under attack from foreign imports, so we have a duty to protect ourselves by buying home-produced products, like XXX, which is wholly owned by citizens of this country.

Answer:

The persuasiveness of this argument rests on the equivocation of the concept 'attack'. In the first sense it refers to military attack and our patriotic duty to defend the country. But in the second sense it refers to economic competition, which we accept as a normal part of foreign trade.

Checklist

For most of us, the problem is how to organise ourselves to check for these things routinely as we read. It will help if you can keep a copy of the following checklist by your side as you work.

1 Arguments
1.1   Are there hidden assumptions in the argument?
1.2   Does the conclusion follow from the reasons given?
Qualifiers
Distributing terms
Converting claims
Affirming and denying
2 Evidence
2.1   Does the author have enough reliable evidence? Untypical examples/insufficient or weighted evidence
2.2   Does he represent the evidence accurately? Statistics
2.3   Does he draw reliable inferences from it? Analogies
Oversimplifying (Stereotypes, Straw man, Special pleading, False dilemma)

	Invalid causal inferences (*Post hoc* fallacy, Cause/correlation, Multiple and underlying causes)
2.4	Are the inferences relevant? (Attacking the person, Popularity, Authority, Fear, Compromise)
3 Language	
3.1	Is the author's meaning clear? Jargon
	Loaded language
	Begging the question
3.2	Does she use words consistently? Equivocation

Nevertheless, this is a lot to look for as you read, so remind yourself what you're looking for before you start and then, after you have read the article, check through the list again. The more you do this the more you retain, until you don't have to remind yourself what's on the list at all. And, ultimately, of course, it will remind you what to avoid in your own writing, when you come to write your review.

 You can download copies of the table and the checklists in this chapter, along with additional exercises, from the companion website (www.macmillanihe.com/greetham-literature-review).

Summary

1. One of the most common problems is generalising on the basis of untypical examples and insufficient or weighted evidence.
2. To strengthen their arguments, authors oversimplify the evidence in four common ways.
3. Once they have presented the evidence, authors often draw inferences that are unreliable and irrelevant.
4. The most effective way of concealing confusion in our thinking is to resort to jargon.
5. Often the most difficult errors to identify are the result of authors using words inconsistently.

What next?

Now that we have completed the critical evaluation of our sources, we can move onto the second stage of processing them. Over the next two chapters, we will learn how to analyse the key concepts in the arguments we read, restructuring the patterns of ideas they represent to reveal in a stand-alone review where effective research might be undertaken, or to lay the foundations of our own research for a dissertation or thesis.

Chapter 10

Analysing Concepts 1: Finding Connections Between Ideas

In this chapter, you will learn...

- how to analyse and redesign the patterns represented by concepts to lay the foundations of further research;
- the power that concepts have to shape our thinking;
- that concepts are more than mere words that you enter into search engines;
- the difference between 'open' and 'closed' concepts;
- that original thinking comes from stepping outside of the routine thinking dictated by our concepts.

The quality of our thinking is determined not by the strength of our ideas, but by the significance of the connections we make between them. New connections produce new concepts that give us a new way of seeing the world. As Steve Jobs once said, 'Creativity is just connecting things.'

What are concepts?

Concepts are the source of all our understanding, our most effective means of interpreting experience and reducing the confusion of life. Through them, we create the understanding we need to shape our environment.

Concepts are general classifications or universals that we create from our experience of particular things. We group all those things that share particular characteristics under one idea or principle, giving us the ability to go beyond the particulars of our world and extend our understanding in ways that would otherwise be impossible, indeed, in the strict sense of the word, 'inconceivable'. The philosopher Bertrand Russell explains, 'Awareness of universals is called *conceiving*, and a universal of which we are aware is called a *concept*.'[1] Each time we use them, we bring our understanding gained from past experience to bear on the present and shape our future.

Without concepts, understanding the world would be 'inconceivable'.

Underlying concepts are patterns of ideas, through which we group and organise experience, and which allow us to see things in a particular way. However, so influential are they that for much of the time we are unaware of the way they manage our thinking: our conclusions and judgements may be influenced in ways over which we have little control. The basis of a concept is a readiness to respond in certain ways rather than others. We may wonder why a problem is so difficult to solve, when all along it is our concepts and the way they direct our thinking that prevents us finding a solution.

This makes it imperative that we analyse them and reveal the way in which they shape the patterns into which our ideas are organised, so we can redesign them, create new concepts and find new ways of tackling the problems that will form the foundation of our own research and reveal in stand-alone reviews where effective research might be undertaken. This is what we will learn to do in this and the next chapter.

Concepts – the driving force within your research

In Chapter 5, we saw that the problem in our research and, therefore, in our review, was to ensure that the abstract concepts we've used to describe our proposition or thesis have been analysed into concrete components, for which we can find evidence.

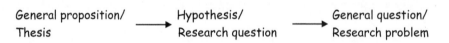

By analysing the concept in the general question into its component ideas, we can create sub-questions that will apply the variables in the concept to the concrete evidence we need to establish the degree to which our hypothesis or research question has been confirmed or falsified.

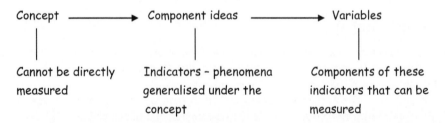

Autonomy and dependency: their influence on learning behaviour and study skills in the 16–19 age group   **EXAMPLE**

In this project, we need to know exactly what concrete evidence to look for in the form of student behaviour to decide whether students are 'autonomous' or 'dependent' learners. An autonomous student, for example, might be someone who displays self-motivation, self-reliance and the confidence to rely on her own judgement. In contrast, a dependent student might need clear instructions about what to do and might be reluctant to challenge those he regards as authorities.

> **A literature review to explore integrated care**   EXAMPLE
> **for older people**
>
> Similarly, in this review, we need to know what is meant by 'integration' and what concrete
> evidence we need to look for to decide the extent to which integrated care for older people is
> achieved in the different forms it takes. What evidence of integration should we look for between
> service sectors, professions, the different settings, types of organisation and types of care?

Words are just the vehicle for the concept

As you can see, concepts are more than mere words. We cannot just feed them into a
search engine and expect the software to do our thinking for us, making connections
between keywords among our sources and noting the similarities and differences in the
way authors use them. This calls for genuine thinking as we use our cognitive abilities
to analyse concepts and then compare, contrast and synthesise the ideas they embrace
into new patterns that will form the basis of our research.

Indeed, the connections we create between ideas come from their similarities and
differences, not because they are known by the same name. This involves more than
mere words. Indeed, for some concepts there are no words.

> *2001: A Space Odyssey*   EXAMPLE
>
> In a chilling scene at the start of Stanley Kubrick's 1968 Oscar-winning film *2001: A Space
> Odyssey*, an ape picks up a bone from the bleached skeleton of an animal and strikes the skull,
> smashing it into pieces. Then, in the moments that follow, quiet and motionless, with the bone held
> in both hands high above his head, he forms a concept. This is no longer just a bone to smash this
> bleached skull before him, but a 'weapon' to strike all the skulls of all his enemies.

In exactly the same way, we see ideas come together to form a pattern. We search
for an existing concept that might fit the pattern. Finding none, we create a new
concept that represents this pattern of ideas.

> **Creating a concept**   EXERCISE
>
> Examine in turn each of the figures below. As you do, you will see a concept emerge.
> For want of a name, let's call it a 'gollet'. Not all of the figures are gollets, so you will
> have to form your idea of the concept and then use it to distinguish between the
> gollets and non-gollets. Once you've done this, answer the following:
>
> 1 Which of the figures are gollets?
> 2 Analyse the concept of a gollet and list three of its core characteristics.

1

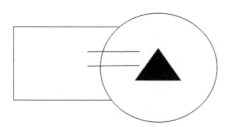

2

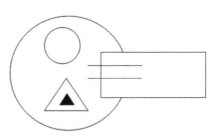

3

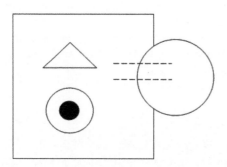

4

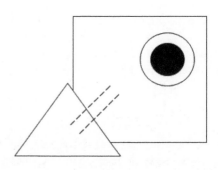

5

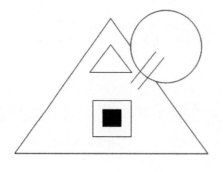

6

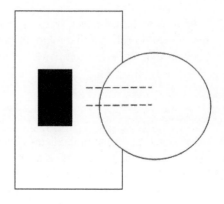

7

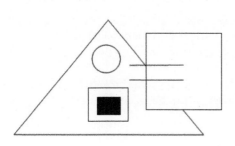

8

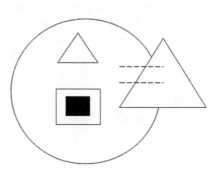

9

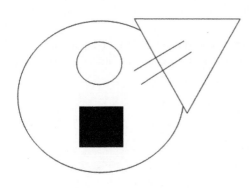

10

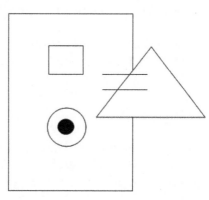

11

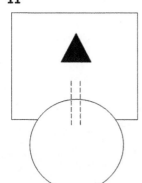

12

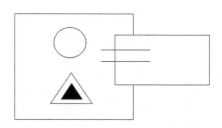

Answers:

1   The gollets are numbers 2, 3, 7, 8, 10 and 12
2   A gollet has the following features:
  2.1 A geometrical figure with another figure coming out of it horizontally on the right.
  2.2 Two other figures are contained within the first geometrical figure.
  2.3 The bottom one contains another figure of the same type, which has black shading.
  2.4 There are two horizontal lines, some continuous, some broken, coming out of the original figure at right angles, overlapping the second figure.

The advantage of using abstract shapes, of course, is that there are no preconceptions and no authorities to tell us what to think. The concept is ours to form without assistance from anyone else. Some people protest that they have no idea how to do this, yet even with the briefest of acquaintances with these shapes, after confronting just four or five examples, most are quite clear about the core characteristics of the concept. Indeed, they can be surprisingly dogmatic as to what is and what is not an example of it just minutes after declaring they knew nothing about it and had no idea how to create and analyse it.

For other concepts the word remains the same, but the concept changes. Indeed, as we'll see, many concepts are constantly evolving in response to the different ways we use them and the different contexts in which we use them.

Telephone   EXAMPLE

Up to the 1980s, a telephone was a large, heavy object that sat in the corner of a room tethered to the wall by a short cable. Today, the word represents quite a different concept. Now it is a light object we carry around with us on which we can check for messages, watch videos, search for information and many other things besides making and receiving calls.

Moreover, some concepts are represented by different words. So relying on a mere search engine to find connections means we are likely to miss many innovative and insightful ideas that will open up new areas of research.

- Concepts are more than mere words.
- For some concepts there are no words.
- In many cases the word remains the same, but the concept changes.
- Some concepts are represented by different words.

Creating and analysing concepts

The first step is to realise that words have more than one meaning, depending on the context and purpose for which they are used. They have no meaning in their own right. Therefore, our concern should be for their actual and possible uses. If we were to look up their meaning in a dictionary, we would find just somebody's picture of what they mean in a particular context, or a mere snapshot, a still in the moving reel of images, each one recording what the concept meant at a particular time and how it has changed and is still changing. Our task, therefore, in analysing a concept is to map out all the different ways in which the word representing it is used.

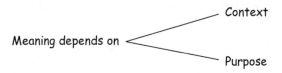

Most of the concepts we use are constantly changing, both because of cultural and social change and because the purposes for which we use them change. The meanings of concepts, like 'progress', 'success', 'luxury', 'necessity', 'poverty' and 'prosperity', are all relative to the person that uses them and the context in which they are used.

Poverty   EXAMPLE

We might be able to agree that in the absolute sense the concept of poverty means someone who has no means of sustenance or permanent shelter from the elements. But in its relative sense it means different things in different circumstances to different people. In some societies today, poverty is more like being without a TV, a refrigerator or even a second car.

Open and closed concepts

1 Closed concepts

Even so, analysing some concepts is, indeed, as straightforward as looking up the word in a dictionary. They are what you might describe as 'closed concepts'. They usually have an unchanging, unambiguous meaning. Words like 'bicycle', 'bachelor' and 'triangle' each have a structure to their meaning, which is bound by logical necessity. We all agree to abide by certain conventions that rule the meaning of these words.

So, if you were to say, 'This bicycle has one wheel' or 'This bachelor is married', no-one would be in any doubt that you've made a logical mistake, and you would run the risk of not being understood. When we use them according to their conventions, we are, in effect, allowing our understanding of the world to be structured in a particular way.

Closed concepts: their structure is bound by logical necessity.

---

2 Open concepts

But with 'open concepts', it's the reverse: our experience of the world shapes our concepts. Their meaning is not governed by a complex set of formal rules, like closed concepts, so they cannot be pinned down just by looking them up in a dictionary. Their meaning responds to, and reflects, our changing experience. As we saw above with the concept of poverty, they change through time and from one culture to another.

Closed and open concepts

1 Closed concepts are governed by complex sets of formal rules, while open concepts adapt to changing circumstances and experience.
2 Closed concepts structure the way we understand our experience, while open concepts are structured *by* it.

Our concern, therefore, is rarely with the words and their dictionary definition, but with the concept and how we use it.

Try this ...

Try it for yourself: create the concept of 'professional'. Think about the concept that the word represents when we use it as a noun and an adjective. Then analyse the common characteristics as you did with the gollets.

Step 1: Gather your typical examples

First, spend some time gathering the evidence: say, five or six examples of the way you use the concept in your everyday life. Try to make them as different as possible. In this way, you'll be able to strip away their differences to reveal more clearly their essential similarities.

1. How do I use the concept?

If you find it difficult to come up with examples, start by asking yourself three questions. First, 'How do I use the concept – do I use it in more than one way?' If you find you do, then you have a structure emerging: each way needs to be explored and its implications unwrapped. The prepositions we use with concepts are in many cases a very useful indicator of different meanings.

Authority   EXAMPLE

We tend to use the concept 'authority' in two different ways: one with the preposition 'in' and the other with the preposition 'an'.

We talk about somebody being 'in' authority, like a police officer, a judge or the head of a school. We comply with their orders either because we respect the institution that they represent or because we fear the consequences if we fail to comply. Police officers have powers at their disposal that can seriously affect us, even denying us our liberty. They are 'in' authority as a result of being given their powers either by being appointed to their positions or by being elected, like members of parliament or local councillors.

In contrast, those who are 'an' authority have earned the respect that we show them. They may be doctors, teachers or experts in certain fields. This respect hasn't been given to them as a result of the institution they represent or because we fear their powers to seriously affect our lives. It comes from the knowledge and expertise they have acquired usually through years of study and dedication to their profession. If they have any power over us, it is the power to persuade us of their point of view as a result of the respect we have for them, their knowledge and years of experience.

2. What sort of thing am I referring to?

If this doesn't help, ask yourself a second question: 'What sort of thing am I referring to when I use the concept?' This means recalling simple everyday situations in which you might find yourself talking about, say, 'authority', even if you don't actually use the word. When you use the word 'bribe', what sort of thing are you referring to?

3. How does it differ from similar things?

To help with this question, it's often useful to ask a third: how does it differ from similar things? When I use the word 'bribe', how does it differ from other things, like commissions, gifts, tips and incentive bonuses? When I use the word 'authority', how does it differ from things like power, force, legitimacy and influence?

Questions

1   How do I use the concept – do I use it in more than one way?
2   What sort of thing am I referring to?
3   How does it differ from similar things?

Step 2: Analyse your examples

Now, using these examples, create your concept: use your conceptual skills to abstract the general from the concrete, just as you did when you created the concept of gollet. In other words, identify the common characteristics in each of your examples, isolating them so that you can then put them together to form the concept. In this way, by recognising the common pattern of characteristics that each example possesses, we visualise what the concept might look like that underlies all the examples.

Answer:

Although perhaps not identical, your concept of 'professional' will no doubt contain many of the same characteristics as mine.

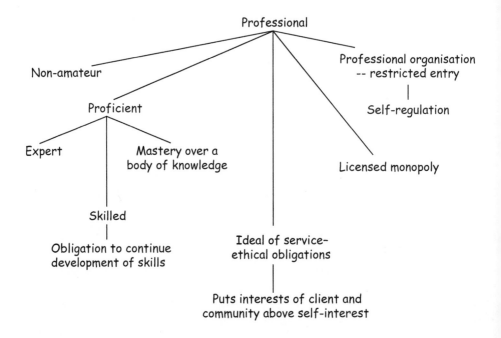

Original ideas – new ways of tackling a problem

Original ideas come from stepping outside our concepts and the routine thinking they dictate. The problem we all face is that in many cases it just seems a rather unnecessary thing to do. It seems obvious: we all know what's meant by words like 'needs', 'poverty' and 'tragedy'. So we have to learn to ask that characteristically philosophical question, 'Yes, but what do we mean by *X*?', particularly when the meaning seems obvious to everyone. In a probing, self-reflective way, we are questioning our own use of these quite ordinary words, which we can no longer take for granted.

 You can download a copy of the tables in this chapter and additional exercises from the companion website (www.macmillanihe.com/greetham-literature-review).

Summary

1 Concepts are the source of our understanding, our most effective means of interpreting experience.
2 For much of the time, we are unaware of the way they manage our thinking.
3 It is imperative to analyse our concepts to reveal the way they shape the patterns into which our ideas are organised.
4 A word is just the vehicle for the concept: for some there are no words, for others there are more than one.
5 The meaning of concepts evolve in response to the different contexts and ways in which we use them.

What next?

Now that we have analysed the concept, we need to redesign it to reveal new ways of approaching the problem that will reveal genuinely original ideas. In the next chapter, we will learn to think outside our concepts and the routine thinking they dictate by restructuring the patterns of ideas they represent to create the foundations of our own research and to recommend, in stand-alone reviews, where promising research might be undertaken.

Note

1   Bertrand Russell, *The Problems of Philosophy*, 1912, (Oxford: Oxford University Press, 1986), p. 28.

Chapter 11

Analysing Concepts 2: Adapting Structures of Ideas

In this chapter, you will learn...

- the importance of learning to think differently;
- four simple strategies to help you see the literature from a different perspective;
- how to change the structure of ideas represented by a concept;
- how to approach the problem from a different direction or start from a different point;
- how to create a new structure by combining other structures or by changing the basic concept.

We like to think that breakthroughs in research are the result of a simple process of gathering evidence, from which we then draw logical inferences. But this is the way the story of discovery is told, rather than how it actually happens. For this, we first need the ability to analyse concepts and, out of them, create new patterns, through which we look at the world and organise our information about it.

Once we've revealed the pattern of ideas at the heart of our concept, we can then manipulate it and form new ones. Many of the most significant breakthroughs in our understanding have come about not because researchers have new or better data, but because of the quality of their thinking and the type of concepts they create. In many cases, when researchers have been faced with obdurate problems that defy solution, the answers have only finally come as a result of being able to think outside the accepted concepts and methods of their disciplines.

Einstein   EXAMPLE

In 1905, Einstein wrote four ground-breaking papers that went beyond orthodox thinking and revolutionised modern physics. He did no experiments of his own and discovered nothing new. All he did was think differently. He challenged established concepts, like absolute space and time, created new, revolutionary concepts, like relativity, and forged unexpected connections between ideas, like mass and energy, producing insights that were to transform our thinking.

As this illustrates, all forms of creativity arise from developing asymmetries between the structures we use to understand the world: unusual contrasts between them, created by being able to see things from a different perspective or interpretation. In this chapter we will learn to use simple strategies to step outside the structures that we normally use, so that we can more easily see different, innovative ways of approaching the literature.

The four strategies

Thinking differently about our structure of ideas involves adapting it and seeing it from different perspectives. You can learn to do this quite simply by using the following four strategies. These place us in the position of being able to think outside the norm, revealing what might otherwise have seemed an inspired way of approaching the problem in the literature.

Adapting structures

1 Change the structure.
2 Approach it from a different direction.
3 Start from a different point.
4 Create a new structure.

The first strategy, changing the structure, involves reorganising the elements and their relationships. By contrast, the second and third strategies involve accepting the structure as it is, but looking at it differently. We either approach it from a different direction, looking at it from different points of view, or we start from a different point. The fourth strategy is perhaps the most radical. This involves creating a new structure, either by combining other structures, or by changing the basic concepts in terms of which the situation is described and interpreted.

Strategy 1: Change the structure

With this strategy, we start with the ideas we have gathered and the structure into which they are organised, and we restructure them. In contrast with the other strategies, you might describe this as a bottom-up strategy. But the most surprising thing about it is that the solution to the problem, or the new way of approaching it, often just appears suddenly and you are struck by the novelty of the solution. The fact that we find this as a result of changing the structure as a whole and not just one or two parts explains why it always appears like a sudden insight with the answer revealed as a complete whole.

T. S. Kuhn, *The Structure of Scientific Revolutions*   EXAMPLE

In this, his most famous book, Thomas Kuhn explains scientific progress in the same way, using the same terms. He explains that the sudden shift between one incompatible paradigm and another comes in the form of a complete revolution; it is not a gradual process.

To make use of this strategy as we design a new approach to the literature, we have to learn to manipulate and change our normal patterns of expectations. The reason we find this difficult in normal circumstances is that the brain allows information to self-organise into patterns, which then dictate the way we use our ideas and understand the world. So the key to this is to learn simple methods to change the structure, to see things from new and more effective perspectives. We can do this in three ways:

Changing the structure

1 Split it up.
2 Rearrange it.
3 Reinterpret it.

1 Split it up

Before you use any of the other methods, it's worth trying this one, which is the simplest of the three. See if you can split up the structure into two or more parts. In many cases, this can convert a bewilderingly difficult problem into two simple problems, whose solution is plain to see. We discover that each one can be solved either by the application of a structure we have used before, or by a parallel structure, an analogy. Failing that, once it's split up we can then use one of the other methods and rearrange or reinterpret the problem to find a solution that way.

2 Rearrange it

However, with some problems the most effective method of finding an answer is to rearrange the structure. To do this see if you can identify a factor that can be moved or changed.

Study skills   EXAMPLE

You may be searching the literature for studies that examine why it is that so many students struggle to take notes, read texts and write essays, so they can meet the demands of syllabuses and exams. If this were the subject of your review, you are likely to look for literature that examines what seems to be the most likely causal explanation, one which suggests that they are not given sufficient or effective instruction in how to do these things.

The structure of ideas that represents this explanation suggests the following causal relationships: study skills instruction shapes the way we use our skills to meet the demands of syllabuses and exams.

study skills ⟶ note taking, reading, ⟶ meet the demands of
instruction   essay writing skills   syllabuses and exams

But then, say you were to discover that in fact with most students this is not the case: that they seem to have very good instruction, yet still manifest the same problems. Given this, you would have to look for a different explanation in the literature. And to find this you would have to identify a factor that could be moved or changed to reveal the most likely solution.

One factor that we could move in this way to rearrange the structure might be the influence of exams and syllabuses, which would then give us an alternative explanation and an interesting hypothesis to explore in the literature:

meet the demands of ———→ study skills ———→ note taking, reading,
syllabuses and exams   instruction   essay writing skills

This suggests a radically different explanation, one that focuses on the influence of syllabuses and modes of assessment, like essays and exams. The way we write them might so shape students' perception of the purposes of learning that despite all the instruction in study skills, they still take notes, read and write in the same way, exhibiting exactly the same problems.

It might be that syllabuses encourage students to believe that learning is largely about knowing things and that exams test how many 'right' answers they can recall and trade for marks. If this is the case, despite taking study skills courses, they are likely to continue to read word-for-word and take verbatim, unstructured notes, fearing that if they leave anything out they might be missing a right answer.

3 Reinterpret it

If rearranging the structure in this way doesn't give you a new way of approaching the literature, try reinterpreting it, changing its meaning. In the last chapter we learnt that the way we make sense of concepts and structures of ideas can itself lead us in the wrong direction. So, without even changing the structure we can sometimes find the most insightful way of reviewing the literature by looking at it naïvely, without any preconceptions, as someone who has never seen it before.

The French Revolution   EXAMPLE

In this example, we did exactly that by questioning whether the French Revolution was really a bourgeois revolution. Instead, we wondered whether it was merely an internal revolt within the ruling class with groups competing for lucrative offices and not striving to be entrepreneurs at all.

As a result, we found an interesting way of reinterpreting the literature, which, as we saw in Chapter 5, will produce some fascinating sub-questions

Strategy 2: Approach it from a different direction

With some problems, it's not necessary to change the structure at all, just approach it from a different direction, from a different point of view. This strategy seems to be routine with some thinkers. Whenever a problem arises, they devise a method of approaching it in a different way from others. Donald Newman, a mathematician who knew John Nash at MIT, said this of him:

[E]veryone else would climb a peak by looking for a path somewhere on the mountain. Nash would climb another mountain altogether and from that distant peak would shine a searchlight back onto the first peak.[1]

The most common strategy we routinely use to approach a problem from a different direction is to reverse the order of things: to turn it upside down, inside out or back to front.

Approach it from a different direction

1 Turn it upside down.
2 Inside out.
3 Back to front.

1 Turn it upside down

This involves reversing the **relations between ideas**; changing the way we think about things so that we think in quite a different way. In what he described as his 'Copernican Revolution', the eighteenth-century German philosopher Immanuel Kant found a solution to the problem David Hume set by turning Hume's argument – that all our ideas develop out of our sense impressions – upside down, reversing the relationship between our sense impressions and our intellect. As Copernicus removed the earth from the centre of creation, so Kant found a solution to Hume's problem by removing the earthly experience of our senses, making it peripheral to the active processing of the mind.

Karl Marx and historical materialism   EXAMPLE

In the same way Karl Marx turned Hegel's argument upside down, arguing that it is not ideas that determine the shape of material forces, but material forces in the form of social and economic factors, like production, that shape society, social relations, the individual and what he believes and values, indeed the whole extent of his freedom.

2 Inside out

With this method, rather than reverse the *relations between ideas*, we reverse our **intuitive assumptions**, turning them inside out. In effect, we approach the problem from a different direction by deliberately thinking the opposite to see what we can find.

Penicillin   EXAMPLE

Before the Second World War, a German chemist was working to discover what we would call today an antibiotic. Each evening he would leave out Petri dishes with bacteria in them so they could grow during the night for him to work on them the next day. But everyday he found them dead with mould spores on them, which he assumed came from the spores in the corners of the laboratory. Consequently, he had everything thoroughly cleaned and decontaminated.

Unfortunately, he was unsuccessful in his search for an antibiotic. Yet, if he had only reversed his intuitive assumptions and seen the spores as a solution, rather than a problem, he might have realised that they were the very thing he was looking for. Eventually the Nobel Prize for the discovery of penicillin went to Sir Alexander Fleming after he discovered it in similar mould that had destroyed his own cultures of bacteria.[2]

As you can see in this example, the asymmetries, the unusual conjunctions and contrasts, created by reversing the way we normally think about things are often the source of the most surprising insights.

3 Back to front

When we use the third method, rather than reverse the *relations between ideas* or our *intuitive assumptions*, we reverse the **order of things**; we turn things back to front. Copernicus argued that the earth moved around the sun, rather than the sun around the earth. Einstein argued that it wasn't that the planets moved in a curved motion through space, but that space itself was curved.

The importance of writing across the curriculum   EXAMPLE

If we were writing a review for this topic, we might begin with our normal assumptions that clear thinking is important because it results in clear writing. But, if we were turn this back to front and consider that perhaps clear writing makes for clear thinking, then we would have an altogether different and interesting hypothesis that we can explore in the literature.

It suggests that by forcing us to think through our ideas with greater clarity and care, writing could play a more important role across the curriculum, even in the sciences and mathematics. By writing about how they come by their ideas and solve problems, students could begin to understand more about the processes of how they think in these subjects.

As we have seen, all three of these different ways of approaching the problem in the literature involve reversing different things:

1 Turn upside down – reverse the relation between ideas.
2 Inside out – reverse our intuitive assumptions.
3 Back to front – reverse the order of things.

Strategy 3: Start from a different point

In contrast, this strategy works by focusing our attention onto different parts of the structure and starting from there. We might start at the end rather than the beginning, but wherever we start, our aim is not to take the ideas for granted but to see them from a different perspective.

As we've seen, by analysing a concept we are able to reveal the structure of ideas at the heart of it. One or more of these ideas are likely to dictate the way we generally use it. But analysing it has revealed clearly those ideas we usually ignore, which give us different points from which to start. They throw different light on the problem, presenting interesting angles from which to approach it.

Counterfactual Thinking and Shakespearean Tragedy: **EXAMPLE**
Imagining Alternatives in the Plays

In this thesis, if you were to begin by analysing the concept of 'tragedy' you might produce ideas similar to the following notes. From this you could find an alternative interpretation of it as something that is self-defeating in that, without meaning to, we destroy the very thing we value most. This may suggest a unique angle of investigation that will give your project an original focus.

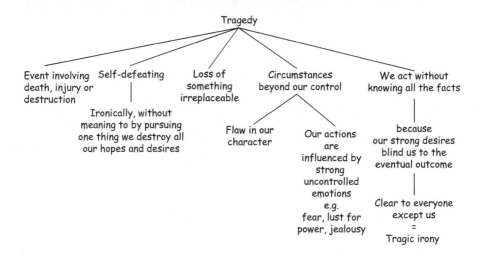

But if the key concepts of your topic don't offer you a way of starting from a different point, try something that might seem disarmingly simple: step back from your topic and approach it from the more general standpoint of someone who is not technically involved in your subject. To adopt this approach, get used to asking questions that might seem too simple or obvious to ask.

Naïve questions   **EXAMPLE**

One reason for the stunning success of Einstein's four groundbreaking papers in 1905 was his habit of starting his work with naïve, simple, almost childlike questions. What would it be like to fly alongside a beam of light? If you flew at the same speed as the light beam, would it, for instance, appear to stand still? What happens to passengers in an elevator when it falls into emptiness?

Sometimes a problem is only a problem because it is looked at in a certain way. Change the way in which you look at it and there is no longer a problem. By just shifting the emphasis from one part to another, the solution becomes so clear that you wonder why you hadn't seen it before.

Try this ...

An equation in mathematics is nothing more than two ways of describing something. Having two ways of expressing the same thing either side of the equals sign gives you a different way of looking at it and the ability to manipulate things and find the answer. With this in mind, find a solution to the following problem.

Barbara is half as old as Clive was when Clive was five years older than Barbara is now. How old is Barbara now?

Answer:

The best way of finding the answer is to represent the statements as an algebraic equation. Then you will have two contrasting representations of the same thing either side of the equal sign.

If you translate the words, 'Clive was five years older than Barbara is now', you get $C = 5 + B$. If you then translate the rest of it, 'Barbara is half as old as Clive was', becomes $B = \frac{1}{2}C$. Now we can begin to adapt these representations by substituting for C, which will give us an equation with just one unknown: B.

$B = \frac{1}{2}(5 + B)$
$2B = 5 + B$
$2B - B = 5$
$B = 5$

So, Barbara is 5 years old.

Strategy 4: Create a new structure

In contrast to the others, this is a top-down strategy, in which a new theory is put in place of the ruling one. There are two ways of doing this.

Creating a new structure

1 Combine structures.
2 Change the basic concepts.

1 Combine structures

Perhaps the most effective way is to import a theory or another way of interpreting things from another discipline, another profession or just from everyday life. Synthesising structures in this way can open up entirely new ways of approaching the literature.

The Crowd in History   EXAMPLE

With the rise of totalitarian leaders in the 1930s and '40s and their mesmeric influence on crowds, some historians began to wonder how significant the crowd and a leader's capacity to manipulate collective sentiment had been in previous periods with leaders like Napoleon. So they combined different structures by borrowing from political science the theory of totalitarianism and re-evaluating their own historical understanding in the light of this. As a result, they were able to open up new lines of investigation with surprising results.

It is often possible to synthesise structures from different sources in this way to create new structures. As you review the literature, look out for different approaches that might usefully be synthesised. It's worth reminding yourself that creative thinking often means disregarding our own cultural conventions. There may be within your subject an accepted way of approaching your topic, but don't let this trap your thinking. It has been said that genius is the capacity for productive reaction against one's training.

● Can you import a theory or a different way of interpreting things?
● Are there different approaches you can synthesise?
● Don't get trapped by the accepted ways of approaching your topic.

2 Change the basic concepts

As we have seen, a concept represents the structure through which we understand a situation; a system of learned responses which we automatically apply to organise and make sense of data. If we can find different ways we use the concept, we will uncover different perspectives through which we can approach the literature. For example, in the last chapter we found that there were different ways of using the concept 'authority', depending on whether someone was 'an' authority or 'in' authority.

Financing the health care safety net   EXAMPLE

In this project, you may have to analyse the concept of patient 'needs'. In an absolute sense, it is something that is necessary for basic survival. But it also has a relative sense meaning those things necessary for a certain quality of life; the product of living in a particular society. From this perspective an altogether more interesting project emerges.

The lesson is 'don't take the concept for granted'. See it from a different perspective, even though this may at first seem absurd; what comes afterwards may not be. So, concentrate on other parts of its meaning and other ways in which it is used, and let these dominate your review of the literature to see where it takes you.

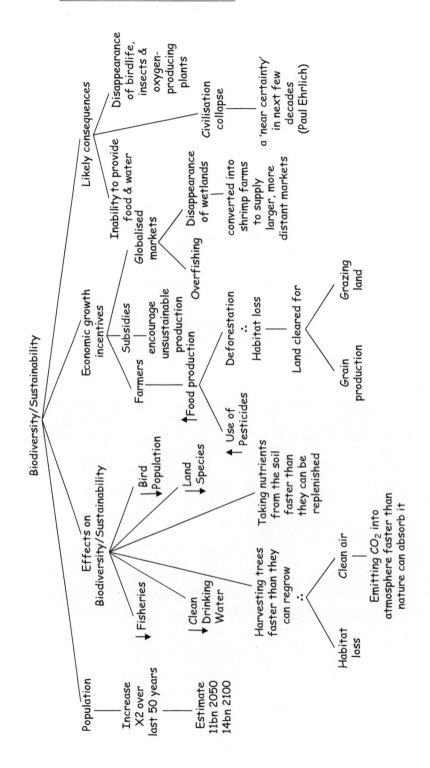

Biodiversity and sustainability   **EXERCISE**

One review article you read suggests that the only solution to this problem, which we examined in Chapter 4, lies in drastic measures to control population growth. You want to challenge this by arguing that there are alternatives. Let's say from your trigger questions and your perspectives and levels you generated the structure of ideas on the previous page. Using one of the four strategies with this structure, come up with an alternative solution.

Answer:

If you systematically use each of the four strategies, you will produce a range of different answers. To take just one of these, I have used the fourth strategy. This involves finding a solution by creating a new structure either by combining structures or by changing the basic concepts of the problem. One solution might be to re-examine the concept of growth. Most politicians insist on the importance of promoting economic growth as the key measure of progress. But the way we define and measure it almost inevitably ties it to the degradation of nature.

So it seems an obvious solution would be to adopt a different definition that decouples growth from the destruction of the natural environment. Alternative measures of progress might be living within the earth's means, reducing the levels of poverty and hunger, reducing the threat of climate change or, perhaps, some measure of happiness. For example, New Zealand has recently passed a 'Wellbeing Budget' and Bhutan has rejected GDP as the only measure of progress, instead measuring it through the formal principles of gross national happiness (GNH).

 You can download copies of the tables in this chapter and additional exercises from the companion website (www.macmillanihe.com/greetham-literature-review).

Summary

1 The answer to many of the most difficult problems comes not from new data, but from thinking differently.
2 We can more easily see innovative ways of approaching the literature if we can step outside the structures we normally use to understand experience.
3 Sometimes a problem is only a problem because it is looked at in a certain way.
4 No matter how absurd it may seem, ask naïve questions and see things from unconventional perspectives.

What next?

In this chapter, we have learnt the importance of thinking differently. In the next chapter, we will build on this by learning a simple, practical method of synthesising ideas, making connections that lead to innovative ideas and insights.

Notes

1 Silva Nasar, *A Beautiful Mind* (London: Faber & Faber, 1998), p. 12.
2 Adapted from Arthur J. Cropley, *Creativity in education and learning* (London: Kogan Page, 2001), pp. 45–6.

Chapter 12

Synthesis: Creating Patterns and Finding Gaps

In this chapter, you will learn...

- the five-stage method for synthesising ideas;
- the seven types of connections to look for as you review the literature;
- how to generate insights;
- how to make the most of your ideas.

The distinguishing characteristic of intelligence is not what you know, but what you do with it: the ability to identify relevant connections and put together what ought to be conjoined. This ability to synthesise ideas can produce the most surprising results. You can bring two unpromising ideas together and suddenly you have an idea of astonishing potential.

In this lies the obvious truth that the properties of the whole cannot always be predicted from the parts. New connections produce new concepts that give us a new way of seeing the world. This is what creative people can do: they can synthesise ideas from different areas of thought and expertise to produce the most surprising results.

Common problems

However, the most common criticism of literature reviews is that they amount to little more than annotated lists of sources, just loose collections of discrete parts with few connections that would help us develop a deeper understanding of the problem. This strikes at the very essence of a review, which is to synthesise sources into a coherent, integrated whole: a meaningful picture that gives the reader a broad and deep understanding of the issues that dominate the topic. It should reveal where the picture is unclear, where parts are missing and where there are gaps that need to be filled.

For a stand-alone review, this reveals where promising research might be undertaken, and for a dissertation or thesis it lays the foundations for our own research: to test a hypothesis, develop new answers to a problem, explore new areas, extend or challenge an accepted line of thought or simply fill a gap. In this way, we reveal the one unifying idea that lights up the way we are to understand the material.

A literature review should synthesise sources into a coherent, integrated whole that gives the reader a broad and deep understanding of the issues.

A practical method

When we doubt our ability to do this, it is tempting to assume that we can allow search engines to do our thinking for us; that we can simply rely on them to make connections between different sources. But you cannot substitute software programs for genuine, creative thinking. Novel and innovative ideas and insights don't come from merely using keywords in search engines to bring up connections between them.

For this, we need a practical method that will use our higher cognitive abilities in a systematic way. This is how many of the most important breakthroughs in our thinking have occurred. The brightest ideas have developed out of systematic work and simple routines. In what follows you will learn a simple, practical method of five stages that you can use routinely to develop connections and synthesise ideas.

Synthesising ideas – a practical method

1 Connect
2 Insight
3 Hypothesis
4 Test
5 Adapt

1 Connect

Start by just taking the pattern of ideas you first generated on the topic in Chapter 4, along with your analysis of the key concepts and, as you read each source, compare them; start to identify connections between them. As you make sense of what you read, note trends and patterns in the literature; note the comparisons between each study. You're looking for different things that might indicate significant connections between them. It helps if you can do this in a systematic way, so work carefully through the following list searching for,

1 Causes
2 Contrasts
3 Seeing parts of the whole
4 Seeing the whole from the parts
5 Seeing extensions of ideas, like logical inferences
6 Divergences
7 Convergences

As you explore each source, you will see connections between the ideas. The important thing is not to take anything for granted: ask the most naïve questions. Search for connections where you might least expect to find them.

> **Einstein**   EXAMPLE
>
> In his attempt to understand the nature of energy, Einstein took the two concepts, mass and energy, both seemingly quite unalike. He thought about the possible connections he could make between them. Then he related them to the things and ideas around him with which he was familiar.

1 Causes

As you read the literature, you will come across ideas that didn't occur to you as you generated your own ideas and analysed the key concepts. When this happens, it helps to lay out as complete an account as you can of the key ideas and their causal connections. Ask simple, obvious questions, like those we asked in Chapter 9:

> Why do we assume that A causes B?
> Is that really a causal connection, rather than a mere correlation?
> Are there more than one cause?

Often we take it for granted that we are aware of everything, so we see no point in doing this. As a result, we not only miss obvious things, but we fail to register the most interesting questions we could ask or hypotheses we could test. So try to be naïve, take nothing for granted, and set down all you know. Often you will see for the first time interpretations you've never considered. Things will simply jump out at you because they are no longer obscured by the veil of your routine thinking.

2 Contrasts

The same is true as you look for contrasts. Make use of simple everyday contrasts to make issues clearer. They are the source of some of our most fruitful asymmetries as you can see below.

> **Organ donations: the effects of the acts**   EXAMPLE
> **and omissions doctrine**
>
> In the course of your research, you come across a statement from the American Medical Association's Council on Ethical and Judicial Affairs that a doctor may omit treatment to permit a terminally ill patient to die, but should not intentionally cause death.

And you wonder how a doctor's omission not to treat a patient can be free of moral culpability, when she knows the patient will certainly die without treatment? So you look around for everyday contrasts between omissions that carry no moral blame, like your failure to contribute to a charity that saves the lives of children starving in the poorest countries, and those that do, like failing to help a child at the dinner table, who dies choking on something. Why is one culpable and the other not? This begins to throw light on issues you can now explore.

3 Seeing parts of the whole
4 Seeing the whole from the parts

Seeing the parts of the whole and the whole from analysing each part can be the source of the most significant insights. The asymmetries we create can open up a topic in ways we barely imagined.

The philosophies of Thomas Carlyle and   EXAMPLE
John Stuart Mill

In this thesis, you begin with the realisation that Thomas Carlyle and John Stuart Mill hold contrasting philosophical views, one heavily influenced by German idealism and the other by English empiricism, respectively. So far you have looked at the whole to see how the parts fit into the overall pattern of nineteenth century thought. But when you begin to look at the parts more closely you notice that there are issues on which they hold strikingly similar positions, in particular their respective theories of history.

The other direction, from the parts to the whole, can be equally insightful:

Novelistic sympathy and distance in the   EXAMPLE
novels of George Eliot

At the beginning of chapter 19 of *Adam Bede*, you come across what appears to be a fundamental contradiction between George Eliot's description of the need for distance and the novel's more general emphasis on novelistic sympathy, which leads you to wonder whether this runs throughout her work.

---

5 Seeing extensions of ideas, like logical inferences

As you read the literature, get into the habit of extending the author's arguments to see where they lead. Do they end in conflicting ideas or unacceptable consequences? As we will see below, the divergences and convergences we find are the sources of inferences we can draw and fashion into new hypotheses that we can test.

6 Divergences

The obvious way to search for connections is to look for **divergences,** those things that clearly contradict one another, and **convergences**, those that are supportive. You may find your topic has been reviewed in the past. Since then, newer work has taken a different, contrasting position, which has not been taken onboard by reviewers and may give you an opportunity to see if either position stands up to examination.

Alternatively, consider the different styles of approach to problems, theories and literature of authors from different countries and cultures. Are there differences between them in the literature? Are there inconsistencies in their respective arguments? You might have come across explanations that work in one country and you wonder how far these can be applied in your own. This might suggest inadequacies in current ideas, practice or evidence.

- New contrasting positions
- Different styles of approach
- Different explanations

7 Convergences

Alternatively, look for issues, interpretations and points of view that have commonalities, those ideas that can be brought together to provide a more unusual insight; a different way of looking at a problem or issue. The first thing to do is try to identify all those things that will *reinforce* each other: that will act in similar ways, perhaps providing the evidence that supports a particular interpretation.

Edmund Burke and his impact on the British   EXAMPLE
understanding of the causes of the French Revolution

In this thesis, the first thing you will explore are the different causes – intellectual, economic, social and political – all reinforcing each other in bringing about the revolution.

Others may *complement* each other: you may find that if A is to be true, there must also be B – one cannot be present without the other. Alternatively, you may find that in the relationship between two elements one is *supplementary* to another: by revealing more clearly its implications or it may be a logical extension of it.

Edmund Burke and his impact on the British   EXAMPLE
understanding of the causes of the French Revolution

As you generated ideas about the causes, you may have listed among the economic causes the pressure exerted on economic resources by the doubling of the population in the 80 years leading up to the Revolution in 1789 and you may also have listed the rise in bread prices in the summer of 1789 as an economic cause. But you quickly realise, as you develop your structure, that the latter is supplementary to the former: that the increase in bread prices was due in part to the rise in population and was, therefore, a trigger for the revolution, rather than an underlying cause.

Convergence

1 Reinforcing
2 Complementary
3 Supplementary

As you work through each of the seven points above, keep track of the connections you make and set them down in a clear structure: a matrix or any form of pattern notes (see Chapter 16) that allows you to see at a glance the connections between the ideas. Diagrammatic representation of your ideas will always allow you to see clearly ways of linking ideas, extending points and revealing insights you may not otherwise see.

2 Insight

At this point, having compared two things from perspectives that we would not normally adopt, we often experience an insight, that shaft of light that sheds the sort of clarity that leaves us wondering where on earth it came from. In *The Structure of Scientific Revolutions*, Thomas Kuhn explains that the shift from one paradigm to another is not the result of a cumulative process, but a sudden transition, a gestalt, that 'emerges all at once, sometimes in the middle of the night, in the mind ... deeply immersed in crisis.'[1]

> Insights come from comparing two things from perspectives that we would not normally adopt.

A similar thing occurred in Chapter 10, when we compared the abstract patterns, out of which the concept of 'gollet' suddenly appeared. This may seem commonplace, but the certainty and clarity of vision are the same.

Einstein   EXAMPLE

Einstein had the same experience. He analysed and then compared the two concepts of mass and energy from a different perspective, as if energy could behave like a solid object. He then experienced the sudden insight, 'Matter is frozen energy.' It is locked even within the smallest fragment of matter: a piece of paper, a stick of wood, an iron filing or a small piece of uranium.

When the subatomic particles that make up the object become unfrozen, they can become enormously powerful as in a nuclear reactor or in the energy released by the sun. Einstein explained this hoarded energy using an analogy: 'It is as though a man who is fabulously rich (i.e. matter) should never spend or give away a cent (i.e. of its energy); no one could tell how rich he was.'[2]

Einstein's greatest insights came from just this type of thought experiment, fuelled by these unusual comparisons of ideas and the most naïve questions.

Students' scientific thinking in higher education: Logical thinking   EXERCISE
and conceptions of scientific thinking in universities

Let's say you are reviewing the literature relating to this thesis and you come across the following passages. What insight would you draw from them about the nature of scientific thinking?

1 Jacob Bronowski, who worked with John von Neumann, the creator of game theory, once suggested to von Neumann, during a taxi ride in London, that chess is a good example of a game. Von Neumann responded, 'No, no ... chess is not a game. Chess is a well-defined form of computation.'[3]

2 Otto Frisch, who worked with the Nobel prize-winning physicist Niels Bohr, explained that Bohr never trusted a purely logical argument: '"No, no," he would say, "You are not thinking; you are just being logical."'[4]

Answer:

You might conclude that logical thinking is not so much thinking, but a form of computation, like chess. If you work according to the rules and follow the right procedure, you will arrive at the right answer. In contrast, in scientific thinking there is a dynamic component. To say that you are thinking means that you are actively processing ideas, whereas thinking logically can be done passively, almost as if the thinking part of you is not there. Scientific thinking involves going beyond what you know, or what you can show logically, to discover something new.

3 Hypothesis

From the insights we have generated, we can now begin to draw inferences to create hypotheses, which we can test and then adapt. At this point, it often appears that the real work begins. At times, the process of finding a workable hypothesis involves this and the next two stages in rapid succession. A hypothesis may be formed, tested, adapted and finally discarded, if it doesn't work, in a matter of minutes. Indeed this rapid sequential framing and evaluation of hypotheses is not unlike the work of scientists as they do their early probing before they settle on a theory.

Darwin   EXAMPLE

Although much of his work was characterised by careful, patient collection of data, rather than being theory directed, Darwin still confessed that he could not resist forming a hypothesis on every subject.

> **Einstein**   **EXAMPLE**
>
> Einstein's insight that matter was frozen energy gave him what he needed to develop his most famous equation in his theory of special relativity:
>
> $$E = mc^2 \ (\text{Energy} = \text{mass} \times \text{speed of light squared})$$

4 Test

The last two stages are in many ways a lot more straightforward. Our aim is not just to test our hypothesis to see if it works, but to reveal whether and in what ways we need to adapt it.

5 Adapt

You may need to adjust the emphasis or qualify the idea you are testing in some way. In many cases there is a prolonged process of iteration between the testing and adaptation stages as the final version of the idea begins to emerge. In contrast to Einstein's discovery, where the real value of his work lay largely in the work done in the first two stages, much of the value in your idea may lie in the last three stages as it is developed, tested and adapted.

Managing ideas

Synthesising your ideas in this way as you read the literature at times will generate more ideas than you think you can cope with. So, make sure you work according to these three simple rules:

1 Analyse and process ideas when they are still fresh in your mind

Avoid procrastination: don't tell yourself that you'll note an idea or a structure of ideas when you have a moment. Note it as soon as it takes shape. As you record them they will generate new ideas and insights. You'll see gaps and inconsistencies in the material. All of this will throw fresh light on your own assumptions.

2 Be prepared for change

Even though the ideas you generate from your reading might be new and innovative, they are not set in stone. Be prepared to refine and adapt them as you come across more ideas in your reading. Test and adapt them.

3 Wherever possible, clarify your ideas visually

Processing ideas as we read texts is always difficult. The mind works to create structures out of what it reads, but these are hidden deep in sequential and unstructured text. It's often not easy to see it, hidden by words and complex sentence structures. So make it easier by displaying the ideas in visual form, in pattern notes, tables and matrixes.

Three rules

1 Analyse and process ideas as you go along
2 Be prepared for change
3 Wherever possible, clarify your ideas visually

Working through the steps described in this chapter will bring you to the point where insights are born and new patterns of ideas created. Consciously or unconsciously, your mind will deliver you at the point where you are able to see things that you were never able to see before.

You can download copies of the tables in this chapter, along with additional exercises, from the companion website (www.macmillanihe.com/greetham-literature-review).

Summary

1 The distinguishing characteristic of intelligence is not what you know, but what you do with it.
2 Synthesising two or more ideas can release surprising potential.
3 Insights come from comparing two things from perspectives that we would not normally adopt.
4 Take nothing for granted: ask the most naïve questions.
5 Keep track of the connections you make, set them down in a clear structure: a matrix or any form of pattern notes.

What next?

Processing our ideas in this way takes time and careful management of the material we generate. In Part 4, we will look at ways you can do this to allow you to process your ideas thoroughly and at a deeper level.

Notes

1 Thomas S. Kuhn, *The Structure of Scientific Revolutions* (Chicago: University of Chicago Press, 1971), pp. 89–90.
2 Albert Einstein, *Ideas and Opinions* (London: Souvenir Press, 1973), p. 340.
3 Jacob Bronowski, *The Ascent of Man*, quoted in William Poundstone, *Prisoner's Dilemma* (New York: Anchor, 1993), p. 6.
4 O.R. Frisch, *What Little I Remember* (Cambridge: Cambridge University Press, 1991), p. 95.

Part 4

Organising Your Work

Chapter 13

Managing Your Time

In this chapter, you will learn…

> - how to create a safety net to give you control over your work and relieve your anxiety;
> - how to avoid problems by building early warning checks into your work schedule;
> - how to break the literature review down into smaller manageable stages;
> - how to design your weekly timetable to get the most out of your time;
> - how to organise your work to keep on track and respond to every shift in your thinking.

The last five chapters have been all about how to use and develop your thinking skills to process ideas. At the heart of this is a constant interplay between what we read and the structures of ideas we create and adapt in response. What started out as a simple proposition of what you thought you might find becomes more developed and nuanced as your understanding deepens and develops.

Like all creative processes, at times this can appear confusing and difficult to anchor in some element of certainty. This is as it should be. So you need to have a system, a safety net, which will assure you that things are under control, despite the apparent confusion. One important part of this is managing your time.

Being in control

Planning your time and building in stage deadlines along the way helps you chart a clear course through your work, so you know what you have to do, in what sequence and when. It gives you control over your work and relieves your anxiety. It's reassuring to know you can complete your review on time if you stick to the plan.

Of course, as you plan you may discover you've been too ambitious, or not ambitious enough. If you've taken too broad a focus, covering too much ground as you try to review too many sources, you will realise that you have to narrow your focus, but it is better to know that at an early stage rather than later when it will be much more difficult to make changes.

You may discover that you need to scale back your review:

- the number of articles you were going to include;
- the different competing methodologies you were going to review;
- the breadth of your research question – the size and range of the population you were going to research, the length of the historical period you were going to cover, the number of novels you were going to review.

Early warning checks

But it's not just at the beginning that planning is important: the reality check you get here is just one of a number you'll need along the way. Building these early warning checks into your timetable will help you avoid the one problem that everyone has with literature reviews: that we spend far too much time on them, leaving us short of time and space for the rest of our work. Having early warning checks within your timetable will help you monitor your time so that you can make adjustments before there is a problem.

Motivation

Equally important, more than any other aspect of your work, having a plan helps maintain your motivation and long-term commitment. Indeed, we often discover an unexpected bonus: that we have more time than we expected as a result of planning. With a clear plan of what we should be doing and how long it should take, we're less likely to take a more relaxed approach to our work and become victim to Parkinson's Law, allowing the work to expand to fill the time available. Unchecked, this can be like a computer virus, invading every aspect of our work without us even realising.

The benefits of planning your time

1 Stage deadlines chart a clear course through your work.
2 Gives you more control over your work.
3 Relieves your anxiety.
4 Gives you early warning checks.
5 Maintains your motivation and long-term commitment.
6 You may find you have more time than expected.

The steps

In the introduction, we said that the simple answer to many of the problems we experience in writing a literature review is to break it down into smaller manageable stages, plan each of one and then carefully work through each of these one at a time. To set up a system that helps you maintain control over your work and manage your time in this way, work through the following steps.

The steps

1 A typical week
2 Planning your timetable
3 The time available for the review
4 Listing the tasks
5 Allocating hours to each task
6 Stage deadlines
7 Keeping to your schedule
8 Constant checks

1 A typical week

The first and most obvious thing we need to do is assess how much time we have available for the review after we have taken account of the other work we have, the relaxation we need to ensure that we work at our best, and the routine commitments we have each week. To do this, it's essential that we have a fairly accurate idea of how we normally use each hour of the week. This may seem excessively thorough, but the clearer we are about how we use our time, the more realistic and workable will be our timetable at the end of the process.

Weekly timetable   EXERCISE

Take a copy of the 24-hour weekly timetable below and record on it as accurately as you can what you do each hour over a typical week. At the end of the week, calculate the number of hours you have devoted to study and other activities.

2 Planning your timetable

Almost inevitably, this exercise will have revealed problems in the way you use time in a typical week. Like most of us, you will probably find that you waste more time than you thought. This is the opportunity to tackle this. See if you can make changes that will maximise the amount of time you have available without sacrificing the time you need for relaxation. You are trying to create the right balance so that your mind has the free time it needs away from work to process the ideas.

First, set aside one day a week free of work. Then, to ensure you get the most out of work, plot those activities that call for the highest levels of concentration at those times you work best. For the same reason, avoid long unstructured periods of study. Divide up each session into manageable periods of, say, two hours, with relaxation in between.

- Try to create a timetable that avoids too much wasted time.
- Create the right balance between work and relaxation.
- Set aside one day free of work.
- Plot those activities that call for the highest levels of concentration at those times you work best.
- Avoid long unstructured periods of study.

Weekly Timetable

	Monday	Tuesday	Wednesday	Thursday	Friday	Saturday	Sunday
Midnight–1.00							
1.00–2.00							
2.00–3.00							
3.00–4.00							
4.00–5.00							
5.00–6.00							
6.00–7.00							
7.00–8.00							
8.00–9.00							
9.00–10.00							
10.00–11.00							
11.00–12.00							
12.00–13.00							
13.00–14.00							
14.00–15.00							
15.00–16.00							
16.00–17.00							
17.00–18.00							
18.00–19.00							
19.00–20.00							
20.00–21.00							
21.00–22.00							
22.00–23.00							
23.00–24.00							

3 The time available for the review

Now that you know the total time available for study, you can decide what you have left for the review each week after you have set aside time for other work. Once you have this figure, you can multiply it by the number of weeks available for the completion of the review and you'll have the total number of hours available for it.

There is a general rule of research that says you should plan to use only 75 per cent of the time available. This allows for the unexpected and for you to adapt your plans if new opportunities arise. However, literature reviews always take longer than you think, so it is wise to play it safe and increase your first estimate, perhaps even double it. At least plan to finish it a couple of weeks early to give you a cushion against the unexpected, like illness and delays.

The general rule of research says that you should plan to use only 75 per cent of the time available.

4 Listing the tasks

As you list all the tasks involved in the review, arrange them in sequence. Be as thorough as you can, listing everything, including bureaucratic jobs and other tasks you think might be good to do if time allows. Until you've been through this exercise, you won't know if, in fact, time will allow for them. The work schedule below gives you an idea of the sort of list you'll need.

5 Allocating hours to each task

We can now allocate hours to each of these tasks. On the work schedule, enter the time required and then plot the start and finish date. Of course, it's difficult to assess accurately how long each one will take, so give yourself longer than you think.

Work Schedule

Stages	Time required	Start date	Finish date	Stocktaking
1. Generate ideas				
2. Pin down your research question/ hypothesis				Submit to supervisor
3. Organise your retrieval system				
4. Search the literature				Stage deadline

5. Critically evaluate sources				
6. Analyse/synthesise ideas				Stage deadline
7. Plan the review				
8. Write first draft				Submit to supervisor
9. Revise structure – check logic, signposting, paragraphs				
10. Revise content 1 – check citing, plagiarism				
11. Reference list/ bibliography				
12. Revise content 2 – check sentences, word use, de-clutter				Submit to supervisor
13. Final presentation – check word count, pagination, tables				Final deadline

6 Stage deadlines

The more you know about how your time will be spent, the more effective you'll be at managing it and monitoring your progress. Begin by working back from key dates, when you've got to submit work to your supervisor or fulfil some other requirement, and set yourself interim deadlines to finish each stage. Breaking up work in this way with manageable stages marked by deadlines helps us avoid the tendency to get too involved in one part and lose sight of the overall picture, which tends to be a particular problem with literature reviews.

Sessions with supervisors

Some of these deadlines will be marked by scheduled sessions with supervisors to take stock of how things have gone. These are immensely valuable both to you and your supervisor. On the simplest level, you'll find them reassuring: you can stand back from your day-to-day work and look back and forward. Looking back, you can both assess how much material has been collected, and its relevance and reliability. But it's also reassuring to look forward to get a good measure of what you've got left to do. It will help you gain perspective, which might otherwise be buried beneath your day-to-day work.

Sessions with supervisors

1 Assess how things have gone
2 Gives you perspective above your everyday work
3 You can check on the relevance and reliability of material
4 Get a good measure of what you've got left to do

Sessions of this type and the opportunities to take stock that stage deadlines give us are invaluable to help us exert control over our work. It's surprisingly easy without realising it to get bogged down in reviewing literature that is not centrally important to your project. If you find this is the case, it may be that your focus has shifted and, along with your supervisor, you need to consider the implications. Stocktaking after an extended period of working with the material is your opportunity to deal with this and give your review a clear focus for the final stages of your work.

Stocktaking is likely to reveal any shift in your thinking.

7 Keeping to your schedule

If you find it's becoming more difficult to keep to your schedule, look again at how you work. Ask yourself whether each of the tasks you've listed has to be done in sequence. It will save you time if some can be done in parallel with others. For example, it is more than likely that you will be able to start planning your review as you process the ideas. As they coalesce, you will begin to see how certain ideas fit with others to make a cohesive whole.

Writing

Similarly, around the same time you can begin writing sections of your first draft as your ideas begin to take shape. This will not only save time, but help you sharpen your ideas. As we saw in Part 3, ideas are organic: they grow and develop the more we work on them. At key moments, they coalesce and you realise to your delight that you now see clearly an important element in your thinking.

Ideas are organic: they grow and develop the more we work on them.

If you don't write at these moments, instead leaving this until the last stages of your review, not only can your ideas seem rushed, but even naïve and poorly developed. In the Introduction we discussed how important writing is to the formation of our ideas. I emphasised then that writing is a form of thinking: the most difficult, yet the most effective, form. It places us at the heart of our ideas, forcing us to pin our ideas down, clarify our thinking, check the consistency of our arguments and then capture all of this in language that conveys it accurately.

It's not until we have actually written about something in an attempt to explain it to others that we realise what we know and what we think about it. Until that moment, we may not be clear about it and whether it all makes consistent sense. Realising that others are going to read what we write forces us to pin our ideas down with complete clarity and accuracy.

- If you don't write up your ideas and instead leave them until the last minute, they can seem rushed and even naïve and poorly developed.
- Writing places us at the heart of our ideas, forcing us to pin our ideas down and clarify our thinking.
- Not until we attempt to explain something to others do we realise what we know and what we think about it.

8 Constant checks

Although the scheduled stocktaking with your supervisor is the most effective way of maintaining control over how your review is developing over the longer term, day-to-day and week-by-week we also need to check that we are meeting our targets. Most of us can easily get sidetracked into comfort zones: those familiar, reassuring activities that give us the impression that we're doing real work, when we might not be. The opposite is equally true: that we get into the habit of trying to do too many things at once. To give you control over these problems you need to review your progress regularly against your schedule.

- Be aware of getting sidetracked into comfort zones.
- Notice when you're trying to do too many things at once.

The simplest and most effective way of doing this is to plot on your weekly timetable a half-hour session each day to check the jobs you have to do the following day and then to have a similar session at the end of the week to check the following week's work. In this way you can make yourself constantly aware of what's been done and what needs to be done. If you haven't been able to complete a piece of work, you can adjust your schedule. Alternatively, if you've completed work earlier than scheduled, it helps to have a list of other unscheduled jobs that you can do in the available time.

> Plot on your weekly timetable daily and weekly checks on what you have to do.

To make these checks effective it helps if you can design a weekly form, like the one below, listing those scheduled jobs that you need to do on each day and unscheduled jobs, in case you finish a job early or one drops out.

Weekly Work Schedule

Days	Scheduled work	Unscheduled work
Monday		
Tuesday		
Wednesday		
Thursday		
Friday		
Saturday		
Sunday		

Maintaining control

Writing a literature review is a complex and, at times, a confusing task. Ideas can come to you from all angles and patterns take shape rapidly, while you struggle to cling to everything and complete the work you have to do. But, as we've seen in this chapter, there are simple things you can do and systems you can set up to manage your work, which will give you more control over it.

 You can download copies of the tables, the Weekly Timetable, the Work Schedule and the Weekly Work Schedule from the companion website (www.macmillanihe.com/greetham-literature-review).

Summary

1 Planning your time and building in stage deadlines helps you chart a clear course through your work.
2 Stage deadlines give you early warning checks in case you need to adjust your schedule.
3 Create the right balance between work and relaxation to give your mind enough time to process the ideas.
4 Sessions with supervisors will help you stand back from your day-to-day work and look back and forward.
5 To avoid getting sidetracked, check day-to-day and week-by-week that you are meeting your targets.

What next?

In this chapter, we have set up simple systems to organise how we go about our work. In the next chapter, we will look at what we need to do to create the same sort of control over the ideas and material that we generate.

Chapter 14

Managing Your Material

In this chapter, you will learn...

- how to keep an accurate record of all your searches;
- a simple way of recording and comparing the findings of each source;
- how to create a retrieval system that catches your brightest ideas and the connections you make;
- how to avoid noting too much detail in long, complex, time-consuming notes;
- a system for managing your notes in preparation for planning and writing your review.

As we analyse concepts and synthesise ideas, creating connections that lead off in unpredictable directions, it can seem confusing, indeed, even chaotic. At times it's difficult to keep track of all the strands to our thinking and the route that our searches have taken. To cope with this, we need a simple system that will do two things:

1 keep a record of all the searches we make;
2 and record all the valuable ideas we generate and connections we make.

With this in place, we can take full advantage of all those insightful moments when we make connections between ideas and see things clearly for the first time. Equally important, with a detailed record of our searches we can avoid doing the same search twice or, worse still, missing out a significant part of the literature, which we have mistakenly assumed we have already covered. Indeed, this is even more important in certain disciplines, where examiners of both stand-alone reviews and some postgraduate dissertations and theses expect to see the detail of how we chose which sources to use, our process of selection and omission, and how we went about looking for relevant material.

1 Keeping a record of your searches

As we search, it's all too easy just to try one thing after another in quick succession without keeping a record of what we've done. As a result, we're likely to repeat the same searches at a later date. More important, we're also likely to overlook useful combinations of words or different forms of the same idea expressed in different words that we might otherwise have seen if we had slowed down a little and recorded each step.

Indeed, often it's only by looking at the record of our searches that we see something important that we've missed. And, of course, this also helps when we decide to repeat a search to see if a new publication or a new edition of a journal has appeared.

Flowchart

In Chapter 6, we saw how useful the flowchart below can be in recording the keywords and phrases you use, along with the Boolean operators, the search engines and the databases and catalogues you search.

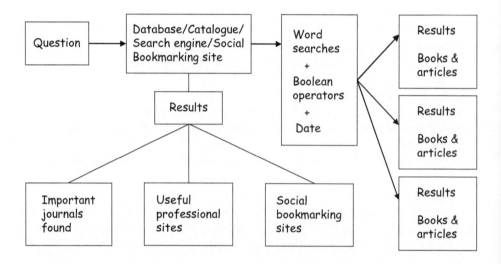

This will give you an accurate record of each search you make and the sources you find. However, at that point you will probably need more space to record and compare your findings from each of your sources. One useful way of doing this is to mark up a sheet of paper with columns under the following headings. Once you've entered the information in each of the columns you can then compare your findings from different sources by working down each column.

Author/s year	Aims or research question	Location of study	Sample size and identity	Data collection methods	Key findings
Source 1					

Source 2					
Source 3					
Source 4					

The headings above are useful for projects that involve empirical research. For those that have a theoretical and textual focus, try the following alternative.

Author/s year	Aims or research question	Key ideas	Similarities	Dissimilarities	Observations
Source 1					
Source 2					
Source 3					
Source 4					

Of course, you can adapt these columns and design the structure to meet your own needs, but you can see how useful this could be. If you enter just essential information from each source on a structured list like this without cluttering it up with irrelevant detail, you can make comparisons and see connections between them more easily. And, of course, when you come to plan and write the review this can form the basis of a section in which you might compare a number of studies.

Reference management software

As for the simpler task of just recording the details of each source, which you can then use to compile your bibliography or reference list, there are a number of software packages that can help you. The most convenient is the Microsoft management tool, which you can find under the reference tab in Microsoft Word. This allows you to store the bibliographical details of references, insert citations as you write and automatically create a reference list.

Other software packages allow you to do similar things, like RefWorks, ProCite, EndNote or Zotero, an open-source, free equivalent. With these you can store the details of references, manually enter data and add your comments on them. And, of course, the advantage of any software package is that it enables you to access the information from any computer.

2 Recording your ideas

As for the ideas we generate from our searches, this calls for a more sophisticated system. Research is a continuous, unbroken process: our ideas are constantly evolving, suddenly appearing in a new form at unexpected times. The quality of our work depends upon whether we can catch these ideas as and when they occur.

However, for much of the time our mental space can be full of irrelevant preoccupations that prowl around and hijack our thinking. In such cluttered minds, there is very little room for serious thought. The thoughts may be there, full of insight and vision, but, if we can't clear a space to think quietly and tap into them, we can easily pass by without even knowing they are there.

> The quality of our work depends upon whether we can catch our brightest ideas and sharpest insights as and when they occur.

Consequently, we need a retrieval system that is sufficiently adaptable to catch the ideas *whenever* and *wherever* they show themselves, and to provide us with a means of accessing them easily. The influence of such a system is never neutral. Get it right and we can find ourselves with an abundance of insightful ideas that are genuinely our own. Get it wrong and our work struggles to rise above the predictable and imitative. The following system will help you record and use more of your brightest ideas.

A retrieval system

1 Notebook
2 Journal
3 Index card system
4 Slip notes
5 Project box

1 Notebook

There is a constant internal dialogue going on in our minds as we think about our research question and search the literature. But good ideas only come to the prepared mind: one that is alive to this dialogue and ready to record insights whenever they appear. These brilliant flashes emerge briefly, disappearing almost as quickly. So getting used to carrying a notebook wherever you go or an electronic equivalent, like *Online Notebook*, which you can access through your smartphone or tablet, are effective ways of recording this internal dialogue and the insights it throws up.

Such a system is invaluable for the work we did in Part 3, where we saw how a successful literature review depends upon our abilities to get to the heart of our ideas by:

- analysing concepts into their parts;
- revealing the structures of ideas at the heart of them;
- adapting the structures to design new ways of approaching a problem;
- synthesising ideas to produce significant, original breakthroughs in what we know.

A notebook is there to catch these sudden insights. It's the way we record the continual analysis and synthesis of our ideas going on beneath the surface. And, equally significant, this is a self-fuelling process: the more you invest, the more you are rewarded. If you allow your ideas to tumble out onto the page or write out a problem that's troubling you, your subconscious will take over and process the ideas in ways you hardly suspected when you set out the issues. When you return consciously to your ideas, more often than not the problem that was troubling you has been resolved and you now see things clearly.

This is a self-fuelling process: the more you invest, the more you are rewarded.

2 Journal

In contrast, a journal gives you a way of being more active, of stimulating your ideas, rather than waiting for them to emerge. Using either a manual or a computer file, work two or three half-hour sessions into your weekly timetable to write about your work. As a student, you may only very rarely allow yourself to write freely about your ideas in this way. Most students normally write having been set an assignment, or while they work with books or notes, so the ideas that are genuinely theirs, untainted by what they're reading or referring to, rarely reach the surface, although they're always there.

Equally valuable, each time we write we plant the seeds of ideas that will develop of their own accord. Like a notebook, the process is self-fuelling. Coming up with ideas is a continuous, unbroken process. Good or bad, they breed other ideas. We may produce an idea that clearly wouldn't work, but it is very likely to produce others that will.

> Each time we write we plant the seeds of ideas that will develop of their own accord.

Another significant bonus is that allowing your ideas to come through in this way will give your review coherent shape. Recording the continuity of your thinking helps you avoid the plight of many reviews that disintegrate into a series of disjointed summaries. Indeed, when you come to write your first draft, much of it will be pieced together from different notebook jottings and journal entries, recording those red-hot moments when ideas just came fully formed with glaring clarity to be written down. As you can see, this is not a tidy process. But your best ideas will come from a continuous process of coherent thought recorded in notebooks and journals.

- Allowing your ideas to come through in this way will give your review coherent shape.
- Coming up with ideas is a continuous, unbroken process.
- Your best ideas will come from a continuous process of coherent thought recorded in your notebook and journal.

3 Card index

A notebook and journal are effective in catching and developing all those ideas that are the product of our continuous thought and the web of ideas we create. But in our work we often come across isolated items: an interesting idea, a useful statistic or a quotation we might read in a journal. These are likely to be lost if we don't record them somewhere.

> The problem: how do we catch valuable isolated material?

The most effective way of doing this is to adopt an index-card system, either manually or online using systems like Dropbox and Google Docs. Using just one card for each item – a quotation, an argument, an idea or a set of figures – with a reference to where it came from, you'll have a retrieval system that makes it very easy to find what you want whenever you want it.

It's also a simple and effective way of recording all your sources, along with a brief note of why they were useful, so that you have a clear idea of how you might use them again. This will save you an enormous amount of time, when you begin to compile your reference list and bibliography. There are few things more frustrating than spending hours tracking down a reference that you failed to record at the time. With all the bibliographical details recorded at the top of the card, you have all the information at your fingertips when you need it.

- A card index is a useful way of recording isolated items we might otherwise lose.
- It is a simple means of recording the bibliographical details of sources.
- It is also an effective system of recording why they were useful and how you could use them again.

With this you will have a remarkably efficient way of lining up all of the details you will need as you come to plan and write your review, particularly if you organise your cards in the same sections and in the same order that you intend to take them in your review.

4 Slip notes

However, the core materials that we find ourselves dealing with most of the time are the longer paper notes we take from articles. This gives us two problems that we all struggle to solve:

1 How can we avoid using up too much time taking long, complex notes as we process our sources, only to discover later that they not only have far more detail than we need, but reflect the author's interests, rather than our own?

2 And then, how do we manage all these notes – what do we do with them? How do we file them so that we can use them when we come to plan and write our review? If we're not careful, the heavy bureaucratic weight of these notes can easily bury our most creative ideas as we try to organise and sequence them.

If you keep hard copies of texts in the form of photocopies of key chapters or articles, you'll find you can process them more flexibly than you can online copies. But to avoid taking long, complex notes try using slip notes attached to each photocopy. These are brief structural notes taken on A4 paper cut into thirds so that they measure around 10 × 21 cm with three or four slips for each article. This forces you to record just the key ideas that form the basic structure of the article without cluttering it up with unnecessary material that obscures the key points.

Then, in a different colour, add your own ideas, opinions, criticisms and cross-references. If you use only one side of each slip for the main structural notes, your own comments can go on the blank side of the previous slip facing the notes that you are commenting on. These notes can then be stapled or paper-clipped onto the front of the photocopy and filed in your project box. Later, when you begin to plan and write your review, you'll find that you have in a manageable form the key structure of the article in front of you, along with your ideas and responses that you can develop into a coherent argument, bringing in other articles that you have cross-referenced.

- Hard copies of chapters and articles can be processed more flexibly.
- Slip notes avoid clutter that obscures the key points.
- They give you, in a manageable form, the key structure of the article, along with your ideas, which you can develop into a coherent argument.

5 Project box

The best way of tackling the second problem of how we organise this is to use a project box with hanging files divided into the sections of your literature review. If you divide up each section using folders for each subsection of your review, you can then file the photocopies of articles with your slip notes attached. In addition, you can also file those notes you might take at a lecture or when ideas come to you in those unguarded moments when you are reading a newspaper article or watching a programme on TV.

When you begin your review, you'll find in your project box a wealth of material you might otherwise have ignored for want of somewhere to store it.

The great advantage of this system is that, knowing you have somewhere to store material like this, the more you will find and the more interesting and insightful your ideas will become as a result. When you begin to plan and write your review each folder you open will be full of material that you might otherwise have ignored for want of somewhere to store it. Even more important, this matches and takes full advantage of the way our ideas evolve. They adapt to new ideas as we come across them, but we first need to register those ideas as significant and worth storing, and for this we need a convenient place to store them.

Resolving an inherent contradiction

Anyone undertaking a literature review at an early stage confronts what appears to be an inherent contradiction: to meet its demands we need a system that catches and records all the detail, while being free of the clutter that hides the structure of our ideas and the connections we create between them. In this chapter, we've seen ways in which we can resolve this contradiction.

 You can download copies of the flowchart and table in this chapter from the companion website (www.macmillanihe.com/greetham-literature-review).

Summary
1 To avoid repeating the same search or missing out a significant part of the literature, we need to keep a record of the searches we make.
2 The quality of our work depends on catching our brightest ideas and sharpest insights.
3 Coming up with ideas is a continuous, unbroken process: good or bad, they breed other ideas.
4 Recording your ideas in your notebook and journal will give your review coherent shape.
5 Slip notes give you the key structure of the article, along with your ideas, which you can develop into a coherent argument.

What next?
In this chapter, we have seen the most effective ways we can record our searches and capture ideas wherever and whenever they appear. In the next chapter, we will examine how we can improve the way we read and process our sources.

Chapter 15

Reading

In this chapter, you will learn…

> - how to read only what you have to in the most efficient way;
> - how to ensure that what you have to read is a reliable source;
> - how to ensure that you only read what is relevant to your needs;
> - the importance of reading purposefully;
> - how to read actively and process the ideas at a deeper level.

A typical literature review could take up to 30–40 per cent of the time for most dissertations and theses, and involve, as a cautious estimate, between 25 and 50 references for an undergraduate dissertation and stand-alone reviews, and anything up to 300 for a PhD thesis. Obviously, this poses the real danger of getting bogged down in texts that turn out only to be peripheral to our main interests, soak up more time than we can afford and leave us with a vast amount of unusable material. So we must make sure that we read only what we have to and in the most efficient way.

1 Reading only what we have to

Deciding what we should read raises two obvious problems – the two Rs: reliability and relevance.

Reliability

Although in Chapter 7 we covered the seven steps we need to take when we check the reliability of sources on the Internet, what follows applies to all sources and authors. Before you start to read a source, ask yourself the questions in the table below. If you can answer satisfactorily more than half, it is probably worth reading, but if you can't, it may not be. And even if it is indispensable and directly relevant to your topic, read the content with these reservations in mind and, perhaps, raise them in your literature review.

Reliability of source material	
Authors	Are the authors named?
	Are their qualifications relevant?
	Are they well-known authorities?
	Do they have other publications?

Reliability of source material		
Sources	Who do they work for?	
	Has the article been paid for?	
	Has it been refereed or edited?	
	Is this a primary or secondary source?	
	What references have been cited?	
	How does it compare with other sources on the same subject?	

The author

Although these questions seem obvious, get used to asking them routinely. Work your way systematically through the list. If no-one is named as the author, it may be that no-one is willing to accept responsibility for the views expressed. Check the author's qualifications. They may be irrelevant to this area of study. Check to see whether the author is a well-known authority, perhaps by entering her name into a search engine. You can also check to see how much she has published in this area and perhaps who she works for, whether it's an academic institution or a commercial body.

Nevertheless, it's still worth exercising some caution before you dismiss a source simply on the grounds that it comes from an author who is not known or who is not an authority. He may still have done some quite remarkable, ground-breaking work, which has placed him outside the conventional thinking in his subject.

Modern physics   EXAMPLE

In 1905, four research papers in physics were published by a lowly, unknown 'Engineer, Second Class' employed in the Patent Office in Bern, who had been rejected by every academic institution and had published nothing before. But now, no-one doubts the significance of Einstein's papers and the impact they had on modern physics.

The source

As for the questions we ought to be asking about the source, here there are fewer caveats to be made. If the article has been paid for, it might be serving other interests than the truth. If it is a secondary source, check for 'selection bias'. Has the author just chosen those parts of the primary source that support his preconceived position? It is, of course, reassuring to know that the author can cite other sources in support of his case. And if it has appeared in a journal that is refereed by the author's peers, this is usually a good guide to its reliability. Still, this is not always a guarantee of excellence.

Postmodernism   EXAMPLE

In 1996, Alan Sokal, a physics teacher at New York University, wrote a hoax paper which parodied the arguments of postmodernist thinkers. Despite the fact it made no sense and was just built around quotes from these writers, his paper was published unchanged by a peer-reviewed journal.

Relevance

Now that you have settled the question of reliability you can decide whether your source is relevant and how much time to spend on it.

Reading purposefully

The key to this is to read purposefully: know what you're looking for so you don't waste your time. Now that you have pinned down your research question and the sub-questions that define the concrete evidence that you're looking for, you can be clearer about those parts you need to read carefully word-for-word and those you can skim and scan. A search of the literature may throw up as many as 100 different sources, so we need to skim and scan them to decide which we need to read and what parts of them.

2 Reading in the most efficient way

As you can see, at this point we begin to address the second question we raised in the introduction to this chapter: how to make sure we use our time economically by reading in the most efficient way.

Books

Our approach to books differs slightly from the way we approach journal articles. Although much of this is common sense, it is worth being clear about the stages we go through to narrow down as clearly as possible what we need to read.

With books it's unlikely that we will have to read them from cover to cover. So we need to pin down exactly which passages look as if they will be useful. Obviously the first thing to do is consult the contents and index pages to locate those pages that deal with the questions and issues we're interested in. But if that doesn't help, read the first paragraph of each chapter, where the author explains what she will be doing in this chapter, and then the last paragraph, where she explains how she has done it.

If that leaves you unsure, quickly skim each page, picking up a general impression of the contents of each chapter, taking note of the headings and subheadings of sections, which are likely to give you an overview of the structure of the chapter. If this doesn't help, scan each page swiftly, looking for key concepts. You may find these are high-lighted in some way, in bold or in italics. See if you can pick out the sequence of ideas as the author develops her arguments.

Check:

- the contents page;
- the index;
- chapter headings;
- the first and last chapters;
- summaries at the end of the chapters and at the end of the book;
- the first and last paragraphs in each chapter.
- **Skim** the text for a general impression of the contents and structure, taking note of headings and sub-headings of sections.
- **Scan** for key concepts.
- Pick out the sequence of ideas.

Journal articles

With journal articles the same approach applies, although here we have a little more help. You'll find that the most useful aspect of most articles is the abstract. It is here that authors explain the main rationale of the study, their intentions, the key results and their interpretation of them. So, as you read the abstract, ask yourself:

- Is the article too general or too specific?
- Is its main focus different from the focus of your review?
- Are there restrictions (limited number of years, locations or people involved) that make it less relevant to your review?
- Does it contain useful information about the research methods employed and the practical problems involved?

This may be enough to convince you that it could be useful. Even so, it's still worth skimming the summary and conclusions. If there is no summary, skim the discussion section, if that's obvious. What you're looking for is whether it's relevant to the question and sub-questions you pinned down as a result of the work you did in Chapter 5.

The importance of purposeful reading lies in the fact that because we make clear why we are reading a source we are likely to read it more efficiently. In Chapter 5, when we were searching for the right research question, our reading was more exploratory as we treasure hunted and mapped out the territory, so we made more use of our skills to skim and scan. But in Part 3, where we were reading in greater depth, critically evaluating our sources, analysing concepts to reveal the key connections between our ideas and then synthesising them into patterns, we needed to concentrate on the detail, reading word-for-word.

Using our reading skills flexibly

At this point, it's worth being sure that we all know what we mean by skimming, scanning and reading word-for-word, so we can use these skills more flexibly to suit the different demands placed on our reading.

Reading strategies

1 We read carefully **word-for-word** when we're reading a text or a passage we know is of central importance to our work, from which we want to extract in our notes the detailed structure of the main points and subsections.

2 In contrast, when we just want to pick up the general impression of the contents, the key ideas and the broad structure of a text or an article, we would do better to **skim** it.

3 And, if we're just looking for an answer to a specific question, say a date, a name, a set of figures or what the writer says about a certain subject, we need to **scan** it.

Reading purposefully   EXERCISE

Faced with the following situations decide which reading strategy would best suit your purpose: do you skim, scan or read word-for-word?

1 You find a long article that may be relevant to your review, but you're not sure.
2 As you write your review you remember a passage from an article you have read that would be useful to support the argument you are making, but you can't remember where you read it, although you know it must be from one of three articles.
3 A new edition of a journal has just appeared in the library with an article, which seems as if it might cover some of the issues that your review addresses.
4 You have found two articles by authors who hold conflicting positions on a problem that lies at the heart of the issues you are analysing in your review.
5 The topic of your thesis is 'George Orwell: *Homage to Catalonia* and the effects of the Spanish Civil War on his writing.' You find an article with the title, 'Writers and the Spanish Civil War.'

Answers:

1 Skim to get a general impression of the contents of the article.
2 Scan the articles to find the passage you're looking for.
3 Skim the article to see if it is relevant to the issues you discuss in your review.
4 Read them word-for-word to get a clear understanding of the issues involved and where the conflict lies.
5 Scan it to see whether it mentions George Orwell and the impact that his involvement in the civil war had on his writing.

Processing ideas – reading actively

However, efficient reading is not just about choosing the right skill, but about how well we process the ideas while we read. In Chapter 8, we drew the distinction between surface-level and deep-level processors.

- **Surface-level processors** read passively without analysing and structuring what they read, and without critically evaluating the arguments, evidence and ideas the author presents. The reviews they produce tend to be mere summaries of their sources.
- In contrast, **deep-level processors** use their higher cognitive abilities to analyse, synthesise and critically evaluate what they read. In effect, they discuss the author's ideas as they read: analysing their implications, critically evaluating them and synthesising them into new ways of seeing and understanding the problem.

Now you know why you're reading the sources left on your list and what sections you need to read, you can begin processing the ideas more deeply as you read. Ultimately, the quality of the work we produce depends upon the quality of our internal processing of the ideas. It is not the speed at which you read these texts that matters, but the depth in which you process the ideas.

- Surface-level processors read passively without analysing and structuring what they read.
- Deep-level processors use their higher cognitive abilities to analyse, synthesise and critically evaluate the ideas.
- It is not the speed at which you read these texts that matters, but the depth in which you process the ideas.

Writing in response to what you read

If something comes to you, clearly insisting on your attention, give in to it. Get into the habit of allowing yourself to respond to what you read by writing in your notebook your thoughts and ideas as they come to you. Never put it off; otherwise the intensity will fade and you'll lose the very thing that will mark your work out as original.

> Write down the ideas as they come to you; otherwise you will lose the intensity in which you first saw them.

Remember what we have said previously about writing: it is a form of thinking, the most efficient form. You may have read carefully and taken the most detailed notes, but it's not until you begin writing that you reveal just how much you understand. This will help you integrate the ideas into your thinking, converting them into your own thought structures, so that you are much more firmly in control of them. As a result, you will be able to forge deeper, more significant connections between the ideas.

There will be times when you struggle to understand a difficult passage. When this occurs step away from your work, leave it for an hour or two and then come back and write out what you understand. It will reveal the gaps in your understanding, which you will have to deal with by going back to the original passage. In this way you build onto your understanding, piece by piece, until you know that you have a deep and comprehensive grasp of it all.

Multiple readings

To make sure you process them deeply, you are likely to find that you will have to read many of your sources more than once, particularly those that are technical and closely argued.

Reading for comprehension

First we might read just to understand the content of the article. It may be full of complex, tightly argued passages that need to be read more than once, or there may be a number of unfamiliar technical terms that you need to think about carefully each time they are used.

Reading for analysis and structure

Once you've understood the arguments, you can take out the organising structure of the article. To do this you need to analyse the passage into sections and subsections, so you can see how you're going to organise it in your notes. You could do this using slip notes that we discussed in the last chapter, using structured linear notes (see Chapter 16), before you then read it again to critically evaluate the arguments.

Reading for criticism and evaluation

In the second and third readings, our processing is a lot more active. In the second we analysed the passage so we could take out the structure, while in the third we're maintaining a dialogue with the author, through which we're able to criticise and evaluate his arguments. If you read Chapters 8 and 9, again you will see the issues to focus on, but the following checklist will help as a convenient guide.

Criticism and evaluation	
Evaluating arguments	1. What are the key claims made by the author?
	2. Does she develop them consistently?
	3. Does she leave some parts undeveloped which could lead to alternative conclusions?
	4. Have any assumptions been made without acknowledging them?
Evaluating evidence	1. Does she use enough evidence to back up her arguments?
	2. What kind of evidence is it and does she describe it accurately?
	From primary or secondary sources?
	Statistical – how is it described? Is it accurate?
	Anecdotal – how reliable/representative is this?
	3. Does she draw reasonable inferences from it to develop her arguments?
	Does she draw conclusions that are too strong?
	Is the evidence relevant to her arguments?
	4. What alternative inferences can be drawn from the evidence?
	5. What do other authors have to say about this?
Evaluating language	1. Is she consistent in the way she uses words or do they mean different things at different times?

Criticism and evaluation	
	2. Is the meaning of her arguments obscured by the use of jargon and abstractions?
	3. Do we need to analyse concepts to reveal the hidden implications of her arguments?

Deep-level processing of your ideas while you read takes time; it can't be rushed. But now that you have narrowed down what you need to read word-for-word, you have the time to integrate what you read into your own thinking and create your own synthesis of ideas.

 You can download copies of the checklist and tables in this chapter, along with additional exercises, from the companion website (www.macmillanihe.com/greetham-literature-review).

Summary

1 It's easy to get bogged down in reading sources and allow your review to take up more time than you can afford.
2 If we're clear about why we are reading a source, we are likely to read it more efficiently.
3 Deep-level processors discuss the author's arguments as they read.
4 It is not the speed of our reading that matters, but the depth in which we process the ideas.
5 Writing about what you have read will help you integrate the ideas into your own thinking.

What next?

In this chapter, we have seen the various ways in which we process ideas as we read. For each of these ways, there is the most effective note-taking strategy to catch our ideas and develop them. In the next chapter, we will see the different strategies you can choose to suit each level of processing.

Chapter 16

Note-Taking

In this chapter, you will learn...

- the importance of being flexible in your use of different note-taking strategies;
- that there are different note-taking strategies for the different levels of processing;
- how to use linear notes and matrixes to reveal the structure and relations between ideas;
- how time lines can be used to piece together elements to create a complete picture of how they are related;
- how pattern notes allow us to work faster and more creatively.

Literature reviews call upon us to use a wide range of abilities. In the last chapter, we saw the complexity involved in processing the ideas we read on different levels. After we have read a difficult source for comprehension, we have to analyse it to identify the structure into which the ideas are organised. And then we must process it more actively at a deeper level, analysing the implications of the author's arguments, critically evaluating them and synthesising the ideas into new ways of seeing and understanding the problem.

For all of these different levels of processing, we need to develop a more sophisticated and adaptable range of note-taking strategies that we can use to record the ideas and our responses to them. We then need to learn to use these flexibly, moving from one to another depending on the level of processing we are recording in our notes.

Flexibility

Unfortunately, most of us get used to using just one method of note-taking and we're reluctant to experiment with alternatives, when it's clear we need a more effective strategy that will meet the different demands on us.

Noting with high-lighter pens   EXAMPLE

Some students prefer to record what they read by using high-lighter pens for all their note-taking. Indeed some develop highly complex systems in which different colours are used for different types of information: one colour for main points, another for subsidiary points, yet another for examples and then one more for their own comments.

While many believe this works for them, it nevertheless poses a serious danger. Such a system gives us the impression that the ideas are being processed in a complex and thorough way, yet in fact quite the reverse might be occurring. It is as if we substitute systematic record-keeping for genuine thinking: surface-level processing for deep-level processing.

In this example, we all recognise a problem that we experience at one time or another. Note-taking can give us the impression that we are working really hard, when in fact we are on autopilot.

Shorthand and stenographers   EXAMPLE

In the age of shorthand, secretaries could take down a letter from dictation with complete accuracy, but if they were then asked to explain what it was about, it would be no surprise if they were to admit they had no idea. Similarly, stenographers today can record with complete accuracy what is being said without ever processing it deeply.

To meet the demands of a literature review, we need to learn methods of creating notes that capture in clear structures the complex ideas we produce from different levels of processing. This means, at the very least, that we need methods that will:

1 capture the organisation and structure of the ideas we read in our sources;
2 and enable us to record and develop our own reactions to them – our criticisms, analyses and syntheses of the ideas.

At the same time, with different methods to choose from, we need to develop the capacity to move flexibly from one strategy to another depending on the nature of each task, rather than being wedded to just one strategy for all our notes. Our note-taking skills should promote our abilities, not stunt them by trapping them in a straightjacket of just one method we use to meet all our needs.

Note-taking strategies

For each level of processing, there is the most effective strategy of note-taking that will help us capture our ideas. Therefore, we have to learn to use a combination of strategies that will help us extract the hierarchy of ideas from the passages we read, selecting and rejecting material according to its relevance and importance. Then we need a strategy that will enable us to adapt these structures in the way we learnt in

Chapters 11 and 12 to reveal new insights and solutions to problems, and synthesise ideas to forge new connections between them.

1 Linear notes

As we read, our first task is to process the ideas we read into structures. Without clear structures, we struggle to use our ideas creatively. We don't have the sort of control over them that we need, so that we can reproduce them, adapt them and synthesise them with other structures.

   Linear notes are particularly good at this sort of analytical task. As you can see in the example below, they are the most common form of note-taking. As we develop the structure, with each step or indentation we indicate a further breakdown of the argument into subsections. These in turn can be broken down into further subsections. In this way, we can represent even the most complex argument in a structure that's quite easy to understand.

A section taken from linear notes on genes and gene therapy

3. Gene therapy:

   (a) Definition: technique for correcting defective genes responsible for disease
   (b) Methods:

      (i) Replacements –
         I. Normal gene replaces non-functional gene
         II. Abnormal gene replaces normal gene thro homologous recombination
      (ii) Repairs – abnormal gene repaired – selective reverse mutation
      (iii) Regulation (i.e. degree to which regulation is turned on/off) altered

4. Common method = I:

   (a) Vector = carrier molecule delivers gene to target cells
   (b) Virus = most common vector:

      (i) Evolved to infect cells
      (ii) Replace disease-carrying genes with therapeutic genes
      (iii) Types:

         I. Retroviruses
         II. Adenoviruses
         III. Adeno-associated viruses
         IV. Herpes simplex viruses

   (c) Non-viral delivery systems:

      (i) Direct intro of therapeutic DNA into target cells
      (ii) Creation of a liposome – artificial liquid sphere with aqueous core – to pass DNA thro target cell's membrane
      (iii) Linking therapeutic DNA to a molecule that binds to special cell receptors
      (iv) Introduce 47th (artificial human) chromosome into target cells

2 Matrixes

Alternatively, if you are writing a review in which you want to lay out clearly and compare the characteristics of the different subjects in your study, a matrix can often be the best strategy, as you can see below. As you read articles and take notes, you may come up with key descriptors that you can organise in a matrix to compare them. You might be comparing:

- the results of particular types of intervention;
- national trade figures for different countries;
- the contrasting features of novels or writers;
- the performances of organisations;
- comparisons of different periods of history;
- or the nature of different political revolutions.

Their contrasting characteristics can be entered onto a matrix, from which you can then draw conclusions. These sorts of complex, multi-faceted comparisons are difficult to draw without a structure, like a matrix, which allows you to lay out the different features in a clear structure.

Try this ...

As you read your sources, you may begin to realise that they fall into different categories. Some may be based on the same working assumption, or they may have selected their research sample from the population using the same sampling method, or employed the same research methodology. If these are significant to your review, you could set them out in a matrix and, when you come to write your review, compare the different studies using the comparisons of these categories as your framework.

A matrix used in this way can be useful both to you and your reader. It's an effective way of creating an overview that will help you organise and summarise your findings.

Developing integrated health and social care services for older people in Europe   EXAMPLE

In this review, the authors examined the main concepts of integrated care in selected EU member states. As you can see below, they listed these concepts and then evaluated how important they were in different countries.

Key concepts of integrated care	A	D	DK	EL	F	FIN	I	NL	UK
Public health discourse	**	**	**			*	***		**
Managed care (health system)	**	**	*		*	*	**	*	***
Horizontal integration (provider mix)	**	**		**	*	*	*	*	*
Vertical integration						**	**		**
Seamless care/transmural care	*					***		**	*
Gerontological co-ordination/networking	*	*			***		*		
Whole system approach									*
Person-centred approach			***			**		***	**

***most important concept being followed and implemented in mainstream provision
**important concept followed (partly implemented)
*concept being discussed and tried out in experimental (model) projects

Electronic forms of note-taking

If you prefer an electronic form of note-taking, you could use the table feature in Microsoft Word to create your matrix, or create it initially in Excel and then copy and paste it into Word once you have finished it. Excel gives you the advantage of being able to plot your findings according to a variety of factors: date, author, methodology and so on.

However, there is one word of caution about electronic forms of note-taking. The one thing you don't want is to allow any intervening medium between you and your ideas: between having an idea and recording it in a structure that best represents it. If you have to negotiate with the technology as you struggle to pin down your ideas and forge connections between them, you will slow yourself down just at the moment when you need to capture the torrent of ideas that come at you rapidly from all directions.

Beware of allowing any intervening medium between you and your ideas.

Of course, you might still prefer to work with electronic forms of note-taking. If so, keep it simple, adaptable and flexible. Anything that detracts from your ability to generate ideas and forces you into working in one particular way will put a break on your creativity.

Migration of skilled labour from Eastern Europe   EXAMPLE
1918–40: the effects on the German economy

At an early stage in this thesis, you would need to chart the levels of migration from Eastern European countries and their occupational structure. You might find the clearest and most useful way of exploring the relationship between these two descriptors is to set them out in a matrix as you can see in the following.

	Profs	Manual	Artisans	Shopkprs	Clerks	Merchants
Poland	35.1	213.7	83.6	14.2	11.6	64.3
Estonia	7.2	21.4	13.7	6.8	9.4	16.7
Latvia	6.8	14.7	11.2	4.2	6.5	11.5
Lithuania	4.6	11.8	8.3	6.7	3.2	7.7
Romania	5.6	13.8	9.1	7.2	2.8	5.8
Hungary	11.7	87.4	57.4	9.4	5.7	10.5
Bulgaria	4.3	9.4	7.2	3.7	4.6	8.5
Albania	3.7	5.4	4.8	2.3	4.5	7.2
Yugoslavia	23.6	137.2	58.6	11.9	7.3	15.7
Czech	31.5	123.8	53.4	10.8	7.1	16.8

All figures are in thousands. These are not the actual figures

3 Time lines

Similarly effective are time lines, particularly if your review takes on a chronological structure, in which you chronicle the trends, patterns or changing nature of opinion that has developed and now dominates a debate in a particular area. If you haven't already used them or seen them used, you'll find they are particularly good at making clear a sequence of events or, more usefully, the developing relations between different people, movements in thought, or organisations.

R.M. Hare and the emergence of preference utilitarianism   EXAMPLE
as the one absolute in ethical theory

In this thesis, you may want to track the way modern ethical theory has developed and how preference utilitarianism has emerged out of this. The most effective way of revealing this and the different forms that utilitarianism has taken, may be a time line that displays the relationships between different ethical theories over the last 300 years as you can see below.

Often we just want to see the whole picture: how the different things we have studied separately all interrelate. However, this sort of synthesis doesn't lend itself easily to most note-taking strategies that are designed principally for analytical work. So, if you want to piece everything together to see the complete whole, use a time line (see pages 168–9).

4 Pattern notes

In contrast, pattern notes are good at both analysis and synthesis. Using these, you will find it is easier to analyse a concept into its constituent ideas as well as synthesise ideas by forging unexpected connections between them. Indeed, by laying out your ideas in simple structures composed of single words or simple phrases you are better able to see the ideas, rather than burying them beneath a weight of words. As a result, because you can see more clearly how a concept might be analysed and how ideas could be related, you are freer to make connections that you might not otherwise have thought about.

Pattern notes come in various forms and are known by different names, including spider notes and mind or concept maps (see below), but the common element is that they allow us to record and develop our own ideas as quickly as they come to us. They are not to be confused with flow charts and other devices we use to represent our ideas graphically so that our **readers** can understand them. Pattern notes are a method we devise for **ourselves** of representing and working with our ideas as they form. So the key is to develop a system through which you can quickly record your thinking without losing any insight that might suddenly appear.

- It is easier to analyse concepts and synthesise ideas, because they are not buried under a weight of words.
- We can see more clearly how a concept might be analysed and ideas could be connected.
- Pattern notes are a method we devise for ourselves to represent and work with our ideas.

Working faster and more creatively

The best pattern notes allow you to work as fast as the ideas appear and as you see their connections with other ideas. As you search the literature and plan your review all sorts of syntheses of ideas will come to you. Not only do you have to record these as fast as they come, but integrate them with the notes you have already taken in order to find connections with other ideas. This is creative work – fast, confusing and difficult to keep track of.

Genuine thinking (and not just recycling received opinions) means we have to keep up with ideas as they come at us rapidly from all angles without any apparent predictability. Our minds can simply produce ideas and connections between them faster than we can find the words to write them down. Pattern notes, like mind maps, not only allow us to keep up but also to work on several lines of discussion simultaneously. In the process they give our own ideas much greater prominence, so that when we begin to review sources we are better prepared to evaluate and select from what we read.

- We have to keep up with ideas as they come at us rapidly from all angles without any apparent predictability.
- They allow us to work on several lines of discussion simultaneously.

Pattern notes – biodiversity and sustainability   EXAMPLE

After we had generated our ideas on this problem in Chapter 4, in Chapter 11 we adapted the ideas in the following pattern notes to see if we could find a solution (see page 170).

TIME

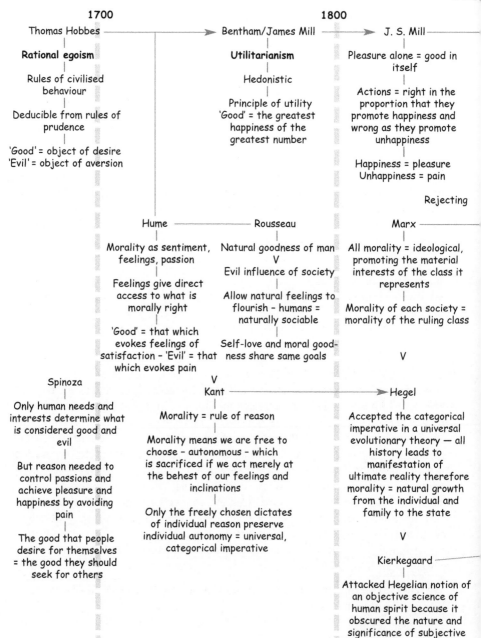

1700   **1800**

Thomas Hobbes ──────────────▶ Bentham/James Mill ──────▶ J. S. Mill ─────

Rational egoism   **Utilitarianism**   Pleasure alone = good in
│   │   itself
Rules of civilised   Hedonistic
behaviour   │   Actions = right in the
│   Principle of utility   proportion that they
Deducible from rules of   'Good' = the greatest   promote happiness and
prudence   happiness of the   wrong as they promote
│   greatest number   unhappiness
'Good' = object of desire   │
'Evil' = object of aversion   Happiness = pleasure
                                                               Unhappiness = pain

                                                                    Rejecting

                Hume ────────── Rousseau   Marx ─────
                  │   │
        Morality as sentiment,   Natural goodness of man   All morality = ideological,
          feelings, passion   V   promoting the material
                  │   Evil influence of society   interests of the class it
          Feelings give direct   │   represents
           access to what is   Allow natural feelings to   │
            morally right   flourish – humans =   Morality of each society =
                  │   naturally sociable   morality of the ruling class
          'Good' = that which   │
          evokes feelings of   Self-love and moral good-
    satisfaction – 'Evil' = that ness share same goals   V
          which evokes pain
                                        V
Spinoza   Kant ────────────────────▶ Hegel
  │   │   │
Only human needs and   Morality = rule of reason   Accepted the categorical
interests determine what   │   imperative in a universal
is considered good and   Morality means we are free to evolutionary theory — all
evil   choose – autonomous – which   history leads to
  │   is sacrificed if we act merely at manifestation of
But reason needed to   the behest of our feelings and ultimate reality therefore
control passions and   inclinations   morality = natural growth
achieve pleasure and   │   from the individual and
happiness by avoiding   Only the freely chosen dictates family to the state
pain   of individual reason preserve
  │   individual autonomy = universal,   V
The good that people   categorical imperative
desire for themselves
= the good they should   Kierkegaard ─────
seek for others   │
                                                           Attacked Hegelian notion of
                                                            an objective science of
                                                            human spirit because it
                                                            obscured the nature and
                                                            significance of subjective
                                                            truth. Problem of morality =
                                                            problem of subjective
                                                            choice and commitment

ETHICS

1900

Henry Sidgwick ⟶ R. M. Hare

Hedonistic utilitarianism

Denied that moral terms could
be defined in non-moral terms

Morality = founded on *a priori*
moral intuition that 'we ought
to aim at pleasure'

Prescriptivism – if a person utters a
moral judgement he is prescribing a course
of action

Preference utilitarianism – what we
ought to do is revealed by calculating the
strength of the conflicting preferences of
those affected

morality

Nietzsche

Moral conduct = necessary
only for the weak who inhibit
the self-realisation of the
strong therefore every action
should be directed to the
development of the superior
individual – the 'overman' or
'superman'

G. E. Moore

Intuitionism

Rightness of an action depends on good or
bad consequences but many sorts of things
apart from pleasure and pain = good in
themselves

'Good'= unanalysable quality – we learn
what it is through intuition

Ethical sentences = descriptive of the world
therefore true or false
=
Cognitivism

V

Logical positivism

Non-cognitivism

Ethical language≠ descriptive – statements
have only emotional or persuasive significance, e.g. A. J. Ayer and emotivism

Existentialism

Religious existentialism
Martin Buber
Paul Tillich
Karl Jaspers

Non-religious existentialists
Martin Heidegger
J-P. Sartre
Human beings = alone in the universe
therefore they are solely responsible for the
choices they make

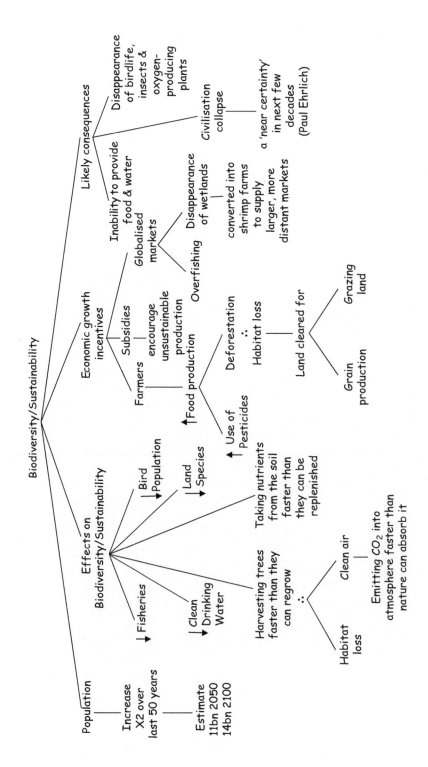

Mind map – rise in world population

Mind map – biodiversity and sustainability   EXAMPLE

Alternatively, as part of our exploration of the possible solutions to the crisis facing biodiversity and sustainability, we could have generated our ideas on the causes of the rise of world population using a mind map, as you can see on the previous page.

Throughout this chapter, we've seen how important it is to cultivate as much flexibility as possible in the note-taking strategies that we use in order to meet the varied demands that a literature review places on our skills. Obviously, our ability to discuss and criticise the implications of the literature we read, and to develop our own ideas, depends first on the skills needed to lay bare its structure and record it, using linear notes, matrixes and time lines. But after this, as we begin to generate our own ideas on sources, our criticisms, evaluations and syntheses, we need a strategy that will respond in a flexible way to capture these as they develop.

Summary

1 For the different levels of processing, we need a sophisticated and adaptable range of note-taking strategies.
2 We need to develop the capacity to move flexibly from one strategy to another, rather than being wedded to one strategy for all our notes.
3 Don't allow an intervening medium between you and your ideas.
4 Pattern notes allow us to see clearly our ideas and the connections between them, rather than burying them beneath the weight of words.
5 They help us work faster and more creatively.

What next?

In the Introduction, I made the point that the important thing to remember is that writing a literature review is not about **what** you know, but about **how** you think. Genuine thinking, rather than merely recycling the ideas of those you regard as authorities, means thinking for yourself and gathering your own ideas and insights.

In Part 4, we have found that to do this we must be flexible in how we organise our retrieval system to catch our own ideas, and in how we read and take notes, so that we can process ideas using our higher cognitive abilities. Now we have to decide which of these ideas we are going to use and how we are going to bring them together in a plan, from which we can write our review.

Part 5

Planning Your Review

Chapter 17

Deciding Which Sources to Use

In this chapter, you will learn...

- the problems associated with a review that is a mere summary of your sources;
- how to avoid this;
- how to decide what sources to use based on how you're going to use them;
- how to decide on the basis of their content;
- the importance of integrating your sources into a coherent whole that your readers can understand.

The dilemma we all face as we plan our literature review is how to describe and demonstrate our broad understanding of the background of our research and the debates that dominate our subject, while only using sources that bear directly on the specific issues raised by our research. The sort of scene-setting implied by the first part of the dilemma must not lead us off into areas that are irrelevant to our research. This makes our decision as to what sources to use particularly difficult.

Synopsis – creating 'background'

Of course, the solution lies in knowing exactly why you're writing a literature review. But more often than not, this is where the confusion begins. Many students are told that they must begin with a synopsis of the literature. But this gets you into the business of summarising all the literature in the area to give some 'background' to your own research or to your stand-alone review, and to impress examiners with how much you've read and understood. Inevitably this results in certain well-known problems.

1 No link between the review and your research project

After the synopsis, when you get down to outlining your own work, the review takes an abrupt change of pace and heads in a substantially different direction, effectively starting again. Indeed, much of what you've mentioned in the synopsis is never mentioned again. This is one of the most common criticisms made of students' reviews, that the link between the literature and their own project is not clear: that they fail to relate clearly the findings of the literature to their own study.

2 The struggle to decide what's relevant

This will leave you so confused that you'll simply have no idea where to start. Most students who are encouraged to approach a review in this way struggle to decide what's relevant, set themselves the task of reading everything remotely related to their topic and waste time on irrelevant and trivial material. Inevitably, as it encourages them to summarise all the findings of each article they read, when they only need comment on those bits that throw light on what they plan to do, they end including in their review a mass of material that is not relevant to their study.

3 Managing the material and your time

Finally, when you come to plan your review you will be left with little clue as to how to organise this mass of material, which is likely to take up far too much time and space. Indeed, if you were not to abandon this strategy, you would have little space for anything else. What should take up, say, 20 per cent of the words in a dissertation or thesis will, in effect, take up nearer 50 per cent. You'll be left with a mass of material, much of it quite irrelevant, which you will ignore in the rest of your work.

Synopsis – creating background

1 No link between the review and your project
2 Difficult to decide what's relevant
3 Waste time on irrelevant and trivial material
4 End up with a mass of material that is not relevant
5 Difficult to organise the mass of material
6 Takes up far too much time and space

How to decide what sources are relevant

Running throughout all of this, as you can see, are two problems, which we will tackle in this and the next chapter:

1 How to decide what sources are relevant
2 How to plan the review

In this chapter, we will tackle the first of these problems. A good literature review will lay emphasis only on the most relevant and significant documents. It is not intended as an exercise in which you demonstrate how much you have read or the breadth of your understanding.

Stand-alone reviews

In Chapters 1 and 2, we found that the problem of deciding which sources are relevant to stand-alone reviews is solved by translating the research question into inclusion and exclusion criteria. These lay out the formal requirements that will have to be met for papers to be reviewed. They address the question of exactly what kinds of studies you're looking for to answer your research question and the sub-questions that you derive from it, which will translate it into concrete terms.

Reviews for dissertations and theses

For dissertations and theses, a literature review is the means by which you lay the foundations on which your own study will be built. In this way you make clear the relevance and broader significance of your research. Consequently, you need only comment on those sections of your sources that throw direct light on what you plan to do.

How to choose

As this makes clear, each source that you use must have direct relevance to your research question. It must impinge upon it: it cannot just be mere 'background' or any of the other terms that are used, like 'theoretical underpinning'. There are two questions you need to ask before you choose to include a source, and for it to be included you must be able to give positive answers to each of them.

1   Abilities – how am I going to use it?
2   Content – how is it useful?

The first question concerns the abilities you are going to use to integrate the paper into your review: how you are going to process the ideas. The second concerns the content: why the ideas it contains are relevant to your review.

1 Abilities – how am I going to use it?

Whatever source you use, it must be composed of those ideas that you are going to integrate into your review by analysing their implications, synthesising them with other ideas or critically evaluating them. It cannot be included for its own sake; otherwise it is merely descriptive padding. It is not enough merely to report what others have done in the field. If your review is part of a dissertation or thesis, you must make sure at some point that you can show that the paper you choose to include has a direct bearing on your research question and the work you plan to do.

Empirical studies   EXAMPLE

You might report the findings of other empirical studies, but only if you are then going on to compare and contrast this work with your own planned research, revealing the limitations and gaps that you plan to address. The point is to integrate it into your review by analysing its implications, synthesising it or critically evaluating it. In this way you make it relevant to your project.

Integrating your sources into your review

One certain way of making sure that you are choosing only relevant sources that you can integrate within your review is to ask yourself each time you come to choose, 'How will I use it? What cognitive ability will I use?' If it is clear that you would be just summarising the article and nothing more, it will amount to mere description, irrelevant padding.

1 Synthesising the ideas

This goes to the heart of a literature review, its main purpose, which is to create a synthesis, to build the different sources that you have assembled into a meaningful coherent whole, which your reader can understand. This is not a mere summary of loosely connected sources, but a synthesis, the result of processing your sources into interconnected structures as you find connections between them. In this way you might reveal:

- a new interpretation of old material;
- where the overall picture is unclear;
- where there are gaps that need to be filled;
- where there are parts that need to be further developed;
- where you can combine old and new interpretations to reveal something new;
- the intellectual progression within a field, perhaps revealing where a certain debate now dominates it, which you can assess.

By synthesising your sources in this way, you can reveal the purpose of your own study and create a coherent picture that the reader can understand and follow.

Try this ...

To get a clear idea of exactly the problem facing a reader of your review, try doing a jigsaw puzzle without referring to the picture of what it should finally look like. Without the picture, you are left holding a piece wondering what to do with it and where it goes. This is the problem that all readers struggle to resolve as they begin to read your review. Writing a review places you in the position of describing to the reader where all the pieces go, what the final picture should look like.

In the process you outline the goals in your own research: to test a hypothesis, to fill a gap with new research, to clarify an area that is unclear, to find a new answer to a problem, to identify a new direction in which you want to take research or to use a new and improved methodology to get a clearer view.

2 Analysing the implications of sources

However, synthesising our sources and their ideas first depends on analysing them, their assumptions and the concepts they use. In this way, we lay bare the ideas we need to work with to find new connections out of which we can create our synthesis. As we discovered in Chapters 10 and 11, by adapting the structures of ideas we find we can design different ways of approaching a problem to find new interpretations and solutions.

3 Critically evaluating sources

The same can be said for the importance of critically evaluating our sources. Without this, the review will be little more than a mere description of sources, a summary. By critically evaluating our sources, we reveal agreements and disagreements between them, their limitations and deficiencies, and the weaknesses in their assumptions, the design of their research and their interpretation of results. In the process, we reveal the gaps in our understanding and lay the foundations for further research.

Autonomy and dependency: their influence   EXAMPLE
on learning behaviour and study skills in the 16–19 age group

In Chapter 8, I suggested that in this study the researcher may have decided to examine the influence of teaching style to see if this promotes greater or less autonomy. So he interviews teachers and examines their lesson plans, in which there are long sessions devoted to discussion, which is likely to promote the autonomy of students.

But you suspect there is a methodological weakness in this strategy, which may make these findings unreliable. While the teacher might plan a lesson believing that at certain times students are doing one thing, in fact they might actually be doing something quite different. The perception of what was happening in the classroom from the teacher's point of view might not match the facts.

So, each time you think about using a source, ask yourself 'How am I going to use it? What cognitive ability will I use?' If you are merely describing or summarising it, it is not likely to be relevant. As a simple guide to help you come to a decision, work through the following questions.

Abilities – how am I going to use it?

1 **Synthesis:**
   Do you know how you will synthesise this article with others to create a meaningful picture that the reader can understand?
2 **Critical evaluation:**
   Have you critically examined the article – its assumptions, design and findings – and compared it with other articles?
3 **Analysis:**
   Have you analysed and considered the implications of the arguments and concepts the author uses? Have you revealed and assessed all the implications of the article's conclusions?
4 **Relevance:**
   Is there a clear link between this article and your own research question? Is it important for laying down the foundations of your own research project or, in a stand-alone review, the work of others?
5 **An alternative view:**
   Does this article represent a contrast to other articles by presenting an alternative interpretation of your research question? Does it represent an alternative approach to it? Does it present different findings that challenge your own view?
6 **Organising structure:**
   Does this article present a general, synoptic point of view that would give your review a way of organising the different elements into a coherent and comprehensive overview?

If the source you are considering is relevant in any of these ways, you have a good reason for including it in your review.

2 Content – how is it useful?

Of course, now that you know how you're going to use an article you may also have decided that the content of the article is relevant. But some articles can be misleadingly convincing simply on the grounds that we know how we could use them, even though their content may not be relevant. So, to be sure, we need to check that its content is relevant to our research question. As with the first question, it helps to make our decision if we have by our side clear criteria. The following list contains seven questions you can work your way through as you consider each source. Each one contains ideas on how you might use the content. If it's not useful in any of these ways, then reject it.

Content – how is it useful?

1   What's in it that gives you **ideas** on which to build your own project?
2   Is there anything in it that reveals the **current debate** on the topic? What are the differences between the contributors? Are there any unsolved problems? Map out the **cross-connections** you find in the articles? If there are references to another article, make a note of where you saw it and record what the first author said about it.
3   Does it outline different **perceptions** of what the problem is and different ideas about how it should be tackled?
4   Does it indicate how many different **aspects** there are to the problem? If so, analyse it. Then, in the review you could pick up and discuss each aspect in turn, making clear what there is in the literature on each one. Out of this, you could develop your own contribution.
5   Is there anything in it that reveals the main **theories** and related **concepts** that are used by different contributors? If there is, in your review make clear the differences and similarities between them. Then you could go on to evaluate each one for their internal consistency. If you're writing a dissertation or thesis, later you could assess them for their consistency with the data you collect and the observations you make.
6   Are there **omissions** in the article? Has the writer overlooked something? In your review, you could make this clear and justify your conclusion. If you're writing a dissertation or thesis, you could then outline what you will be doing in your own research that doesn't overlook the same thing.
7   Is the article useful in identifying the different **methodologies**? You could review the different ones, identifying their key features, before you then indicate the sort of strategy that would best meet the demands of the topic you have chosen.

These seven questions give us clear criteria on which to base our choices, but to be effective we need to have a clear research question or hypothesis from which we have derived sub-questions. As we discovered in Chapter 5, armed with these we can then decide what indicators and variables we are going to look for: the specific outcomes that will confirm or falsify our hypothesis or research question. Armed with these, we have a much clearer idea of which of those articles that have passed the seven questions should go into the review.

Using the criteria

At times, the literature may divert you down a different path or persuade you to adopt a different emphasis in your review. There may be good reasons for doing this, but nevertheless keep in mind the original insight that first grabbed your attention and which will, similarly, grab that of your reader. Keep it somewhere on a card to remind you whenever you find your focus becoming less sharp.

 You can download copies of the checklists in this chapter from the companion website (www.macmillanihe.com/greetham-literature-review).

Summary

1   A literature review is not intended as a means of impressing examiners with how much you've read and understood.
2   A mere synopsis of your sources will leave you with a mass of irrelevant material that takes up too much space and time.
3   The main purpose of a literature review is to create a synthesis of your sources into a coherent, meaningful whole.
4   Without critical evaluation of your sources, your review is left as a mere descriptive summary of them.
5   Choosing relevant sources depends on a clear research question or hypothesis, from which we derive the indicators and variables we should be looking for.

What next?

In this chapter, you have learnt how to answer two key questions that will simplify what can otherwise be a difficult and confusing decision. This provides the basis for creating the structure for your review, as we will see in the next chapter.

Chapter 18

Planning the Review

In this chapter, you will learn…

- the important benefits of planning;
- how to plan the different types of literature review;
- essential guidelines to planning your review;
- the five sections of a review;
- the different ways of structuring the findings of your review.

In the last chapter, we tackled the first of two problems we need to solve as we organise our material: how to decide what sources are relevant. Now we turn our attention to the second of these: how to plan the review.

The benefits of planning

As you begin to see connections between ideas and synthesise them into a coherent whole, it's important to develop them and give them clearer shape by writing them down in your notebook. At this point, it's tempting to assume that you can skip the planning stage and go straight into writing your review. But there are significant benefits to be had from just stepping back, assessing your material and planning the structure into which everything will go.

1 Reduces stress and confusion

Not least of these is that you avoid the stress and confusion that comes from planning while you are writing. By planning in detail before you begin to write, you get a better idea of the scale of the review and where everything will go. For most of us, this is very reassuring: we get a clear sense of what we have to do and how we can cope with it in the time.

2 Thinking about the details

Second, getting ourselves to this stage has involved thinking largely about the big issues: an original idea that interests us and where it sits in the literature of our subject. In our concern for these, we tend to overlook the details: where should each of our sources go and how can we organise them so that we end up at the point we want to be, where we have created the platform for our own research or, in a stand-alone review, revealed where effective research might be undertaken?

3 Confidence

Resolving these problems will give you the sort of confidence you need as your attention turns to writing your review. Knowing that you have planned it in detail and you know where everything is going will relieve any stress you might be feeling. With a clearly devised, detailed plan, you can reassure yourself that you are in control.

Benefits of planning

1   Reduces stress and confusion
2   Gives us a clear sense of what we have to do
3   Reassures us that we can cope with it in the time
4   We know where all our sources have to go
5   It gives us confidence knowing that we are in control

Planning the different types of review

To plan our review well, we obviously need to know what we're trying to achieve, and this, in turn, depends upon the type of review we're writing.

Stand-alone reviews

As we discovered in Part 1, a stand-alone review is a critical evaluation of the literature in a field, in which we analyse key issues and concepts, identify trends and highlight the gaps in the research. Consequently, most stand-alone reviews tend to be structured more like an empirical dissertation or thesis with an introduction followed by sections on methodology, findings and discussion. In the section on structure below (pages 187–90), you can see a detailed description of each of these.

Integrated reviews

By contrast, in dissertations and theses that are theoretical or text-based, common in the humanities and in theoretical research in the social sciences, the subject matter *is* the literature itself in the form of novels, plays, philosophical texts, and theoretical and historical works, so a literature review can be quite an alien concept. All of the citations and references you make to the literature will be spread throughout your thesis or dissertation, so there will be no need for a discrete literature review.

However, in the introduction, you analyse the literature that is the subject of the study, identifying the key issues and themes, which you then address in the body of the dissertation or thesis. Each time you pick up one of these themes to discuss it, the significance of it is made clear to the reader either by dedicating a chapter to it or by using sub-headings within a chapter, as well as by referring back to your analysis in the introduction.

> **Moral Thinking**   **EXAMPLE**
>
> In the introduction to this thesis, the writer explains that he examines Hare's claim in *Moral Thinking* (1981) to have found the foundations of moral thinking in moral language and in his prudential account of moral motivation, in particular his claim that moral prescriptions are merely expressions of preferences. To do this, he focuses on three key elements of Hare's theory and devotes a chapter to each of them: what it is 'to know' in the sense required by his theory, his concept of rationality as prudence, and his theory of representation.

In effect, your analysis in the introduction lays out for readers an interpretative structure they can follow as you work on the literature. Then, as you begin the critical discussion and pick up each of these, they know exactly what you are doing and that it is consistent with your analysis.

Reviews for empirical dissertations and theses

However, in empirical research, things are different. Here you will almost always have to do a discrete literature review. The challenge is to avoid the large, time-consuming synopsis, which sends you off in a largely irrelevant direction, using up your valuable time and burying you beneath a mound of unusable material. To avoid this, keep in mind the four main functions of a literature review:

1 to show that you've developed a sound understanding of the **debates** taking place around your topic and a deep grasp of the issues it raises;
2 to acknowledge the **work of others**;
3 to lay down a **platform** for your own research and point you in the right direction;
4 to show that you've got a good critical understanding of the **theories and ideas** that may provide the basis for much of your critical evaluation of your findings in the discussion chapter.

To ensure your review does not become just a list of disjointed descriptions of your sources, you have to make sure that you dictate to your sources, rather than letting your sources dictate to you. The key to this lies in detailed planning. Charting your structure with clear subheadings and subsections, you can avoid deviation as you make your way to the platform of your own research and to the specific questions at the heart of your research. Your aim should be to progress from the general to the specific texts and from the theory to the practice.

Planning your review

As you plan your review, it is useful to keep in mind five essential guidelines.

1 The context

So much is said about the importance of developing the 'background' to your research. However, your aim should not be to show how much you know and understand. This can lead you into low level descriptive work, in which you cover sources that later turn out to be irrelevant and are never mentioned again, as your review heads in a completely different direction. Moreover, you can get so locked into showing examiners how much you know that you don't get round to analysing the strengths and weaknesses of your sources.

- low-level descriptive work
- irrelevant sources that are never mentioned again
- no analysis of the strengths and weaknesses of your sources

Although it's useful to set your work in the broader context of work done in the area, beware of going into too much detail. All you are doing is showing the scope of your study and how it relates to the most significant studies that impinge on your work.

2 Your own contribution

It's important to know what is likely to be your own contribution. Your review should build up naturally to your own specific questions at the heart of your project as you move from the general to the specific texts and from the theory to the practice. Many of the most serious problems students have with literature reviews stem from not making explicit their own particular way of approaching the material. This should inform your selection of the literature you review and run throughout as you present your critical evaluation of it.

> Your own way of approaching the material should inform your selection of the literature to review.

3 From the general to the specific texts

From the general texts, you build naturally to the specific texts that directly touch on the issues that interest you. These, of course, you deal with in more detail. Through them, you might indicate the gap in the literature that you're filling. They will provide the platform on which your research will be built. There might be key works that you need to evaluate critically from the particular perspective of your own research. Finish with a direct lead that establishes clear contact with your work.

General ───────────▶ Specific

Theory ───────────▶ Practice

4 Filling it out

To help you develop your review in this way, now begin to fill out your structure with clear details of what you plan to put in each section. The one problem you should aim to avoid is allowing the review to become just a mere list of disjointed descriptions of sources – use your sources, don't allow them to use you.

Try this ...

Fill out the structure with provisional subheadings and subsections, giving an approximate word count for each one. Subsections not only help you avoid deviation, keeping you on track as you make your way to your own particular perspective, but they give a sense of proportion to each set of contributions that make up each subsection. As you break the review down between the general and specific sources, within each of these perhaps break it down further between, say, theoretical and empirical studies.

5 Direct lead

Finally, end your review with a direct lead that establishes clear contact with your own work, even though this might also be provisional. As we will see in the next chapter, this might change as you synchronise your review with your discussion chapter or conclusion. Some sections might no longer be relevant, while new directions might open up that make discarded sources relevant now. So you will have to edit your review to reflect this.

The structure

However, even though some aspects of your plan may be provisional, it always helps to plan in more detail than you might think necessary. It will make your review more manageable if you know where you are going and what you need to do to get there. So, break your plan down into the follow sections:

1 Introduction
2 Methodology
3 Findings
4 Discussion and conclusion
5 References

1 The introduction

Your main purpose in the introduction is to give readers a map of your review, so they can follow you without getting lost. Let them know what you are doing and why it is important. This means making clear your thesis and the hypothesis or research question that you have derived from it. In Chapter 5, we discussed the importance of this in that it makes clear what you're looking for and the types of research methods you will use to find it. In the process, outline the context of your review by giving information about the field of study and the importance of your topic within this field.

2 Methodology

In this section, your main aim is to describe the criteria you used to select the literature you have reviewed. At the heart of your hypothesis or research question lies the abstract concepts that you have used to describe it. In this section, you will need to analyse these concepts to reveal the concrete variables you will use to find the evidence you need to confirm or falsify your hypothesis or research question.

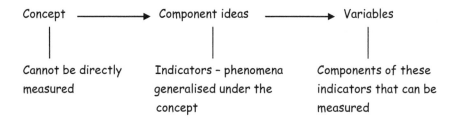

Concept ⟶ Component ideas ⟶ Variables

Cannot be directly measured

Indicators – phenomena generalised under the concept

Components of these indicators that can be measured

By analysing the concept into these variables, you can then outline the sub-questions that you will use to apply them to the concrete evidence.

Autonomy and dependency: their influence on learning behaviour and study skills in the 16–19 age group EXAMPLE

In this project, we need to know exactly what concrete evidence to look for in the form of student behaviour to decide whether they are 'autonomous' or 'dependent' learners. So, in this section we would explain our strategy of reviewing articles to see what sub-questions the authors asked to find the evidence for the autonomy and dependency of students. These might be about how self-motivated and self-reliant they were, and how confident they were in their own judgement.

A literature review to explore integrated care for older people   EXAMPLE

In the same way, in this stand-alone review, we need to know what concrete evidence of 'integrated care' for older people to look for in the literature we review. We need to explain what sub-questions we looked for that the authors might have asked to reveal this evidence, sub-questions about integration between service sectors, professions, the different settings, types of organisation and types of care.

In this way, we can justify how we chose the literature we did and why we excluded others.

3 Findings

If your review forms part of a dissertation or thesis, your main aim is to set your research in the context of the current thinking in your subject and to show how it will make a useful contribution to this. Although stand-alone reviews are not used by researchers to lay the foundations for their own research in the same way, they are nevertheless used to see what the literature says about a particular problem and where effective research might be undertaken. In both cases, you're arguing that according to the current literature there is a problem that needs to be addressed, or a lack of information, or an unanswered question, or a misconception about something and so on. In your review you are making it clear that you know:

- the current thinking;
- the main issues involved;
- the way opinion divides;
- the gaps in the research;
- and the most recent publications on the problem.

You're also showing that you've taken account of all the competing research methods and chosen the most effective tools and techniques.

To do this, you must avoid producing a mere list of sources, each explained in succession without discussion: without making comparisons between different approaches to the problem, different theories and research methodologies, finding agreements and disagreements or weakness and strengths. Your aim, as we have seen in previous chapters, is to synthesise your sources by identifying patterns, trends and major issues that bind them together. There are two common ways of organising this, depending on the nature of your topic and what you find in the literature.

1 Thematic

If your research hinges on a key theoretical concept, like freedom, authority, autonomy, dependency or needs, the main body of your review will be organised around the themes you have been able to draw out of your analysis of the concept. You would examine the literature on the basis of how authors have dealt with these themes and then focus readers' attention on the new perspectives you have been able to throw on the problem.

Autonomy and dependency: their influence on learning behaviour and study skills in the 16–19 age group   EXAMPLE

In this project, the key theoretical concepts are 'autonomy' and 'dependency', and our main focus is on the different ways in which researchers have been able to find evidence of their influence on learning behaviour. You might discover that researchers have approached this in a limited number of ways, which you explore in this section, before outlining what you believe is a new, more effective way of exploring them.

A literature review to explore integrated care for older people   EXAMPLE

Likewise, in this review, the authors' concern is with the different ways in which the concept 'integration' and other key concepts have been analysed into themes in the literature they review and the evidence that researchers have found of the extent to which integration has developed. In this way, they hope to create the 'foundation for enquiry and analysis' by developing the questions that an empirical study would seek to answer.

2 Chronological

Alternatively, your review might fall naturally into a chronological structure. It may be necessary for you to outline how the research on your topic has changed over a certain period and how this has had an important role in shaping the significance of your project. The structure of the review follows the order in which the literature was published as you reveal how the ideas have developed and how research has contributed to this. Typically, the literature is grouped together and discussed in the order of their publication, reflecting the change in opinion from one period to another.

4 Discussion and conclusion

In this section, you are fulfilling the promises you made in the introduction and coming full circle, delivering readers back where they started. For readers, it is deeply satisfying to realise that an author has fulfilled the promises made at the start and brought them full circle. To achieve this, work through the following structure:

1 First, emphasise the broader significance of what you have found: the most significant contributions to the debate and the ideas you take from these – the main themes that have emerged, the major trends and the gaps that need to be filled.

2 Then, discuss the direction that you think future research should take. You might emphasise the gaps in our understanding, the most significant agreements and disagreements that shape the discussion, the limitations of current research and the inadequacies of the research methodologies used in previous studies.

3 Then, finally, if your review forms part of a dissertation or thesis, make clear the contribution you can make to the existing understanding, or, if yours is a stand-alone review, the contribution that needs to be made by future research, and re-emphasise the significance of this.

5 References

The last section deals with your list of references. As we will see in Chapters 25 and 26, it should include accurate and full information about those sources you have used with page numbers and details of the sections of articles that you have discussed.

Summary

1 By planning, you can see the scale of the review and where everything will go, thereby reducing your stress.
2 The review should build naturally from the general to the specific texts.
3 Once you have completed your research and come to your conclusions, some sections of the review might need to be changed to reflect the changes in your thinking.
4 In the introduction, give readers a map of the review that they can follow without getting lost.
5 There are two ways in which you might organise your findings: thematic and chronological.

What next?

If your review is part of a dissertation or thesis, its content will depend on the conclusions your research produces. In the next chapter, we will examine how you can synchronise your review with other chapters.

Chapter 19

Integrating Your Review with Other Chapters

In this chapter, you will learn...

- how to rewrite your review as you complete other chapters;
- how to integrate the review with the rest of the dissertation or thesis;
- the effects on your review of integrating it with other chapters;
- that how well you integrate it depends on how well you have processed the ideas;
- the importance of developing a critical understanding of your sources.

Although it might appear that the subject of this chapter is more relevant to the concerns of those working on a dissertation or thesis, as you read it you will see that its content is also relevant to the needs of those faced with the challenge of doing a stand-alone review.

Even though you have now planned your review in detail, as you work on your dissertation or thesis, or write each section of your stand-alone review, your ideas will crystallise, revealing new insights that will mean you will have to go back and re-write sections of your review. New issues will emerge that must now form part of your project and questions that you thought you had clarified in your review will adapt to reveal that there is more to them than you first thought.

New ideas and publications

This is the evolutionary nature of our thinking. As we conduct our research and write about our ideas, we not only clarify what we already know and begin to see clearly the structure into which we need to organise our ideas, but we reveal new ideas, new ways in which they are connected and gaps in our understanding that we hadn't seen. Ideas will inevitably come to you in the middle of your research that you hadn't thought of when you were reading the literature. Your thinking changes and you see new ways of synthesising ideas, new unexpected connections.

- We clarify what we know.
- We see the structure more clearly.
- We see new ideas, connections and gaps.

As you go back to the most important journals, it's quite likely that you will find new articles in the latest editions that have ideas that are useful to your project. They may reveal different theories or research methods that would make your approach more effective. As a result, you may have to change your project, shifting the focus within it to take account of an aspect that you had originally thought to be less important. Indeed, you may have to include in your review literature a topic that you hadn't considered at all.

New articles may reveal new ideas, theories and research methods that may shift the focus of your review.

Rewriting the plan

As this makes clear, although we may have planned and written our review, we have to accept that it is still necessarily provisional. This presents two problems that can be difficult to manage.

1   Defending a position

With a great deal of careful thought and effort invested in your review, it can be easy just to adopt, unwittingly, a defensive posture. Inevitably, as you read more and your ideas crystallise there will be moments when you experience those blinding insights that suddenly throw new light on a problem that nobody else seems to have seen with quite the same clarity as you do. Understandably, you hold on to this and set about searching for more evidence to support and defend it. Such a situation can be difficult to manage.

Obviously, it is sensible to develop your insight to see where it might lead. You will need to discover more to reveal its strengths and weaknesses. But we have to avoid committing ourselves to a theory, which we then just resolutely defend come what may. Beware of those who tell you that you must develop an argument and then use your sources to defend it. This is deductive, not inductive. In this situation, things are not up for grabs in the way that is central to genuine research. It must be possible for the outcome of your research to be different than you envisage, otherwise you are proving nothing.

- Your research should be inductive, not deductive.
- It should be up for grabs.
- It should be possible for the outcome to be different than you envisage.

2   Over theorising

Connected with this is the all too familiar problem of over theorising. To bolster our idea we might create a theory, which then dominates all our searching as we try to amass evidence that will prove it right. On the face of it, there may seem to be nothing wrong with this. After all, as we saw in Chapter 5, this is what academic authors seem to do: they develop and set out their theories, and then test them, only to find they were right all along. But this is often the way the story of discovery is told after the event. As the Nobel Prize winner Sir Peter Medawar says, it is how we like to appear before the public when the curtain goes up. But it is not how new theories and ideas are discovered.

> We might think it sensible to develop a theory and then set about proving it right. But this is often the way the story of discovery is told after the event.

This is an unavoidably iterative process. A provisional theory is put forward and tested, then re-worked in line with the results and tested again. This process continues until there is a tight fit between theory and results.

So, whether your project is empirical or text-based, don't spend too much time locking yourself into a position that you are reluctant to change. Of course, you've got to pin your ideas down, as we have done in the plan of the review, but learn to accept that this may be provisional and will undergo change and adaptation as your thoughts crystallise under the influence of your research and writing other chapters.

Tying the review in with other chapters

One of the most common criticisms made of dissertations and theses is that students fail to create a clear link between the findings of the literature review and their own research. Indeed, each chapter can seem quite detached from the rest, when in fact our aim should be to create a coherent dissertation or thesis, in which everything is related and performs a clear, well-conceived role.

Main purpose	To create a coherent dissertation or thesis, in which everything is related and has a clear, well-conceived role.

Theoretical, text-based dissertations and theses

With theoretical, text-based research projects, the problem is how to tie your analysis of the literature in the introduction in with to the conclusions reached at the end of each chapter and with the final judgements that you come to in the conclusion.

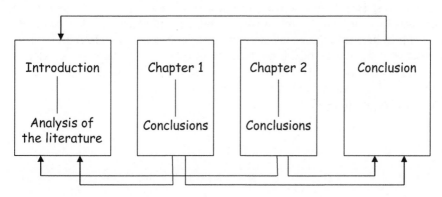

Empirical dissertations and theses

With empirical research projects, the focus shifts slightly. Here we need to tie the literature review in with the introduction, the methodology chapter, the research findings, the discussion and the conclusion.

1   Introduction

Only after you have collected and analysed your data will you be able to write the discussion chapter and then come to your final judgements in the conclusion. Once you've completed this, you may then have to rewrite both your literature review and the introduction.

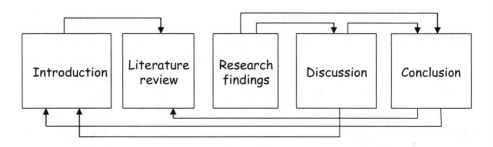

2   Methodology

In contrast, it is, perhaps, this chapter more than the others that can seem detached from the rest. So to bind it in with the rest, you will have to tie the methods you've chosen to your research question and sub-questions, which you explained in your literature review by using some of the references there to the approaches adopted by other researchers.

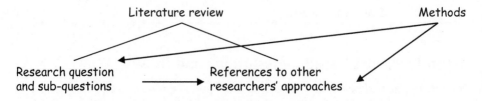

Your key concerns in this chapter are to show that you have a good grasp of the epistemological issues that underpin your research – that you have a clear idea of what should pass for knowledge in your research – and that you have a sound working knowledge of the methods, techniques and instruments you've used to collect it. For this, you will need to draw heavily on the arguments and explanations you developed in your literature review and on the sources you used to justify your choices. If, however, as a result of your research, you have changed your approach, you will have to rewrite your review to reflect this.

3   Research findings

Similarly, in this chapter your main aim is to interpret your findings in the light of the problems and questions you outlined in the introduction and developed in more detail in your literature review. To integrate these chapters closely, you will need to show how your work answers these questions by reminding your readers of the questions and sub-questions you developed in your review.

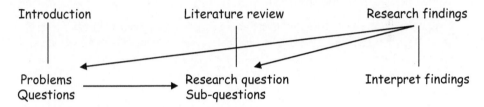

Your key concern in this chapter is to confirm that everything you've done has been relevant, so if things have changed as a result of your research you will need to rewrite your review to reflect this. This may involve changing the emphasis within your project to highlight some aspect that you had considered to be less important. To adapt the review to reflect your research findings, you may have to introduce something that you have not considered at all in the review.

● To integrate this chapter with your review, show how your work answers the questions raised in the review.
● If things have changed as a result of your research, you will need to rewrite your review to reflect this.

4   The discussion

However, this is where much of the integration really takes place. Your main focus will be to assess your findings in the light of the different perspectives you have drawn from the literature. But at the same time you may need to rewrite your review to make sure that in the light of your findings you establish clearly where your research fits into our understanding as reflected in the literature.

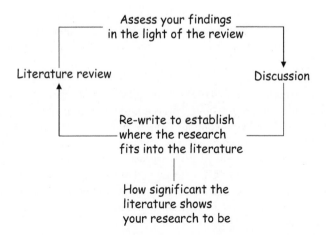

Effectively, this is your opportunity to show how significant your research is and how important the literature shows it to be. To make this clear to the reader, it will be necessary to summarise significant sections of your review and cross-reference them to show how integrated your review is within your project.

Using the theoretical framework   EXAMPLE

In your literature review, you have probably developed the theoretical framework for your research. So, while you are using this in the discussion chapter to reveal the significance of your findings, in the literature review it may be necessary to rewrite this section to ensure that what you are saying in the discussion chapter is clearly reflected in the review as you pick up the same issues and follow the same structure.

But it's not just a question of establishing where your research fits into the framework that you have established in the review. The other important way of integrating your review is to compare your findings with those you have identified in the review. Other researchers may have similar results which would endorse your project and place it in a wider perspective. Alternatively, you may find differences that give you the opportunity to explain why.

Comparing your findings with others in your review   EXAMPLE

After you have revealed your findings, you can assess the organisation and methods you've used. At this point, you can refer back to those researchers you have mentioned in your review who have adopted similar methods. Alternatively, you may have adopted a slightly different research question. If this is the case, you will have to discuss and explain why your results are, perhaps, more significant as a result.

The obvious importance of this lies in the opportunity it gives you to underline the significance of your contribution to current research. By integrating your literature review in this way, you can explain your findings and reveal their wider significance.

5   The conclusion

In the conclusion, your focus shifts to two things: the significance of your work and any recommendations for future research. This is another point in your dissertation or thesis where you will draw heavily on your literature review. Obviously, your first concern will be to make sure that your review supports your conclusions by using sources that endorse them. But research of any kind is unlikely to answer all the questions it addresses. More often it raises new and more interesting questions. Therefore, the conclusion gives you the opportunity to draw on your review to indicate new avenues of research that will address similar issues in the future.

Already in the review you have drawn attention to the significance of your research. Now, by integrating your review with your conclusion you can make recommendations about how your work can be improved. You can also point to other areas that your research suggests deserve further investigation. In this way, you'll show that you have developed an awareness of the importance of your work and its broader implications for related fields.

Use your review to draw attention to future avenues of research, while you emphasise the significance of your project.

The effects of integrating your review

When you've completed your research and know what conclusions you're going to draw, you will know what your final draft of the introduction will look like. At this point, you will know what parts of the literature review are no longer relevant. As a result, you will need to change your review accordingly, editing quotations, deleting others and removing those references that you don't refer to later.

Synchronising your review with the results of your research might mean some sections are no longer relevant.

By the same token, you may find, as the evidence comes in and your ideas develop, that you see more things to explore, which are important to your project. This might mean you will have to go back to the literature to re-examine papers and articles you rejected at the time.

At this point, you may wonder whether it might have been better to have included them in the first place. However, using them now is a lot easier to cope with than finding you've devoted an inordinate amount of time that you couldn't afford on something, only 30 per cent of which is relevant. Ruthlessly editing an overweight and irrelevant literature review is not only time-consuming, but dispiriting and frustrating.

New directions might also open up that make discarded sources now relevant.

By discarding some sections that are no longer relevant and pursuing new directions that open up, you will improve your review considerably. Not only will you demonstrate that you have exhaustively covered all the issues raised by the problem, but your review will be more convincing as a result of each part of it cohering closely with other parts. Similarly, by integrating it with other chapters, it will be supported and its arguments reinforced by these other chapters.

Making the ideas your own

However, your ability to integrate your review convincingly with other chapters will depend upon how well you have processed the ideas; the extent to which you have made them your own. If you find yourself using large sections of the texts, it's almost always a sign that you haven't got to the heart of these ideas. So try to avoid just quoting or paraphrasing the contents of articles and, instead, weave them into your own arguments. Wherever possible, use them alongside your own ideas and arguments.

> If you find yourself using large sections of the texts, it's almost always a sign that you haven't got to the heart of these ideas.

Try this …

The key to this is to develop your critical understanding of your sources, so you can demonstrate to your reader that you know just how much weight you can reliably place upon them. Although we will cover this in more depth in the next chapter, to help you develop this, ask the following 10 questions each time you use one of your sources.

1 Where does the author get her data/evidence?
2 Is it relevant? Is it sufficient to support her arguments?
3 Has she represented it accurately?
4 Has she drawn the most relevant and consistent inferences from it?
5 Is the argument balanced? Is it fair/biased, objective/subjective?
6 Has she omitted anything?
7 Is the argument consistent?
8 Does she use language accurately? Does she mean different things at different times, when she uses a word?
9 Does she reveal all her assumptions when she uses language, or does she take things for granted?
10 Do her arguments support or contradict what others have said? If so, why?

Summary

1 As you write sections of your stand-alone review, or undertake research and write chapters of your dissertation or thesis, your ideas will change and you will have to rewrite your review in response.
2 It's easy to over theorise and then let this dominate all your searching as you try to amass evidence that will prove your theory correct.
3 Our aim should be to create a coherent thesis or dissertation, in which everything is related and has a clear, well-conceived role.
4 By discarding some sections that are no longer relevant and pursuing new directions that open up, you will improve your review considerably.
5 Integrating your review convincingly with other chapters will depend on how well you have made the ideas your own.

What next?

In this chapter, we have seen how important integrating the review with other chapters is for producing a coherent review. But this depends upon showing a good critical understanding of your sources. In the next chapter, we will learn more about how to use and develop this understanding as we discuss our sources in the first draft.

Part 6

Writing Your Review

Chapter 20

Discussing the Literature

In this chapter, you will learn...

- how to analyse the different types of argument;
- how to organise your discussion so that you move from the general to the specific;
- how to critically evaluate your sources in your discussion;
- how to develop your discussion from analysis to critical evaluation to synthesis;
- how to finish with a synthesis that lays the foundations for future research.

The discussion of your sources in a review is one of the most difficult tasks you face. You have to demonstrate that you can use a wide range of cognitive abilities at the same time. Not only do you have to show that you understand your sources and the implications they have for your project, but you have to meet complex, often conflicting demands on your thinking and writing skills. You need to analyse your sources, critically evaluate them and synthesise them into a new way of approaching a problem that will lay the basis of your own research or, in a stand-alone review, show where effective research might be undertaken.

Research: assessing your ability to think

This explains the importance of research of any kind as a mode of assessment. It gives examiners a window into the minds of students. As we write, we're forced to take a hard look at our thinking to pin down our ideas, organise them rationally and present them clearly. If we can force ourselves to think clearly, we'll write clearly. At each point, we ask ourselves two questions:

1 Is this really what I want to say?
2 Is this the direction in which I want to develop this argument?

As you can see, this means that to make sure we do our best thinking as we write, we must be self-reflective. Good thinkers think about their thinking while they think. But the same goes for the authors of the literature we review. As we discuss the literature, we must check that their arguments are consistent too. We must evaluate their evidence and the way they use it, and analyse their use of concepts and language to reveal their hidden implications.

Good thinkers think about their thinking while they think.

We all make mistakes when we write, no matter who we are. We fail to apply elementary tests of logic to determine whether one idea does in fact lead to another. We rely on partial, untested evidence. We use language in a misleading, inconsistent way without reflecting on its hidden implications. These three types of mistake cover virtually all of the points of criticism you need to identify as you discuss your sources, so develop the habit of checking for them routinely by using the following checklist.

Criticism and evaluation	
Evaluating arguments	1. What are the key claims made by the author?
	2. Does she develop them consistently?
	3. Do her conclusions follow from the reasons she gives?
	4. Does she leave some parts undeveloped, which could lead to alternative conclusions?
	5. Have any assumptions been made without acknowledging them?
Evaluating evidence	1. Does she use enough reliable evidence to back up her arguments?
	2. What kind of evidence is it, and does she describe it accurately?
	From primary or secondary sources?
	Statistical – how is it described? Is it accurate?
	Anecdotal – how reliable/representative is this?
	3. Does she draw reliable inferences from it to develop her arguments?
	Does she draw conclusions that are too strong?
	Is the evidence relevant to her arguments?
	4. Are her inferences relevant?
	5. What alternative inferences can be drawn from the evidence?
	6. What do other authors have to say about this?
Evaluating language	1. Is she consistent in the way she uses words or do they mean different things at different times?
	2. Is the meaning of her arguments obscured by the use of jargon and abstractions?
	3. Do we need to analyse concepts to reveal the hidden implications of her arguments?

Discussing your sources

When we planned the review in Chapter 18, we broke it down into the following sections:

1 Introduction
2 Methodology
3 Findings
4 Discussion and conclusion
5 References

We found that the main purpose of the introduction is to make clear your thesis and your hypothesis or research question that you derived from it. In the methodology section, you outline the criteria you used to select the literature that you have reviewed.

It is in the third and fourth sections that you analyse and discuss your findings and conclusions as you move from the general to the specific. In the third section, you summarise the sources you have selected. Then, in the fourth section you develop your analysis, critical evaluation and finally your synthesis, where you lay the basis of further research, either your own in a dissertation or thesis, or the research of others in a stand-alone review.

Summary ⟶ Analysis ⟶ Critical evaluation ⟶ Synthesis

As you move from the general to the specific, you reproduce the thinking you did in Part 3, when you processed the ideas. In other words, you work through the following stages:

1 Summary of your sources
2 Analysis
3 Critical evaluation
4 Synthesis

1 Summary

However, this is no mere list of your sources, each described and listed without connection or comparison. The content and structure of your summary should be dictated by your analysis of the themes and ideas you found in the literature, and the patterns you developed as you synthesised them in Part 3.

2 Analysis

From your summary you can then begin to develop your discussion, working through the other three stages as you draw upon all those skills we developed in Part 3. To lay the basis for your critical evaluation of the author's arguments, the first thing you must do is analyse the author's argument by asking the question, 'What sort of argument is it?'

An argument can be a mixture of fact, value and concept. So we have to be able to analyse it and identify what it is before we can decide how to critically evaluate it. The author may have presented the argument as exclusively about facts, whereas it may also be about values and concepts. As a result, he may have smuggled in without us noticing a value judgement or the meaning of a concept he has taken for granted.

2.1 *Facts and values*

An argument of fact purports to represent the way things *are* and, therefore, can be assessed in terms of its truth or falsehood, whereas an argument of value is about how things *should* or *ought* to be and, therefore, cannot. One is descriptive, the other prescriptive. With many of the value judgements we make, there is no objective criterion to which we can appeal to settle the issue.

Fact	Value
An argument about what *is* the case	An argument about what *ought* or *should* be the case
Descriptive	Prescriptive

The question we need to ask an author, therefore, is whether he has confused the two and deduced a conclusion containing a value judgement from purely factual assumptions, smuggling in his own opinions under our radar as if they are just statements of fact. You might find someone argues:

1 All major engineering projects go over budget.
2 The new high speed train link is a major engineering project.
3 Therefore, it should be stopped.

The first two assumptions are both statements of fact, whether or not they are true, but the conclusion is a value judgement. Deductive arguments of this type are valid only as long as they draw out by way of a conclusion what is already contained in the assumptions. The key principle to remember is:

> Nothing can be drawn out by way of a conclusion that is not already contained in the assumptions.

This means that no value judgement can be deduced from any set of assumptions which do not themselves contain a value judgement. In the argument above, we could only have drawn out this conclusion if the first assumption had been instead:

All major engineering works should be stopped because they go over budget.

This reveals a common weakness in many arguments: that authors make unstated assumptions like these without making clear that they're doing so.

2.2 Concepts

However, an argument can also involve concepts as well as facts and values. Look at the following arguments and see if you can distinguish between those that are arguments of fact, value or concept or, indeed, a mixture of all three.

What sort of argument is it?   **EXERCISE**

1 The football team I support lost 4-0 at the weekend.
2 They played very badly.
3 They have no idea how to play modern attacking football.
4 After four consecutive defeats the manager should lose his job.
5 The problem is he has only been in management for two years and he has very little experience of how to manage a big club.
6 He selects all the wrong players.
7 He finally realised this at half time and made changes, but by then it was too late.
8 It made very little difference.
9 For most of the game, there was no pattern to their play.
10 Under previous managers, they played possession football really well, but in this game they had only 30 per cent of the play.

Answers:

1 Fact
2 Value
3 Value/Concept
4 Fact/Value
5 Fact/Value/Concept
6 Value
7 Fact/Value
8 Value
9 Value/Concept
10 Fact/Value/Concept

You can now see the potential problems that lie in all arguments and the importance of determining what sort of argument it is, before you critically evaluate it. So, as you complete your analysis, check that you have covered everything by working through the following list:

> 1 Are the assumptions purely factual?
> 2 Are there value judgements that the author hasn't revealed?
> 3 Are there concepts about which you should ask, 'But what does he mean by this?'
> 4 Has he made clear all of his assumptions or does he rely on some that are unstated?

3 Critical Evaluation

Our critical evaluation of the literature breaks down into the three elements we listed in the table above:

1 Arguments
2 Evidence
3 Language

3.1 Arguments

Now that you know what kind of argument you are dealing with, you will know where to direct your critical evaluation.

1 Arguments of fact

Obviously, to critically evaluate arguments of fact, we have to evaluate the evidence the author gives to justify them. We will examine this and the steps we need to work through in the next section (Section 3.2) on evidence.

2 Arguments of value

As for value judgements, the first thing we need to acknowledge is that they cannot be avoided. Not everything is objective, so evidence has to be weighed and value judgements made about its strength.

Verifiable value judgements

Even so, there are some that are ultimately verifiable by reference to an objective criterion. If we were both to look out of my study window and I were to judge that the tree opposite was 30 yards away and you were to judge that it was more like 50 yards, the difference in our judgements could ultimately be settled by using a standard measuring tape. There is, in other words, an objective standard that we both accept, to which we can appeal.

No objective criterion

However, for most value judgements there is no objective standard, so they cannot be settled so easily. We might not be able to agree over whether it was right for Jane to lie to her boyfriend to protect his feelings, or whether Verdi's *Requiem* is a great piece of music. All we can do is ask:

1 What is the criterion on which this is based?
2 Is it a reasonable value judgement and well thought out?
3 Does the author reveal all the evidence?
4 Has any evidence been withheld to lend support to his conclusions?

3 Arguments of concept

As for concepts, this tends to be more complex. In Chapter 10, we found that underlying them are patterns of ideas, through which we group and organise experience and which allow us to see things in a particular way. When we use them, we tend to allow one of these ideas to dominate our interpretation of experience. When an author does this, it places limits on his argument that we should make plain and point to our alternative use of the concept to highlight the issues we want to explore in our own research.

Autonomy and dependency: their influence   EXAMPLE
on learning behaviour and study skills in the 16–19 age group

In this project, the author may have concentrated on assessing how self-reliant students were as a measure of their autonomy. In contrast, you can reasonably point out that there are alternative, perhaps more important, characteristics, like self-reflection, that are more reliable indicators of autonomy.

Similarities and dissimilarities

By comparing and contrasting the different analyses of concepts, theories and arguments in this way, we begin to lay the basis for our recommendations of where future research should be directed or begin to develop the foundations of our own research. Remember, you are not drawing conclusions here – just raising questions that you think should be the subject of further research.

1 Finding gaps

On the one hand, you are critically evaluating an author's arguments to see if they are valid: that he has drawn his conclusions from the reasons given in a logically consistent way. As you do this, you will find it helpful to work through the checklist above and refer back to Chapter 8.

You are also drawing attention to the alternative interpretations of concepts that may open up avenues of research the author may have overlooked. By identifying the flaws and limitations of the arguments in this way, you draw attention to gaps and questions that need to be answered.

2 New connections

On the other hand, by drawing attention to similarities between your sources, you can begin to lay the basis for your own synthesis of ideas and arguments to find a new way of approaching the problem. You can create structures of ideas by finding new connections between them and then begin to adapt the structures as we did in Chapter 11.

3.2 Evidence

However, as we saw above, if you have identified an argument of fact, you will have to critically evaluate the author's use of evidence:

1   Does she have enough relevant and reliable evidence?
2   How does she describe it? Does she exaggerate or understate it?
3   Does she draw reliable inferences from it?
4   Does she draw relevant inferences from it?

1 Enough relevant and reliable evidence

For this, refer back to Chapter 9 and use the checklist above. Where you suspect weaknesses in the argument, discuss whether you think the generalisations the author makes are based on sufficient evidence, which represents a fair sample.

2 How does she describe it?

Critically evaluate whether she exaggerates it using simple absolutes as qualifiers, like 'all', where the evidence will only support qualifiers, like 'some'. Is her use of statistics reliable? Work through the following list of questions.

1   Are her generalisations based on a sufficient number?
2   Are they a fair sample?
3   Is there a reasonable probability that they are true?
4   Has she used simple absolutes, like 'all', where other **qualifiers**, like 'some', would be more accurate?
5   Has she presented her evidence with enough precision?
6   Where she uses them, is it clear what she means by 'typical', 'normal' and 'average'?
7   Where she uses **averages**, has she chosen the right type: mean, median or mode?
8   Where she uses **statistics** are there:
    8.1   hidden qualifications;
    8.2   uniformity between the comparisons she makes;
    8.3   confusion between absolute and comparative figures?3

3 Reliable inferences

Next move on to the inferences she draws from the evidence: are they reliable? If she uses **analogies** to draw her inferences, evaluate them on the basis of the three things that we discussed in Chapter 9:

1   the connection between the analogy and the inference;
2   the numbers involved;
3   the relation between the analogy and the inference drawn from it.

Then assess whether she has oversimplified her evidence by using **stereotypes**, the **straw man fallacy**, **special pleading** and the **fallacy of false dilemma**. Similarly, evaluate the causal inferences that she draws: are they invalid; are they irrelevant? Ask yourself ...

1   Has she committed the *post hoc* **fallacy**?
2   Has she confused a **cause** with a **correlation**?
3   Has she assumed that there is a **single cause**, when in fact there may be many? And, obversely, where she has assumed that there are many causes operating, is there just one single underlying cause?

4 Relevant inferences

Alternatively, where you think she may have drawn irrelevant inferences, check whether...

> 1 she has sidestepped the weaknesses in her argument by **discrediting those who drew attention to them**;
> 2 whether she has appealed to **popular opinion** to bolster her argument;
> 3 diverted attention away from criticism by appealing to an **authority**;
> 4 attempted to promote her own argument by raising **fears** about accepting her opponent's;
> 5 or encouraged you to accept her argument on the basis that it is the most reasonable **compromise** between two undesirable extremes.

3.3 Language

Finally, evaluate her use of language. Is it clear and consistent or do the arguments contain language and concepts that are poorly defined? Does their meaning change in the middle of the argument, allowing her to draw unjustified conclusions?

1 Clarity

As you consider these things, check her use of ...

1 **jargon**;
2 **loaded language**;
3 or where you might think she **begs the question**.

Unfortunately, at university many of us are inducted into a way of expressing ourselves that leads to obscurity, rather than clarity. We are encouraged to read turgid, polysyllabic, badly written prose that drowns us in a mire of convoluted sentences and misleading **jargon**. Often, it seems, the assumption is that a simple style is a sign of a simple mind, whereas in fact it is the result of harder thinking and harder work. So wherever you come across it ...

1 convert the jargon into concrete words that ground the ideas in everyday reality;
2 ask yourself whether she is deliberately obscuring a weakness in her argument beneath a camouflage of jargon, rather than think her ideas through to resolve it.

Similarly, where you suspect words are **loaded** ...

1 translate them into neutral terms;
2 then ask yourself, is the argument still convincing?

In a similar way, as we discovered in Chapter 9, authors can manipulate our thinking by **begging the question**, where they encourage us to accept as an assumption what they are arguing for as a conclusion. In other words, they manipulate readers without them knowing it by smuggling into their assumptions the conclusion they are about to deduce.

So, in all of these cases, evaluate the arguments by asking ...

1 what is the cash value of what the author is saying;
2 what do these words stand for?
3 what is their objective meaning?

2 Consistency

Beyond the clarity of the language an author is using, we also have to be concerned with its consistency. In Chapter 9, we found that authors commit the fallacy of **equivocation** when they use a word to mean one thing in one part of their argument and something else in another part. So, in your discussion, where you think this has occurred ...

1 draw attention to it by suggesting that the persuasiveness of the argument depends upon this inconsistency;
2 and then replace the doubtful word with others that consistently maintain the same meaning to reveal the actual strength of the argument.

4 Synthesis

Finally, you come to that section of your review in which, out of your critical evaluation of your sources, you lay the foundations for your own alternative approach to the problem you first laid out in the introduction. To help you do this, you will find it useful to work through different stages in your synthesis:

1 First draw connections between your own research topic and the sources you have reviewed to show how your topic fits into this.
2 Briefly sum up your evaluation of the strengths and weaknesses of the main sources and the gaps they leave.
3 Now create your own structure of ideas out of the differences and similarities you found in your sources. In this stage use the ideas we created using the methods we learned in Chapter 12, where we synthesised the arguments, ideas and analyses of different sources to lay the basis of our alternative approach.
4 We then adapted these structures, using the four strategies we learned in Chapter 11 to find a new way of approaching the problem either by...

     1 changing the structure;
     2 approaching it from a different direction;
     3 starting from a different point of view;
     4 or by creating a new structure.

5 Finally, show how your alternative approach, the new ideas, methods and procedures, represents a significant advance and will fill the gaps you have identified.

As you can see, you are not developing these ideas as you write, but reproducing the thinking you did in Part 3, when you processed the ideas.

 You can download copies of the checklists in this chapter and additional exercises from the companion website (www.macmillanihe.com/greetham-literature-review).

Summary

1 Good thinkers think about their thinking while they think.
2 Your discussion must move from the general to the specific, where you lay the foundations for your own research or indicate in a stand-alone review where effective research might be undertaken.
3 An author can smuggle in a value judgement or take for granted the meaning of a concept without us noticing, unless we learn to distinguish between different types of argument.
4 By comparing and contrasting the different analyses of concepts and arguments, we begin to lay the foundations of our own research or, in a stand-alone review, of our own approach to the literature.
5 In the synthesis, create new structures of ideas out of the differences and similarities you have identified.

What next?

Now that we know the detail of what we must do, in the next chapter we will examine how best to write our first draft.

Chapter 21

The First Draft

In this chapter, you will learn...

- that writing is the most effective way of gaining control over our ideas;
- the importance of starting to write your first draft early;
- how to create a clear rationale in your review that makes coherent sense;
- how to structure each paragraph;
- how to use transitions to indicate what you are doing and why it is relevant.

The success of a literature review depends upon two things. First, it should be written clearly and concisely in a style that is simple to understand and interesting to read. Second, there should be a clear rationale behind the literature you have chosen and planned to use – it should make coherent sense.

1 Writing

As we will see, these two problems are necessarily connected: by writing about our ideas we begin to fashion a clear rationale through them that gives our review coherent shape. The problem is that we tend to spend most of our time reading with little devoted to writing and developing the ideas we form. Yet writing is the most effective way of gaining genuine control over our ideas and of working towards the centre of a problem.

1 **Revealing errors in our thinking**
   We can see our false starts, our inconsistent conclusions, our misuse of evidence and the unexamined assumptions that lurk unnoticed in the concepts we might otherwise use unreflectively.
2 **Developing more ideas**
   What's more, it engages our imagination, intellect and emotions, all of which are different ways of generating insights and developing our understanding.

As I've said in previous chapters, we cannot easily separate thinking from writing. To do our best thinking, we must write about our ideas. No other activity is so effective at forcing us to think clearly. It places us at the heart of our ideas, forcing us to pin them down, clarify our thinking, check the consistency of our arguments and then capture all of this in language that conveys it accurately.

Write early in your notebook and journal

In view of this, it makes sense to begin early. Record in your notebook and journal the constant dialogue you will be having with yourself on your ideas. Whenever a new idea comes to you, give yourself time to write it down and empty out your mind on it. This is your opportunity to express complex ideas and, in the process, form a deeper understanding of them, before you begin writing your first draft. In this way you will structure your thoughts, develop your arguments and evaluate your ideas as you go along.

- Record in your notebook and journal the constant dialogue you will be having with yourself on your ideas.
- In this way you can express complex ideas and develop a deeper understanding.

The effects of this on your thinking are significant, but so too is the impact on your writing. A piece of writing that glides effortlessly across the page in light, elegant prose doesn't occur all in one session as one piece of thought. It will be pieced together from different notebook jottings, journal entries and those red-hot moments when ideas just come fully formed with glaring clarity to be written feverishly into your notebook and then worked on until it does finally glide across the page effortlessly.

Start your first draft early

By the same token, it also makes sense to begin your first draft early. As with all forms of writing, it's better to start when the ideas are most familiar and vivid. So, don't leave long periods between carrying out your search and processing the ideas, and then writing it up; otherwise you might forget details and your impressions will lack the same freshness.

Equally important, you are likely to discover early whether you have too much material or too little, and whether your ideas are coming together as you expected. If this means you will have to change your approach, it's better to know this early, rather than discover it when it's too late to do anything about it. Moreover, not only will you write when you are most likely to produce your best work, but you will avoid the dispiriting effects of seeing a mountain of work building up, all of which needs to be written and revised.

> You are likely to know early whether you have too much material or too little, and whether you will have to change your approach.

Write freely

As for the actual writing, allow yourself to write freely as you develop your ideas. To make it easier, banish all fear that what you're writing may not be up to standard. Otherwise you might find yourself suffering from the legendary writers' block, which often comes from your internal editor stepping in to pass judgement on what you're doing. To allow your ideas and your writing to flow in this way, keep your inner editor at bay. Just tell yourself that this is only a draft. You can leave the editing until later. You're just sending out a reconnaissance party to see what you've got and how it shapes up.

- Banish all fear that what you're writing may not be up to standard.
- To allow your writing to flow, keep your inner editor at bay.
- Tell yourself this is only a draft – you're just sending out a reconnaissance party to see what you've got.

Your own voice

The more you allow your words to flow onto the page without worrying at the moment about style and whether you've written complete sentences, the more your own voice will come through. You will find your own natural rhythm and there will be a lot more energy in your writing. Indeed, when you come to revision you will have to be careful not to kill this off. Too much editing can deaden your writing.

The key to success here is to remind yourself that the best writing reads as though it is talk in print. The smoother the rhythm and the closer it is to our normal speech, the easier it is to read and understand. You'll get your ideas across more effectively and you'll hold the attention of your readers.

- The more you allow your words to flow onto the page, the more your own voice will come through.
- You will find your own natural rhythm, closer to your normal speech.
- Therefore, the easier it will be to read and understand, so you'll hold the attention of your readers.

2 A clear rationale that makes coherent sense

As we have seen in previous chapters, one of the most common criticisms of literature reviews is that students merely list and summarise their sources without establishing a link between them, an overall structure that ties them together to create a coherent review, and, even more serious, without linking them with their own ideas. There is little analysis, critical evaluation and synthesis of sources out of which they develop and impose their own structure of ideas.

As a result, the review is dominated by the authors that have been chosen as sources. Your purpose in using these sources and your own ideas are left in the background. The solution to this is twofold:

1 Careful, detailed planning

In Chapter 18, we planned and rehearsed our arguments and ideas in detail. In this way you allow your own structure, formed from your analysis of the key concepts, theories and ideas, to dictate what sources and parts of sources you will use.

2 Structure each paragraph

By structuring each paragraph, you can indicate clearly for readers the structure of your plan, so they know where you will be taking them and why. You can do this quite simply by making sure that each paragraph has three parts:

1 *The topic sentence*

This picks up a topic from the plan, thereby clearly establishing for the reader the subject of the paragraph or section and why it is relevant.

2 *The development of the argument*

Having made clear to the reader the topic you are discussing and why it is relevant, you can now develop your own argument by analysing and critically evaluating the ideas in the source.

3 *The evidence*

Rather than leave your argument as just an assertion of opinion, you support it with evidence drawn from your sources. In this sense, a literature review is no different from any other academic work, in that your interpretation and critical evaluation of the literature must be backed by evidence to substantiate your arguments.

By ensuring both of these things – that your review is carefully planned and your paragraphs are clearly structured – you make sure that it is you and your ideas that dictate the shape and content of your review and not your sources.

Organ donations: the effects of the acts and omissions doctrine   EXAMPLE

In this literature review, the author used the following paragraph to present a source challenging the view that omissions are free of moral culpability:

However, when we look for the cause of an event we look for something that has changed in the environment, something that has departed from normal expectations. If an act is omitted that we would normally expect to be done, this disruption of normal functioning is what we would describe as the cause. This suggests that our omissions do have causal consequences when they represent a deviation from normal expectations. For example, at one time, if the parents of a newly-born infant with Down's syndrome made it clear that they didn't want the infant, doctors would often allow it to die if it developed a life-threatening condition, like pneumonia (Rosenthal, 2004). Of course, the official cause of death might be pneumonia, but from the causal background it could not be this that made the difference, because in all cases of infants without Down's Syndrome this would have been treated.

In the topic sentence the subject of the paragraph is picked up from the plan and introduced; in this case an analysis of the concept of 'cause'.
In the next two sentences the argument is developed by drawing out the implications of this analysis.
Then, in the rest of the paragraph, the author presents the evidence, a source that supports and illustrates the argument.

1 Topic sentences

As you can see, the topic sentence allows you not only to present your own argument drawn from your detailed plan, but the opportunity for your own voice to come through clearly. With your own voice at the start of the paragraph, you avoid your sources dictating to you and dominating both the structure and the writing of the review.

Transitions

The other key element in the topic sentence is the transition, in this case the word 'However'. Although they may seem inconsequential, transitions are in fact important indications of the logic of your plan. Your readers need to know at the beginning of each paragraph where you are taking them and why. This single word or phrase does that. In effect, they form the logical scaffolding of each section by which you indicate to the reader the links between each idea and each paragraph and the changes in direction that you're taking.

> Your readers need to know at the beginning of each paragraph where you are taking them and why.

Now that your plan has been carefully rehearsed and structured, the one remaining problem is how you're going to create fluent links between paragraphs that will signal to your readers the structure of your plan, so they will know what you're doing and won't get lost. For this, you will need effective 'transitions' at the beginning of each paragraph. This can be a short phrase, like 'As a result', or a single word, like 'Nevertheless'. They will help you create a taut, cohesive piece of work, with a clear connection between each paragraph.

Transitions ...

- indicate the logic of your plan;
- which way you are taking readers and why;
- create a cohesive literature review.

Logical indicators

As you can see, transitions work as 'logical indicators' telling your readers what you'll be doing. You might be striking a contrast with the previous paragraph ('In contrast', 'However'). You may simply be extending the argument you've already developed in a slightly different way ('Moreover', 'Therefore'). You may want to strengthen your argument by developing a point that reinforces it from a different angle ('Similarly', 'Likewise'). Or you may want to illustrate your point with an example ('For example', 'For instance'). In some paragraphs, it will be obvious what you're doing and there will be no need to announce it, but if in doubt, use a transition.

In Chapter 24, you will find an exhaustive list of transitions and what they're used for. However, for a quick reference you may find useful the following list of commonly used transitions. As you come across examples in your reading, note how other writers link their paragraphs and add them to the list. Some of the most effective are the most simple, indeed so simple that we hardly realise they're there at all. Demonstrative pronouns, like 'this', 'these' and 'those', slipped into a topic sentence create a bridge between two paragraphs, while hardly disturbing the flow of ideas.

Section transitions

To reinforce the logic of what you are doing and indicate where you are in the overall structure of your plan, you will also find it useful at the end of important sections of your review, or at the end of a chapter if it is an integrated review, to look back and summarise the key points so far and then look forward to what is to come. In this way, you can ensure that at key moments your reader can take stock by recapping and reviewing the most important points from the sources you have cited before you begin the next section.

Similarities	In the same way, Likewise, Similarly, Correspondingly
Contrast	However, On the other hand, Yet, But, But at the same time, Despite, Even so, For all that, In contrast, In spite of, On the contrary, Otherwise
Illustration	For example, For instance, That is, In other words, In particular, Namely, Specifically, Such as, Thus, To illustrate
Extension	Similarly, Moreover, Furthermore, In addition, By extension, What is more, Above all, Further, In the same way.
Conclusion	Therefore, Consequently, As a result, Thus
The next step	Then, After that, It follows
Emphasis	Above all, After all, Equally important, Especially, Indeed, In fact, In particular, Most important, Of course

Causal relations	As a result, Consequently, For that reason, So, Accordingly, Owing to this, Due to this, Because of this, Under these circumstances.
Temporal relations	In future, In the meantime, In the past, At first, At the same time, During this time, Earlier, Eventually, Meanwhile, Now, Recently, Simultaneously
Summarising	Finally, In brief, In conclusion, In short, In simpler terms, In summary, On the whole, To summarise
Qualification	However, Nevertheless, Even though, Still, Yet
Alternatives	Alternatively, On the other hand, Rather
Explanation	That is to say, In other words, Namely, This means, To put it in another way, To put it simply

2 Development of the argument

After we have presented in the topic sentence a point or argument taken from a source, we can develop our argument. In this part of the paragraph, we discuss the topic by processing the ideas in each of the ways we talked about in the last chapter: analysing its implications, critically evaluating these and then synthesising the ideas we develop out of it.

$$\text{Analysis} \longrightarrow \text{Critical evaluation} \longrightarrow \text{Synthesis}$$

Of course it may not be possible to do all this in one paragraph. Instead you might analyse the implications in one paragraph and then pick up each of these in the following paragraphs, where you critically evaluate them. Then, after you have evaluated them all, you might follow this up at the end of this section of your review by bringing this all together into your own original synthesis. Alternatively, you could do this in the conclusion of the review, if that works better.

Integrated reviews

If you are writing an integrated review, you could bring all these strands together at the end of the chapter you're writing. Each of the sections in the chapter could deal with a significant issue and then at the end of the chapter you could bring all those strands together and reinforce the most significant points from the sources you have cited.

3 Evidence

In most paragraphs, as you can see from the one above, you will have to back up your interpretation and critical evaluation of the literature with evidence and, in a literature review, this means, for the most part, citations from the texts you have used. But, if not in each paragraph, this will have to come later when you bring all the strands together.

Nevertheless, avoid burying your reader beneath quotations piled one on another. Of course, if it is something that an author says in a way that has impact, which you cannot match, use one, but keep it short. Remind yourself of the point that was made in Chapter 19, that long quotations suggest that you haven't made the ideas your own: you haven't processed them deeply.

Analyse a paragraph   **EXERCISE**

> Take a paragraph you have written and analyse it, first to see how you have written the topic sentence to indicate what you will be doing in the paragraph and why it is relevant. Are your intentions, which you made clear in your plan, dominant in the paragraph? How have you developed the analysis and evaluation, and have you supported it with evidence? Then, second, assess which voice is most dominant – yours or the authors' you are citing.

 You can download a copy of the table in this chapter from the companion website (www.macmillanihe.com/greetham-literature-review).

Summary

1 Writing is the most effective way of gaining genuine control over your ideas.
2 Start your first draft early when your ideas are most familiar and vivid.
3 Writing in your own voice you'll find your natural rhythm. As a result, it will be easier to read and understand.
4 A topic sentence at the beginning of a paragraph allows you to impose your thinking on your sources.
5 Transitions are important indicators of the logic of your plan.

What next?

Much of this chapter has been about how to place your own voice and your own ideas at the forefront of your literature review. However, letting your own voice come through is not just a question of the way we use references and the structure of paragraphs, as we will see in the next chapter.

Chapter 22

Finding Your Own Voice

In this chapter, you will learn...

- how to avoid becoming just the anonymous translator of the view of others;
- the five things you can do to assert your own voice;
- how to write more freely;
- how to write in the first person while avoiding statements of mere opinion;
- how to write clear, direct, concise prose.

The very nature of a literature review means that for much of the time you are presenting the ideas of others. Consequently, it is all too easy to become submerged in all this, allowing yourself to assume the passive, anonymous position behind the text as if you are just some neutral translator of the views of others. To avoid this, you have to ensure that your voice is at the centre of what you write, controlling, directing, adjudicating and evaluating each source you consider.

In this way, you will reclaim your mental space and the unique way in which you express your ideas. It will bring a lightness of touch to your expression, a naturalness to your writing, nearer to the spoken word, that will help you present your ideas and develop your arguments clearly, simply and economically.

- Avoid assuming the passive, anonymous position of a mere translator of other people's ideas.
- Reclaiming your mental space will help you present your ideas clearly, simply and economically.

The anonymous reader

Unfortunately, in much of our academic writing, our ideas seem to be targeted at some unknown, anonymous reader, which encourages us to adopt a more universal, less personal form of communication. We are encouraged to believe that there is a style, a method of thinking and writing, which we must imitate. So we abandon our own voice and allow our own thoughts and ideas to recede into the background, while we settle for just recycling the ideas of authorities, using their terms and forms of expression, even though they may mean very little to us.

Despite our best efforts, this inevitably results in poor thinking and poor writing. In effect, we express ideas that are not ours in a language we do not command. And not even the most accomplished writer can write well when she is expressing ideas that have no meaning for her. She will struggle to give shape to the ideas; her fluency of expression will break down; her sentences will no longer mean what she meant them to mean; she will become illiterate.

> We express ideas that are not ours in a language we do not command.

Asserting your own voice

However, there are simple things you can do to assert the primacy of your own thinking and write in your own voice. By working on the following five things, you will begin to hear your own voice coming through in everything you write.

1 Know your audience
2 Make contact with everyday reality
3 Write freely
4 Use the first person
5 Wherever possible, avoid passive writing

1 Know your audience

No matter how you are communicating, it makes obvious sense to have a clear idea of who you are talking to. Visualise your readers as a group of friendly critics; intelligent non-specialists, who might need just a little more translation of the technical aspects of your work. By translating them into more complete explanations, you avoid the easy reliance on jargon and other literal shortcuts.

Jargon used without this sort of explanation turns your writing into a foreign language that must be translated before sense can be made of it. This will alienate readers, the cardinal sin in any form of communication, particularly writing. Write in a way that is accessible to any intelligent reader: you're not writing to be read by an exclusive set of code-breakers.

2 Make contact with everyday reality

To achieve this, every time you find yourself just recycling the complex abstractions and jargon you have read, remind yourself to break it down into simpler, more concrete language that makes contact with our everyday experience. Each time we fail to do this we make it difficult, if not impossible, to understand what we're saying. Once our work has been stripped of its alien jargon, our own voice and our own ideas begin to shine through in a way that often surprises us.

Meaning is what your words actually forbid

If there is one statement that deserves to be placed nearby as you work, it is one that reminds you constantly that if you don't forbid anything by using a word it won't mean anything. The information content of an argument is directly proportional to the range of possibilities it excludes: the more it excludes, the more information content it has. Writing that is full of abstractions with few concrete referents holds very little actual meaning. Or more precisely, it could, in fact, mean anything.

> The information content of an argument is directly proportional to the range of possibilities it excludes.

Like any scientific theory, an argument must forbid something from happening to allow it to be tested. If it cannot be tested, it could mean anything: it holds no meaning. Using concrete language excludes possibilities; it forbids certain things from happening, so we can assess how probable it is that the argument is true. If it is composed just of abstractions, we cannot test it in this way, so we have to conclude that it is meaningless: it could mean anything.

- The information content of an argument is directly proportional to the range of possibilities it excludes.
- If an argument does not forbid something from happening, it cannot be tested.
- Consequently, it could mean anything: it holds no meaning.

Abstractions   EXERCISE

Read the following passage taken from the prospectus of a new political party and count up the number of concrete words in it.

It will be liberal because it will stand for the maximum of individual liberty, for tolerance of all honest diversity of opinion. It will be conservative because it believes in conserving the great constructive achievements of the past. And it will be reactionary in its opposition to ignorant and reckless efforts to destroy traditional values in the name of alleged 'progress'.

Answer:

In fact, there are no concrete words in this passage, so nothing is forbidden: it could mean anything. You are left with the conclusion that it all depends what is meant by 'honest', 'constructive', 'ignorant' and all the rest.

Nevertheless, as we have discovered, abstract concepts play an important part in the arguments we develop. They give us the ability to go beyond a concern for particulars to create universal claims that enable us to advance our knowledge and solve fundamental problems. However, they must be grounded in the concrete reality of our lives; otherwise the author is free to say what he likes, as is the case in the passage above.

> Whenever you use abstract concepts, ask yourself, 'What difference do they make to our lives: how are we to come to understand the way they work in our experience?'

3 Write freely

Equally effective in asserting the primacy of your own thinking is to allow yourself to write freely. As we discovered in the last chapter, this injects more fluency into your writing and brings your own voice to the surface. But to do this you have to keep your inner editor at bay. Once you have completed a difficult section, resist the temptation to read it all through so you can bask in the glow of your achievements. At moments like these, we are all tempted to allow our editor in to give us his or her approval.

Remind yourself that the best writing reads as though it is talk in print. The smoother the rhythm and the closer it is to our normal speech, the easier it is to read. You'll get your ideas across more effectively and you'll hold the attention of your readers.

- Don't revise as you go along.
- Concentrate on writing fluently – don't stop to correct things.
- Keep your editor at bay.
- The best writing reads as though it is talk in print.

4 The first person

However, perhaps the most obvious way of reclaiming your mental space is to write in the first person. Unfortunately, many departments at universities disapprove of this, so it would be sensible to discuss it early with your supervisor to see what's required of you. Students are told that in academic writing they cannot place themselves at the centre of their writing; that they must avoid all forms of the first person pronoun 'I'.

Instead, you are told you must disguise your identity by talking about 'the author's opinion', 'in the opinion of the present writer', 'the author assumed that' or similar hedging devices, like 'It was thought that' and 'It was decided that'. As a result, your writing becomes anonymous. And with no identity, your own voice is silenced. Not only does this rob you of your own voice, but it makes very little sense.

1 First, it introduces unnecessary ambiguity into our writing. At times when you refer to 'the author' it's not clear if you're referring to the last mentioned reference or to you, the writer of what's being read.

2 And, second, despite all your attempts to disguise your identity by referring to a third party, it is rare that anybody is actually deceived. After all, your name is on your work. To suggest otherwise is to claim that someone else is writing your review, as if you are shirking the responsibility for what you are saying.

> Your writing becomes anonymous. With no identity, your own voice is silenced.

Objectivity

However, the reason such advice is given is that our main focus in academic work is objectivity: we judge an argument on its consistency and how well it is supported by the evidence, and not on the individual who has made the argument. So we cannot accept an argument that only rests on someone's subjective conviction. We want the reader to take onboard our arguments as something that deserves to be thoroughly assessed and considered, and not dismissed as just our own point of view with no more credibility than that.

Nevertheless, as we said in Chapter 20, not everything is objective. Unavoidably, you will have to weigh the evidence and come to your own judgement as to how convincing you think an argument might be. Indeed, these are important events in your literature review and in your research, when you take responsibility for the evaluations and choices you have made.

If you are writing a stand-alone review, you will have to justify the inclusion and exclusion criteria you used, how you evaluated the methodological quality of the literature you chose and the basis on which you synthesised the ideas and arguments you found in the literature. If yours is an empirical dissertation or thesis, you will have to explain and justify...

- your **methodology** – the tools and instruments you used – the questions you asked in an interview – how you designed a questionnaire – why you chose one subject for a case study, rather than another;
- your **findings** – why they were not as conclusive as you had hoped;
- the **experiences** that affected your results – how you handled a difficult interview – how you managed a focus group without imposing your own ideas and values on the discussion.

To call upon subterfuge to disguise this behind the unconvincing phrase 'in the opinion of the author' flies in the face of everything we say about upholding the highest standards of academic integrity. You can quite reasonably argue that if academic writers are expressing their own opinions, they should uphold these standards of honesty and own up that this is 'my' opinion, 'my' judgement, and you may not agree with it.

> We should uphold the highest standards of academic integrity.

So, instead of disguising it, address the problem that an argument should not rest merely on someone's subjective conviction by making explicit your justification for arriving at these value judgements by answering the same questions we asked of our sources in Chapter 20. In other words, as far as you can, make clear the grounds on which your judgement is based and why you think this is reasonable. By acknowledging in the first person your own responsibility in this way...

1 your writing will be more direct, clear and effective;
2 and your intentions will be clearer, too, as you present your own ideas, conclusions, analyses and evaluations.

Avoiding potential problems

Nevertheless, there are moments in a review when you might find yourself using a personal pronoun, which is likely to leave you with the problem of how to avoid the charge of subjectivity.

1   Statements of intention

This is the sort of statement that we might make about what we will do or have done. We might begin a sentence with phrases like,

I do …
I have done …
I consider …
I discuss …
I will focus on …

Sentences beginning like this run the danger of undercutting any claim to be objective. They appear to present an approach which is largely personal and beyond objective criticism. The only way they can work is if you show through argument and analysis that these are the only logical alternatives or if you demonstrate that it is the most sensible way of approaching the problem.

Moral Thinking   EXAMPLE

I examine Hare's claim that his is an entirely formal, neutral account of the canons of moral reasoning and whether in fact he introduces substantive assumptions into his account, which lead him to claim that moral prescriptions are merely expressions of preferences.

In this thesis, the author begins in the first person, but then reveals that his approach is not merely a personal choice by setting out the two logical alternatives: either a formal, neutral account of moral reasoning, in other words one that is free of all substantive judgements as to what should and should not be the case, or one that does indeed hold substantive assumptions.

2   Statements of opinion

By contrast, statements that are more obviously open to the charge of subjectivity are those that appear to be straightforward statements of opinion.

I believe …
I suggest that…
I argue…

If they are substantiated now or later in the body of the literature review by argument or evidence, then we do take responsibility, but if no substantiation is offered, then it leaves these points as mere opinion. They must be verified either through evidence or through argument and analysis that shows them to be the only logical conclusions.

5 Wherever possible, avoid passive writing

As with writing in the first person, similar advice is given to some students that in academic writing they must adopt a passive writing style. Like avoiding the first person, this too can rob your writing of its clarity and introduce unnecessary ambiguity. It is also more impersonal and indirect, which makes it more difficult for you to use your own voice in your writing.

The distinction between the passive and active forms is as follows:

Passive form	The receiver of the action or the action itself is the subject of the sentence.
Active form	The doer of the action is the subject of the sentence.

In the active form there is less ambiguity, whereas the passive form not only lacks precision, but is almost always less direct, positive and concise.

Active writing   EXAMPLES

1 In the passive form, you might say,
   'The test was carried out on the subjects of the experiment by the psychologist.'
In contrast, in the active form, you would say,
   'The psychologist tested the subjects of the experiment.'
2 Instead of saying,
   'The survey was undertaken and the results published by the author of this report',
in both the active form and in the first person you would say simply,
   'I conducted the survey and published the results.'

Using a sentence like, 'An experiment was conducted', introduces ambiguity, leaving you unsure who conducted the experiment. By using a pronoun or noun at the beginning of the sentence to identify the person involved and an active verb to describe what she did, you can visualise the actual event in specific detail.

Passive	Introduces unnecessary ambiguity
Active	Helps you visualise the event

So, to make your work clear, concise and more direct, remind yourself of the same principle we used in our analysis of abstractions, where we insisted that we must be able to cash them in to see what difference they make in our lives; how they work in our experience. Wherever possible, avoid distancing your ideas from your readers' daily reality by using passive, impersonal, abstract forms. Otherwise, your arguments will be difficult to understand and, therefore, less persuasive.

Writing as lightly as you can

To avoid these problems place yourself and your own voice at the heart of your writing and resist the temptation to take the easy route by just recycling the language and style of specialists. This is likely to drown the reader in ambiguous terms and convoluted sentences. Let your own voice come through. Write in light, unambiguous prose. The result is likely to be a memorable, effective piece of writing that your reader will not forget.

Summary

1 By recycling the ideas of others, we express ideas that are not ours in a language we do not command.
2 Jargon will alienate readers, the cardinal sin in any form of communication.
3 Meaning lies in what your words forbid.
4 When you use an abstraction, ask yourself how are we to understand the way it works in our experience.
5 Acknowledge in the first person your responsibility for the value judgements you make.

What next?

As this chapter makes clear, our aim should be to express our ideas clearly, concisely and unambiguously. In the next chapter, we will learn how we can improve our style to achieve this.

Chapter 23

Style: Simplicity and Economy

In this chapter, you will learn...

> - how to avoid losing readers in long, complex sentences;
> - the importance of using punctuation to indicate the structure of your sentences;
> - how to de-clutter your sentences;
> - the importance of relying on strong nouns and verbs;
> - how to express your ideas with an economical use of words.

If you struggle to write your ideas clearly and you worry about having a good style, you are not alone. Even the greatest thinkers have struggled to convey their ideas clearly and logically. Despite all his published work, including the monumental *On the Origin of Species* and many other books and papers, Charles Darwin freely admitted how difficult he found it to express his ideas on paper:

> As long as it consists solely of description it is pretty easy; but where reasoning comes into play, to make a proper connection, a clearness & a moderate fluency, is to me ... a difficulty of which I had no idea.[1]

An idea converted into words often takes on a different form than we intended. An argument put down on paper goes in a different direction than we expected. The problem is that the flexibility of language means that words have a capacity for holding many shades of meaning, or even several separate meanings. So, while the essence of reasoning is precision, language normally tends toward imprecision. Two opposing forces are at work. The sharpness, clarity and constancy of meaning that are important to consistent reasoning are at odds with the ambiguity of language, the lack of sharp and stable definitions.

The solution lies in learning to write what you want to say in the fewest possible words: in other words, cultivating simplicity and economy in the way you use language. This is what is meant by style.

1 Simplicity

Unfortunately, the more we struggle to understand the complex words and sentences in our sources, the less inclined are we to believe that simplicity could possibly play a role in all this. Yet, along with economy, it is the key to effective writing and communication.

Sentences

When we write sentences, our main concern is not to lose our readers. A complex sentence full of multiple clauses is difficult to follow. Not only are you likely to lose readers as they gingerly pick their way through it, but by the time they reach the end they will have forgotten your original point. To prevent this, try to do two things:

1   keep sentences relatively short;
2   and use logical indicators to indicate what you are doing.

1 Length

Long sentences are good for developing an argument, as long as their structure is clear and easy to navigate, whereas short sentences tend to be abrupt and are useful to give your point the sort of impact that will make your reader think carefully about it. Obviously, shorter sentences are easier to follow, so wherever you can use them.

Punctuation

However, when you are developing a long and complex argument, this is not always possible, so in cases like this remind yourself that your primary goal is to enable your reader to navigate your ideas without getting lost. To avoid such confusion, use logical indicators and the signposts of punctuation to indicate the structure.

In addition, think about using your punctuation to create a rhythm that is nearer to the spoken word. As we've said before, the nearer you can approach this, the easier it is to understand what you've written.

Use punctuation to...
- indicate the structure of sentences;
- create the rhythm of the spoken word.

2 Logical indicators

Although we discussed the importance of logical indicators in Chapter 21, the problem is not just that we fail to use them, believing that readers can follow our train of thought without difficulty, but that they get lost in our sentences. When you read over your work and find that the logical structure is not as clear as it should be, try moving your logical indicator to a more important position in the sentence, say, to the beginning.

Sentences
1. Avoid losing your reader in long sentences.
2. Wherever possible use short sentences with clear structures.
3. Use your punctuation and sentence length to create the rhythm of talk in print.
4. Use logical indicators to help the reader follow your train of thought.
5. If the logical structure is not clear, move them to a more prominent position.

Words

As you read your sources, it's easy to conclude that along with long sentences more complex ideas and arguments also call for more complex and subtle vocabulary to convey them. However, this doesn't mean that we're driven to using a plethora of multi-syllabled words or the most convoluted sentences that appear to conceal more than they reveal.

Settling for 'near enough'

Without interrupting your flow of ideas, the first thing to do as you choose your words is not to settle for one that just captures your meaning 'near enough'. This will edge you into the clutches of jargon and farther away from what you want to say, sending your argument in a direction you don't want to go.

If you fail to pin down exactly what you want to say, readers might conclude that you simply haven't got the intellectual determination to pin your ideas down precisely or, worse still, that you have few interesting ideas of your own at all. Either way, readers are likely to assume that the words you use mean one thing when you really mean another.

Settling for 'near enough'...

1   Can send you off in a direction you don't want to go.
2   Readers might conclude you haven't got the determination to pin your ideas down.
3   Suggests you have no interesting ideas of your own.

To give your ideas real impact and ensure that your readers appreciate how really interesting and original they are, avoid any word or phrase that doesn't do them justice.

Rely on strong nouns and verbs to carry your meaning

However, perhaps the clearest way of determining whether your prose lacks the simple clarity it needs for your meaning to be clear is to check how much clutter there is in your sentences. This includes the plethora of adjectives and adverbs we use to shore up weak nouns and verbs, respectively, which only obscure our meaning.

Verbs

Wherever possible, build your sentences around verbs that are specific and active; otherwise, you will find yourself having to shore them up with adverbs and adverbial phrases that water down the image. In the following examples, you can see that the sentences are sharper and their meaning clearer by just replacing the weak verb and its adverb with a stronger verb:

We might be right in *thinking suspiciously* that behind all this information lies a covert message.
We might be right in *suspecting* that behind all this information lies a covert message.

Our respect for authority has given advertisers an effective way of *deceptively taking advantage* of us to promote all manner of products.
Our respect for authority has given advertisers an effective way of *exploiting* us to promote all manner of products.

Nouns

Make sure your nouns are also specific and definite. They must produce a clear image. Like verbs and adverbs, if you find yourself having to shore them up with adjectives and adjectival phrases, you've probably chosen the wrong one. As a result, your meaning will lose impact or be difficult to see beneath the camouflage of adjectives. You can see this in the following sentence. When we replace the noun and its adjective with a single, strong noun with a specific meaning, a clearer image is produced, one which carries more meaning:

By appealing to their *strong tastes,* advertisers successfully by-pass the consumer's capacity to make rational choices.

By appealing to their *passions,* advertisers successfully by-pass the consumer's capacity to make rational choices.

It's not just 'tastes' you're discussing, but 'passions'.

Strong nouns	EXERCISE

Read the following sentence and replace the noun and adjective in italics with a stronger, more specific noun that needs no adjective to make its meaning clear:

They may give us information on the latest technology, but advertisers are also covertly suggesting that we can't afford not to keep up with the *latest developments.*

Answer:

They may give us information on the latest technology, but advertisers are also covertly suggesting that we can't afford not to keep up with *progress.*

It's not just the 'latest developments', but the whole idea of 'progress' and whether this is necessarily a good thing.

Replace prepositional phrases with prepositions

Like adverbs and adjectives, too many prepositional phrases can also clutter up your prose and obscure your meaning. Your readers will struggle to sift through it all to get a good grasp of your ideas. Instead, give your readers a clear image by stripping out the clutter, replacing prepositional phrases with simple prepositions.

Replace	'with regard to' with 'about'
	'for the simple reason' with 'because'
	'on the part of' with 'by'

This is not to say that such phrases should always be avoided, but you should ask yourself, 'Can I replace these with a simpler preposition without any loss of meaning?' At the same time, start listing the propositional phrases that appear regularly in your writing. In the next chapter you will find lists of prepositions, transitions and strong nouns and verbs to help you convey your ideas clearly and concisely and develop your arguments in the direction you want them to go. You'll also find lists of the phrases and unnecessary words we all use, which clutter up our sentences and make our meaning obscure.

Complex and technical subjects

However, it is sometimes argued that some subjects are just too technical and complex for simple, concrete words and sentences. Moreover, students need to show in their writing that they have a good working knowledge of the key concepts and jargon of their subjects. Before you convince yourself of this, consider two points:

1 No subject is too complex.
2 There is a difference between concepts and jargon.

1 No subject is too complex

There is not a single complex idea that is so complex that it cannot be expressed in simple, concrete language that we can all understand. No matter how complex the subject, it can be expressed simply, in clear, accessible English. Writing is a form of thinking, so if we can think clearly we will write clearly. In the best academic writing you will find:

1 passages close to the spoken word, with our normal rhythms of speech;
2 words chosen to express precise meaning – vivid nouns, working adjectives and strong verbs;
3 no flab – authors saying what they want to say in as many words as they need and no more.

There is not a single complex idea that is so complex that it cannot be expressed in simple concrete language.

If you doubt this, just read any passage from Einstein's *Relativity: The Special and General Theory*, or Bertrand Russell's *The Problems of Philosophy*. Each of them explains the most esoteric and difficult subjects, yet in a simple, elegant language that makes the most complex idea accessible to all.

Significantly, in the acknowledgements to *A Brief History of Time*, Stephen Hawking concedes that the subject of his book is often made unreadable, not because of the difficulty of the subject, but because of poor writing. Referring to a book he himself had written on the same subject in 1973, he says:

> I would not advise readers of this book (*A Brief History of Time*) to consult that work for further information: it is highly technical, and quite unreadable. I hope that since then I have learned how to write in a manner that is easier to understand. [2]

2 The difference between concepts and jargon

As students, we are presented with a particularly difficult dilemma. A large part of learning any subject is learning its language, but then we should also be developing our ideas with absolute clarity and precision. As I said in a previous chapter, there is no better way of exposing the gaps in our understanding than by writing down our ideas, but, equally, the most common and effective way of concealing these gaps is to resort to jargon. So how do we distinguish between concepts and mere jargon?

Concept

A simple way of answering this is to say that a concept can always be analysed with clarity and precision into its parts, each of which can be expressed in language grounded in our everyday lives.

Jargon

In contrast, jargon is the language of specialists who have convinced themselves that their ideas cannot be expressed in any other way.

Jargon immunises ideas from criticism and evaluation

On occasions, using jargon seems like deliberate obfuscation in the hope that it will pass for depth and meaning.

English   EXAMPLE

In her account of her time studying English at a top US university, Helena Echlin describes the long sentences, received with awe and thoughtful silence, which sounded like English, but lacked all meaning:

> 'The ode must traverse the problem of solipsism before it can approach participating in the unity which is no longer accessible.'[3]

As she says, 'How can one "traverse" a problem, or "participate" in a unity?' Indeed, how can you participate in something which is no longer accessible? Words are adorned with suffixes for no other reason than to make them seem more obscure and arcane: 'inert' becomes 'inertial', 'relation' becomes 'relationality' and 'technology' is substituted for 'method' as in the sentence,

> 'Let's talk about the technology for the production of interiority.'

Such obfuscation immunizes the sense of what's being said from all evaluation and criticism. As Echlin says, 'Where there is no paraphrasable meaning, dissent is impossible, because there is no threshold for attack.' However, as writers we have an obligation to ensure our readers see our ideas clearly through the words we use.

Try this ...

Compare the following two passages. The first comes from a book by a famous sociologist, cited in William Zinsser's book, *Writing to Learn*.

> The third major component of modeling phenomena involves the utilization of symbolic representations of modeled patterns in the form of imaginal and verbal contents to guide overt performances. It is assumed that reinstatement of representational schemes provides a basis for self-instruction on how component responses must be combined and sequenced to produce new patterns of behaviour.[4]

The second comes from Bertrand Russell's book *The Problems of Philosophy*.

> But if we are to be able to draw inferences from these data – if we are to know of the existence of matter, of other people, of the past before our individual memory begins, or of the future, we must know general principles of some kind by means of which such inferences can be drawn. It must be known to us that the existence of some one sort of thing, A, is a sign of the existence of some other sort of thing, B, either at the same time as A or at some earlier or later time, as, for example, thunder is a sign of the earlier existence of lightning. If this were not known to us, we could never extend our knowledge beyond the sphere of our private experience; and this sphere, as we have seen, is exceedingly limited.[5]

As you can see, while the first passage is incomprehensible, the second can be immediately understood. Russell uses one concept that you might regard as jargon in his profession ('inferences'), but only after he has first converted it into concrete terms. Beyond that, everything is accessible the moment you read it. Nothing needs to be translated like some piece of foreign prose.

2 Economy

Once you've thought your ideas through, your major concern thereafter should be to express them clearly and concisely, with an economical use of words. Each component of a sentence should have a reason for being there: it should have a clearly defined function. There should be no wasted effort: no unnecessary word or phrase that obscures the meaning of the sentence. Otherwise, the clarity of your thoughts will be lost, leaving the reader wondering what it all means.

There should be no unnecessary word or phrase that obscures your meaning.

Indeed, knowing what to leave out is as important as knowing what to include. Therefore, if clauses and phrases can be summed up in a word, replace them. If they add nothing to the meaning of the sentence, delete them: words like '*ongoing* progress' (progress), '*successfully* avoided' (avoided), 'this moment *in time*' (this moment) and 'it will be fine *going forward*' ('will be' is the future tense so there is no need for 'going forward'). Start a list in your notebook and get into the habit of de-cluttering your work of all those wordy phrases. Keep a sign near your desk reminding you that:

> The readability of my work increases in proportion to the unnecessary words I eliminate.

As a result, the really significant words will no longer be smothered. Your points and arguments will no longer be obscured by unnecessary words and phrases. They'll stand out more, and they'll have impact to make the reader think and wonder. So, get into the habit of asking yourself, 'Is this word or phrase necessary and does it convey my meaning exactly?'

 You can download a copy of the table in this chapter and additional exercises from the companion website (www.macmillanihe.com/greetham-literature-review).

Summary

1 A good style means saying what you want to say in the fewest possible words.
2 If the structure of a sentence is not clear enough, move the logical indicator to a more prominent position.
3 Don't settle for a word that merely captures your meaning 'near enough'.
4 Reduce the clutter of prepositional phrases, adjectives and adverbs in your sentences.
5 There is not a single complex idea that cannot be expressed in simple concrete language.

What next?

It's easy to say 'De-clutter sentences and rely on strong nouns and verbs', but where can you find these? In the next chapter, you will find a wealth of examples to help you.

Notes

1 Quoted in Adrian Desmond & James Moore, *Darwin* (London: Michael Joseph, 1991), p. 183.
2 Stephen W. Hawking, *A Brief History of Time* (London: Bantam Press, 1988), p. vii.
3 Helena Echlin. 'Critical Mass' in *The Sydney Morning Herald*, 10 February 2001.
4 William Zinsser, *Writing to Learn* (New York: Harper & Row, 1989), p. 68.
5 Bertrand Russell, *The Problems of Philosophy*, 1912 (Oxford: Oxford University Press, 1986), p. 33.

Chapter 24

Finding the Right Words

In this chapter, you will learn…

- how to ensure your meaning is clear and concise;
- how to indicate the logical structure of your sentences and paragraphs;
- how to identify the overused and unnecessary words we use;
- how to avoid overstating and understating the strength of your ideas;
- how to create your own compound transitions.

In the last chapter, I made the point that the flexibility of language, its capacity to hold many different shades of meaning, is at odds with the sharpness, clarity and constancy of meaning that are important to consistent reasoning. This raises not just the problem of how we can express our ideas to reflect our thinking accurately, but how we can avoid the danger of the words we use controlling our ideas and the way we develop them.

To solve both of these problems, we need to choose our words carefully. In the last few chapters we have:

1 learnt the importance of **simplifying** our writing to ensure that our arguments come across clearly and effectively;
2 stressed the importance of **economising** our use of words;
3 seen how the clarity of our writing improves as we avoid the overuse of adjectives and adverbs, relying instead on **strong nouns and verbs**;
4 learnt the importance of using **transitions** and **qualifiers**, which we first discussed in Chapter 9, to create consistent and accurate arguments that readers can understand easily.

Practical solutions

But still, to get started, it helps to have an easily accessible source of these words to use as you deal with these problems each time you come across them. This is what we will do in this chapter.

Here you will learn how to de-clutter your sentences, using lists of all those words and phrases we all use without much thought. You will find lists of alternative words to choose from, including strong nouns, verbs and prepositions. There will also be lists of useful transitions and qualifiers, the scaffolding of our arguments that signpost what we are doing and which way we are developing our arguments, so readers can follow them confidently without getting lost.

De-cluttering

Before we choose alternative words and phrases to convey and develop our arguments clearly and consistently, we have to take out all those things that obscure our meaning. Here there are three things that we should do routinely:

1   Cut out empty phrases.
2   Replace prepositional phrases with prepositions.
3   Identify all the overused, unnecessary words in our work.

1 Cut out empty phrases

This includes all those phrases that appear in our work, which add little or nothing to the meaning of what we want to say. They occur most frequently when we speak, where they do less harm, but the danger is that once we become accustomed to using them, they will infect our writing. When you take these out, you will be surprised how much clearer your ideas have become and how much more impact they have on the reader. In the following list, you will find phrases that you use, which will no doubt trigger others that you can add to the list.

All things being equal	In my opinion
All things considered	In the event of
As a matter of fact	In the final analysis
As far as I am concerned	Kind of
At the end of the day	The point that I am trying to make
For all intents and purposes	Type of
For the purpose of	What I am trying to say
In a manner of speaking	What I want to make clear

2 Replace prepositional phrases with prepositions

In contrast, the following phrases do add something to the meaning of a sentence, but they could be said in far fewer words, making the sentence clearer and more direct. Again, you will probably recognise those you are in the habit of using and these will no doubt trigger others that you can add to your list:

Ahead of schedule – early	Give an indication of – show/indicate
Arrived at an agreement – agreed	In close proximity to – near
As a consequence of – because of	In spite of the fact – although
At the present time – now	In the direction of – to or toward
At this point in time – now or at this time	In the vicinity – near
Bright in colour – bright	Large in size – large
Came in contact with – met	Located at – at
Costs a total of – costs	On the part of – by
Due to the fact that – because	Smooth to the touch – smooth
During the time that – while	With regard to – about
For the simple reason – because	With the possible exception of – except

3 Overused, unnecessary words

Despite all our efforts, we all have words that we are in the habit of using that add nothing to the meaning of our sentences. To check just how reliant you are on these, enter them into the search function of your word processor and check a piece of work to see just how many times you use them. Then ask yourself whether there are alternative words that convey your meaning more accurately.

The obvious targets are the jargon of our subjects that we are accustomed to using without ever thinking about whether we are clear about what we mean by them. But there are others that we use in conversation every day, which seep into our writing, clouding our meaning and robbing our arguments of the impact they should have, words like:

Appropriate/Inappropriate	Kind of/sort of
Going forward	A lot
Iconic	

You could then add to these all those combinations of words we use, which contain unnecessary elements that we could strip out to make our sentences clearer and more concise:

absolutely essential/necessary	*joint* collaboration
advance warning	later *time*
added bonus	look *ahead* to the future
alternative *choice*	meet *together*
assemble *together*	might *possibly*
basic fundamentals/necessities	*mutual* cooperation
brief moment	*mutually* interdependent

brief summary	mutual respect *for each other*
careful scrutiny	*natural* instinct
close proximity	*necessary* prerequisite
collaborate *together*	never *before*
compete *with each other*	*new* beginning/innovation/initiative
completely destroyed	none *at all*
confer *together*	*originally* created/built
consensus *of opinion*	*over* exaggerate
contributory factor	*past* experience/history/records
cooperate *together*	period *of time*
crisis *situation*	*personal* opinion
depreciate *in value*	pick *and choose*
during *the course of*	plan *in advance*
each *and every*	*polar* opposites
eliminate *altogether*	postpone *until later*
emergency *situation*	present *time*
end result	protest *against*
entirely eliminate	reason is *because*
eradicate *completely*	reason *why*
estimated at *about*	refer *back*
evolve *over time*	*regular* routine
exactly identical	repeat *again*
favourable approval	revert *back*
fellow colleague	*safe* haven
few *in number*	small *size*
filled *to capacity*	spell out *in detail*
final conclusion/outcome	*still* remains
final ultimatum	*sudden* impulse
first *of all*	*sum* total
foreign imports	time *period*
free gift	*true* facts
future plans	*two equal* halves
general consensus	*unexpected* surprise
general public	*usual* custom
grow *in size*	*very* unique
had done *previously*	warn *in advance*
integrate *together*	whether *or not*
join *together*	write *down*

Unnecessary words   **EXERCISE**

> Rewrite the following sentence, taking out all the unnecessary words and phrases so that its core meaning can be written more clearly and economically. As you decide what to remove, ask yourself whether the word or phrase adds any meaning to the sentence. If it doesn't, remove it.
>
> In the final analysis, our current understanding with regard to the universe makes it more plausible, all things being equal, that something can arise over a period of time out of nothing.

Answer:

Our current understanding of the universe makes it more plausible that something can arise out of nothing.

Strong nouns and verbs

In the last chapter, we saw the dramatic impact we can have on our sentences by removing the clutter of adjectives and adverbs. Immediately our sentences were made sharper and more concise. By using strong nouns and verbs, we were able to catch the image of what we wanted to say precisely. It's worth remembering the key difference between adjectives and adverbs on the one hand and nouns and verbs on the other.

- Adjectives and adverbs *tell*
- Nouns and verbs *show*

Nouns and verbs are the most important words in a sentence. Nouns give your sentence a clear image, the sound foundations on which you develop your ideas, while verbs give your sentence its movement, its momentum. When your nouns are weak, your sentences are unclear: the subject of the sentence lacks clarity. When your verbs are weak, your sentences are sluggish. Consequently, by choosing the best words your writing becomes clearer, more vivid and memorable.

1 Strong nouns

To create a clear visual image, first ask yourself whether you really need to use an adjective with your noun. If you think you do, ask yourself, 'Is there a noun that says exactly what I want to say without having to use this adjective?'

In many cases, the noun we are accustomed to using is weak because it's a nominalisation: a noun that has been derived from a verb. Usually, this is accompanied by a weak verb, so by replacing the nominalisation with the original verb we strengthen the sentence by making it more direct and specific.

Nominalisations   EXAMPLE

Rather than 'make a decision', we 'decide';
rather than 'show a reaction' we 'react'.

In the following list, you will recognise those you use most. When you come across others, add them to it.

Derive a conclusion	–	conclude
Present an argument	–	argue
Have admiration	–	admire
Conduct a review/investigation	–	review/investigate
Make a discovery	–	discover
Put up a resistance	–	resist
Have a belief	–	believe
Enter into discussion	–	discuss
Give a demonstration	–	demonstrate
Made the arrangement	–	arranged

2 Strong verbs

To give your sentence a clear direction, choose your verb carefully to ensure you move it in the direction you want and your readers can understand clearly where you are taking them. This often means stopping and thinking a little more than you might normally. If you find yourself shoring up your verb with adverbs, this in itself will indicate that the verb doesn't say exactly what you want to say. In this case, replace it. Getting your verb right will invigorate your writing, making your ideas and arguments clearer.

Think   EXAMPLE

If you say that 'Brown *thought* about the proposition', ask yourself, 'What did he really do?' Did he 'reflect', 'judge', 'deliberate', 'assess', 'speculate', 'ponder', 'imagine', 'conceive', 'consider', 'contemplate', 'recollect', 'rationalise', 'realise', 'digest'?

This type of verb and others, like 'talk', 'say' and 'argue', are weak: they don't say precisely what we want to say. We just get used to using them without asking ourselves whether this is precisely what we want to say. When you find yourself using them, stop and think, then ask yourself if there are other verbs that more accurately say what you want to say. Where you have your favourites, list the alternatives that you should think about each time you find yourself using them. In the following table are examples of the most common weak verbs.

Weak verb	Strong verbs
Criticise	censure, condemn, disparage, compare, appraise, consider, judge, discern, estimate, evaluate, appraise, rate, conjecture, ponder, review
Talk	converse, communicate, discuss, confer, negotiate, inform, confide, speak, utter, confess, acknowledge, concede, criticise, pronounce, dictate, recite
Say	state, declare, announce, maintain, mention, assert, affirm, express, pronounce, communicate, disclose, convey, divulge, report, claim, suggest, insist
Argue	discuss, debate, dispute, question, reason, challenge, claim, insist, maintain, assert, contend, uphold, suggest, imply, allege
Develop	derive, progress, promote, generate, undertake, initiate, cultivate, instigate, start, establish, originate, foster, extend, elaborate, broaden, amplify, augment, enlarge

Qualifiers

In Chapter 9, where we were discussing how to critically evaluate our sources, we found how easy it is to use the wrong qualifier and understate or overstate the strength of our evidence. Overstating a claim is likely to lead to its rejection, while understating it is likely to rob it of its significance. So, it's worth having by your side a list of the most useful qualifiers to ensure that you choose the best one.

In the following table, I have listed qualifiers that express certainty, either positive or negative, and all those that express degrees of certainty between these two. As you come across others that you think might be useful, add them to the list.

Certainty	Uncertainty
All/every	many, most, some, majority, numerous, countless, abundant, copious, profuse, multitude
None/no	few, minority, some, not many, hardly any, sparse, rare, scarce
Always	often, frequent, recurrent, repeated, common, incessant, perpetual, usual, sometimes, customary, habitual
Never	infrequent, uncommon, sporadic, occasional, rare, seldom, sometimes, intermittent
To be (it is, it was, I am, I was, we are, we were)	may be, may have been, might be, might have been, conceivably, perhaps, possibly, could have been, can be, perchance, appears, seems, indicates
Will	may, might, could, possible, likely, probable, feasible, plausible
Will not	improbable, unlikely, doubtful, unforeseeable, implausible, unimaginable, inconceivable, contingent on
Definite	probable, possible, potential, viable, arguable, feasible, attainable, likely, presumable, foreseeable
Indefinite	unlikely, improbable, doubtful, questionable, debatable, controvertible

Transitions

In Chapter 21, we discussed the importance of topic sentences and transitions in creating the connections between our ideas and, equally important, indicating what we are doing and why as we move from one paragraph or section to another. By signposting the logic of our arguments in this way, we establish their relevance and ensure the reader can follow us without getting lost. Transitions are the key to this as we create a coherent review that makes logical sense throughout, whether we are:

1 striking a contrast;
2 extending or concluding an argument;
3 explaining something;
4 identifying the causal relations between two things;
5 drawing attention to similarities between two sets of arguments;
6 or just summarising the points we have made.

In the table below, you can find transitions that will meet all these needs and more. Make a copy and keep it by your side as you write.

Similarities	In the same way, Likewise, Similarly, Correspondingly, By the same token, Equally, For the same reason, Complementing this
Contrast	However, On the other hand, Yet, But, But at the same time, Despite, Even so, For all that, In contrast, In spite of, On the contrary, Otherwise, Although, Whereas, Unlike, By way of contrast, Conversely, Having said that, That said, Nonetheless, There again, All the same, Contrastingly
Illustration	For example, For instance, That is, In other words, In particular, Namely, Specifically, Such as, Thus, To illustrate, As an illustration, As an illustration, In this instance/context, A case in point, A clear example of this
Extension/ Addition	Similarly, Moreover, Furthermore, In addition, By extension, What is more, Above all, Further, In the same way, Also, Apart from, Besides, As well as, Indeed, Not only this but, In fact, Equally important, Reinforcing this point
Logical sequence	Therefore, Consequently, As a result, Thus, Hence, Accordingly, So, This means, To conclude, As a final point, Eventually, Finally, In the end, Lastly, It follows that, Given these points, It follows then
Chronological sequence	Then, After that, It follows, Subsequently, Eventually, Previously, Next, Before this, Afterwards, After this, Then, Following this, Meanwhile, At the same time
Emphasis	Above all, After all, Equally important, Especially, Indeed, In fact, In particular, Most important, Of course, Namely, Notably
Causal relations	As a result, Consequently, For that reason, So, Accordingly, Owing to this, Due to this, Because of this, Under these circumstances, Since, As, Hence, Thus, As a consequence, Therefore, As a result, Subsequently
Temporal relations	In future, In the meantime, In the past, At first, At the same time, During this time, Earlier, Eventually, Meanwhile, Now, Recently, Simultaneously, Now, Shortly, Recently, Thereafter, Consequently

Summarising	Finally, In brief, In conclusion, In short, In simpler terms, In summary, On the whole, To summarise, To conclude, So, Thus, To sum up, Overall, Briefly, Given these points, In all, In summary, Altogether, Thus, Hence, Throughout it all
Qualification	However, Nevertheless, Even though, Still, Yet, Nonetheless, Whereas, Admittedly, Despite this, Notwithstanding this, Albeit, Although, In spite of this, Regardless of this, And yet
Alternatives	Alternatively, On the other hand, Rather, As an alternative, Otherwise, Then again, Instead, Apart from that, On the contrary, In another way, Contrastingly, Conversely, On the other side, In contrast, In many ways, In different ways
Explanation	That is to say, In other words, Namely, This means, To put it in another way, To put it simply, That is, By way of explanation, To explain

Compound transitions

The more you are aware of these words, the more of them you are likely to find to help you navigate just the right passage through your arguments. Indeed, you will also see how you can create your own compound transitions by combining words and phrases. These are enormously helpful in catching all the subtleties of your ideas, so that you can navigate just the right changes in direction and emphasis as you create your arguments.

Conjunction	And moreover, And although, And in one respect, And once, And so, And while some, And as it is, And even though
Extension	So even though, In this way, From that angle, By the same token, On that account, Given this
Emphasis	Not surprisingly, Of course, And moreover, Most important, Even more, In particular
Contrast	But instead, But at the same time, And yet, But even, But then again, But perhaps, Yet still, But while, Even though, But even so, And though, But even if, But otherwise, Yet even
Chronological sequence	Following this, And after that, But then, So began, But so far, More recently, But at the same time, And while, And there continues to be, In so doing
Illustration	Consider for instance/for example

You can download copies of the lists and tables in this chapter, along with additional exercises, from the companion website (www.macmillanihe.com/greetham-literature-review).

Summary

1 The words we use can control our ideas and the way we develop them.
2 The empty phrases we use infect our writing and obscure our meaning.
3 Nouns and verbs are the most important words in a sentence.
4 By using transitions, we create the scaffolding of our arguments, indicating their logic, so readers can follow them confidently.
5 By choosing the best qualifier, we can avoid overstating our claims, which will lead to their rejection, or understating them, which will rob them of their significance.

What next?

Once you've finished writing your review, you will need to identify all the material you've borrowed from the texts you've used. In the next chapter, you will learn how to avoid plagiarism and decide which sources you need to cite.

Part 7

Using Your Sources

Chapter 25

Plagiarism

In this chapter, you will learn...

- what is meant by plagiarism;
- why we need to avoid it;
- how to distinguish between what needs to be cited and what doesn't;
- how to avoid accidental plagiarism.

Most human progress has come from building upon the work of others. Perhaps the clearest expression of this is a literature review, which, by definition, involves using the literature and research of others. In each stage, we have depended heavily upon our sources:

- we have analysed their ideas and then used them with our own to create an original synthesis;
- we have taken passages from the literature, which we have critically evaluated;
- and we have used tables, figures and statistics to support and illustrate our own arguments.

Of course, all of this is entirely acceptable as long as we acknowledge it. And in this lies the problem of plagiarism. In broad terms, it involves presenting someone else's work and ideas as your own without acknowledging it.

Why do we need to avoid it?

Later in this chapter, we will reveal exactly what this implies in practical terms. But first, why do we need to avoid it? There are two sets of reasons:

1 Ethical obligations
2 Self-interest

1 Ethical obligations

As you can no doubt see from what we have already said, we have an ethical obligation to acknowledge the help of all those from whom we have borrowed material in the form of ideas, arguments, quotations and the results of their research. If we fail in this, we are guilty of dishonesty by any standard.

To borrow somebody's work without acknowledging it may not be intellectual 'theft', as it is often described; after all, it hasn't actually been taken away from them so that they can no longer use it themselves. However, it is intellectual 'fraud' in that it involves trying to gain unfair advantage by passing off as your own the ideas or words of someone else. And, even more ethically significant, having invested so much thought and care in their work, those from whom we borrow deserve to have their work and their achievements acknowledged.

- It is intellectual 'fraud', in that it involves passing off someone else's work as your own.
- The authors of our sources deserve to have their work and achievements acknowledged.

2 Self-interest

However, beyond ethical concerns, it is simply not in our interests to plagiarise. There is little educational value in it. Copying work and presenting it as our own avoids the task of processing these ideas as we did in Part 3, where we learnt to analyse our sources, critically evaluate them and then synthesise them into our own original thoughts. In this way, we make them our own by testing them against, and integrating them within, our own thought structures.

> We fail to process the ideas, integrating them within our own thought structures.

Equally important in terms of our self-interest, thorough and detailed referencing is a good indication of just how widely we have read over a range of different types of sources. This gives examiners the confidence to award high marks, although, of course, this is no reason to inflate your references just to impress them. They will quickly spot a reference that does no real work.

Not only will they be assured that we have comprehensively covered the literature, but with an extensive list of the literature we have used, examiners and readers in general will be able to check that we have used our sources well: that we have respected the author's claim to intellectual property and drawn reasonable conclusions from the material. For similar reasons, the information is also useful to us in that, if we want to follow up on our work in future, we will need to know where the material came from.

- There is no educational value in plagiarism.
- Thorough referencing is a good indication of how widely we have read.
- Examiners and readers can check that we have used our sources well.
- We can follow up on our work in future.

What is plagiarism exactly?

However, although most students know what the word means, there are still a number of things we do which we often don't recognise as plagiarism. For example, few of us would have any doubt that the following things need to be cited and failure to do so would amount to plagiarism:

1 if we were to take direct quotations from someone's work;
2 if we were to write a summary or paraphrase that was close to the original;
3 if we were to take from a source statistics, data and other information that are specific to that source;
4 or if we were to use someone's unique ideas that have influenced our thinking.

All of these examples are quite obvious, but most examples of plagiarism occur in the grey areas, and many are accidental. It seems likely that these come about as a result of students failing to organise their work well enough. As a result, when they read their sources they take notes in a rushed and careless manner, mixing passages they have borrowed with their own notes. As they do this, they may fail to put these ideas into their own words, so that the paraphrases and summaries they use in their reviews are not sufficiently different from the original.

How can we distinguish between what needs to be cited and what doesn't?

Unfortunately, although it would make it much easier to decide, we cannot just say that certain types of information need to be cited, like figures, statistics and quotations, while other types need not be.

Citing   EXAMPLE

In your work, you might write any of the following:

1 In the First World War there were about 40 million casualties, of which there were around 17 million deaths.
2 Profit maximisation occurs when a firm produces up to the point where marginal revenue is equal to marginal costs.
3 The speed of light is 186,282 miles per second.
4 In the Saar plebiscite in 1935, to the surprise of many, over 477,000 voted for unification with Germany, in other words over 90 per cent.
5 The nine warmest years on record have all occurred since 2005 and the five warmest since 2010.

The first four would not need to be cited. As for the fifth, although there is some room for doubt, it would be safer to cite it. However, you would need to cite the fourth, if you were to present it in the following way:

Choice	Votes	%
Unification with Germany	477,089	90.73
Status quo	46,613	8.87
Unification with France	2124	0.40
Invalid/Blank votes	2161	–
Total	**527,987**	**100**
Registered voters/turnout	539,542	97.99

Distinctive contribution

In this lies the important principle: where there is specific information that has been organised in a distinctive way, you will have to cite it. You may have known what percentage of voters in the Saar plebiscite voted for unification with Germany, but you may not have seen it presented in this form before. You will no doubt have found it in a particular publication, so your reader will need to know who gathered it and where to find it.

> Whenever the author has given something distinctive to the information or its organisation, cite the source.

When you cite a source, what you are acknowledging is the author's distinctive contribution. This applies to all information, whether it's a phrase, a passage quoted verbatim, or numerical and statistical information presented in tables like the one above. If it has its own distinctive form, you must acknowledge it. Even cite a single word if this is distinctive to the author's argument.

Distinctive contribution   EXERCISE

Keeping in mind this principle, read the following five statements and decide which would need citing:

1 Supporters of the 'double effect' argue that a bad act which produces good consequences can never be condoned, whereas a good act done in the full knowledge that bad consequences will ensue can be.
2 The English mathematician G.H. Hardy compared a mathematical proof to that of a chess problem: to be aesthetically satisfying it must possess three qualities – inevitability, unexpectedness and economy.
3 Sigmund Freud maintained that, 'A group is extraordinarily credulous and open to influence, it has no critical faculty, and the improbable does not exist for it.'
4 In contrast to Newton's understanding of gravity, Einstein argued in the theory of general relativity that it was not a force, but the consequence of the distortion of space and time.
5 While women represent about half of the world population, they perform getting on for two-thirds of all working hours, receive about one-tenth of world income and own less than one per cent of world property.

Answers:

2, 3, 5.

Common knowledge

However, with many ideas the situation is not so clear. There may be nothing particularly distinctive about them or their organisation, so you might reasonably assume that, although you found the ideas in a source you had read, you can use them without acknowledgement. One important justification of this is that all knowledge in the public domain, all 'common knowledge', need not be referenced.

Common knowledge	All knowledge that is familiar or easily found in common reference works.

Nevertheless, this seems to do little more than give the problem a different name. So what do we mean by 'common knowledge'? This brings us back to the original distinction. Common knowledge is all those facts, figures, quotations, indeed any idea or opinion, that are not distinctive of a particular author or that are a matter of interpretation. They may be familiar ideas or just easily found in common reference works, like dictionaries, textbooks and encyclopaedias.

Common knowledge   EXAMPLE

You could use any of the following statements without citing them, because they are all common knowledge: they can all be found in common reference works.

1   All public companies have an obligation to submit their accounts to an annual audit.
2   Quantum mechanics deals with the motion and interaction of particles.
3   The Wannsee Conference in January 1942 cleared the last obstacles to the Nazi's Final Solution for the whole of Europe.
4   The carotid artery, found on the side of the neck, carries blood to the brain.
5   Surrealism is a twentieth-century movement in art and literature, which aims to express the unconscious mind by depicting the phenomena of dreams.

Indeed, it wouldn't even be necessary to cite a source if you were to use a distinctive contribution made by someone in a particular discipline, if this is well-known within that discipline and has become common currency within it. In politics and sociology, for example, it wouldn't be necessary to give a reference for Marx's concept of 'alienation', or in philosophy for Kant's 'categorical imperative', but if you were to refer to an author's particular interpretation of either, this would need to be cited.

Paradigm   EXAMPLE

The word 'paradigm' means a dominant theory in an area of study, which sets the conceptual framework within which a science is taught and scientists conduct research. It was first used in this sense by T.S. Kuhn in his seminal work, *The Structure of Scientific Revolutions* (1962). Since then, the term has spread throughout the social sciences and philosophy. But in none of these areas would you be expected to cite the reference to Kuhn if you were to use the term, so common has it become within each of these disciplines.

Other types of common knowledge come in the form of common or familiar opinion. It may seem undeniable that the vast majority of your fellow citizens are in favour of staging the next Olympic Games or the World Cup in your country, but no survey may ever have been done or referendum held. Similarly, it might generally be held that the elderly should receive special treatment, like free bus passes and medical care. In appealing to such common knowledge you would have to judge how familiar it is. The rule is: 'If in doubt, cite.'

Common knowledge
1. Familiar ideas found in reference works
2. Ideas well-known within a particular discipline
3. Common or familiar opinion

Common knowledge   **EXERCISE**

Read the following statements and decide which of them are common knowledge and, therefore, need not be cited.

1　Senescent cells secrete substances that infect healthy cells and bring about age-related disease.
2　The public provides more than $1m per minute in global farm subsidies, yet just 1 per cent of this is used for the benefit of the environment.
3　Sociobiology aims to explain social behaviour in terms of evolution.
4　Karl Marx's 11th Thesis on Feuerbach says, 'Philosophers have hitherto only interpreted the world in various ways; the point is to change it.'
5　By using disjointed and meaningless dialogue, the form of drama known as the 'Theatre of the Absurd' emphasises the absurdity and purposelessness of human existence.
6　Solipsism is the belief that only oneself and one's experience exists.
7　42 people hold as much wealth as the 3.7m who make up the poorest half of the world's population.
8　The Poor Law Amendment Act was passed in 1834.
9　Logical positivism is the doctrine that the only meaningful propositions are those that can be verified empirically, therefore, metaphysics, religion and aesthetics are meaningless.
10　'It is not the most intellectual of the species that survives; it is not the strongest that survives; but the species that survives is the one that is able to adapt to and to adjust best to the changing environment in which it finds itself.' Charles Darwin, *On the Origin of Species*.

Answers:

1, 3, 5, 6, 8, 9.

The six-point code

To make it easier for you to decide exactly when you need to cite, use the following simple six-point code. This is another of those notes worth keeping near you as you work. Wherever you keep it, make sure it's just a glance away.

When to cite
1. Distinctive ideas – whenever the ideas or opinions are distinctive to one particular source.
2. Distinctive structure or organising strategy – even though you may have put it into your own words, if the author has adopted a particular method of approaching a problem, or there is a distinctive intellectual structure to what's written, for example to an argument or to the analysis of a concept, then you must cite the source.
3. Information or data from a particular source – if you've gathered information from a source in the form of statistics, tables and diagrams, you will need to cite the source, so your readers will know who gathered the information and where to find it.
4. Verbatim phrase or passage – even a single word, if it is distinctive to your author's argument. You must use quotation marks and cite the source.
5. If it's not common knowledge – whenever you mention some aspect of another person's work, unless the information or opinion is widely known.
6. Whenever in doubt, cite it! – It will do no harm, as long as you're not citing just to impress the examiner.

Avoiding plagiarism

Nevertheless, even with this simple code by your side, there is always the possibility that you might accidentally overlook the need to cite. Most accidental oversights are likely to be the product of poor organisation, so we need to ask how we can organise ourselves better to avoid them.

1 Organisation

With poor organisation, you can easily find yourself confusing your own ideas with those you have borrowed from a source. But there are simple practical steps you can take to avoid this.

Record borrowed material in a different way or place

Take time to devise a method of distinguishing between quotations, summaries, paraphrases and commentary, so you're aware of what you are using at any time. To distinguish from your own notes the ideas you borrow, record them in a different colour, on different sheets of paper, or in different computer files.

Record the details of sources prominently

At the top of the page record the title of the text, the author's name, the page numbers and the date of publication. This will not only save you the stress of trying to track down a single reference to a quotation or an idea that you took down hastily, but it will also serve to remind you that you are working with a source.

2 Processing our ideas

Processing, too, can help you to avoid accidental plagiarism. In Part 3, we learnt the importance of processing the ideas we find in our sources by analysing their implications, critically evaluating them and synthesising them into a new way of looking at the problem. Not only does this reduce the amount we're likely to borrow, but, more important, we integrate the ideas into our own thinking, imposing our own distinctive organisation and structure on them.

The quality of your literature review will ultimately depend on the ideas you find in your sources and how you process them. This applies to stand-alone reviews as well as those that form part of a dissertation or thesis. Indeed, if you are building a platform for your own research, you owe your sources even more. Either way, the authors deserve to have their work acknowledged as we need to recognise our debt.

 You can download copies of the six-point code and additional exercises from the companion website (www.macmillanihe.com/greetham-literature-review).

Summary

1 Plagiarism is presenting someone else's work as your own without acknowledging it.
2 For both ethical reasons and self-interest, we need to avoid it.
3 Most plagiarism occurs in the grey areas and accidentally.
4 Whenever an author has given something distinctive to the information or its organisation, cite the source.
5 All common knowledge found in common reference works need not be cited.

What next?

Now that we know *what* we must cite, in the next chapter we can turn our attention to *how* we cite.

Chapter 26

Citing Your Sources

In this chapter, you will learn...

- the three cardinal objectives of all reference systems;
- how to use extracts from your sources;
- the five most widely used reference systems;
- how to avoid appearing to hide behind your sources;
- how to compile a bibliography.

In the last chapter, we dealt with what seem to be the most difficult decisions we have to make about how we deal with our sources. Nevertheless, it can seem that referencing, with all its arcane rules and details, is just as difficult a problem.

Conventions

However, it may be that you have no choice as to how you cite your sources. Your department may have its own rules and preferences that you are expected to observe. Some have a style guide outlining how you should arrange and punctuate the details of each entry. So, the first thing to do is check with your supervisor.

Failing that, check the dissertations, theses and stand-alone reviews of previous years to see how other students did it. Then take a look at the journals in your field and the articles they have published. They will make clear exactly what they expect from their authors. But whatever system you use, remind yourself why you're doing this:

1 to give credit to the author for the original ideas;
2 and to give readers clear and sufficient details for them to locate the reference themselves.

To do this, keep in mind the three cardinal objectives: your referencing must be clear, accurate and consistent. If you need help to get all the details consistently right, use referencing software, like *RefWorks* or *EndNote*.

Three objectives

1 Clarity
2 Accuracy
3 Consistency

Three elements

Whatever referencing system you choose, there are three elements that you must decide how you're going to organise:

1 the extract from the source, which might be a direct quotation, a paraphrase or a statement of your own that you've derived from it;
2 the marker you insert into your text to direct the reader to the details of the source;
3 the actual details.

Extracts

Direct quotations incorporated into the text often create problems if you fail to be consistent in observing certain simple conventions. If your department doesn't insist on any particular style, you'll find the following simple rules helpful in reminding you exactly what you must do.

1 **Short extracts**
   If they're no more than, say, three to four lines (30–40 words), incorporate them within your text and enclose them in quotation marks.

2 **Long extracts**
   Indent them from both sides, or just from the left. Usually these are single spaced. With the quotation blocked in this way and separated from the main text, there is no need to use quotation marks. With some style guides, it's customary to reduce the font size, say, from 12 to 11.

3 **Shortened extracts**
   3.1 When you shorten an extract to include only that which is relevant, indicate where you have taken words out by inserting 'ellipsis' marks, which consist of three dots.
   3.2 Where you have to insert your own words to ensure the shortened extract reads grammatically, enclose your own words in square brackets [ ].
   3.3 If a word which was formerly inside a sentence now begins it, make the first letter of the word a capital and enclose it in square brackets.
   3.4 The one obvious rule that governs all these changes to the original text is that you must take care not to alter the author's meaning.

The marker and the details

As for the other two elements, these are governed by the conventions of the different referencing systems you or your department choose. There are five widely used systems:

• MHRA – Modern Humanities Research Association
• Vancouver style – commonly used in medicine and science
• The Harvard System – often called the 'Author-Date System'
• MLA – Modern Language Association
• APA – American Psychological Association

They are broadly divided between those that use footnotes or endnotes and a number in the text to represent the reference, like the MHRA and the Vancouver style of referencing, and the rest that are parenthetical systems, like Harvard, which place short citations in the text enclosed in brackets.

Footnote system

Systems like the MHRA and Vancouver are variously known as 'Footnote', 'Endnote' or 'Numerical' systems. We're all familiar with this system as book publishers tend to use it more than any other. It's also commonly used in the humanities, medicine, science, some social sciences and in law. It uses a superscript number in the text or a number in parentheses for each reference cited. This refers to the details of the source found either in a footnote at the bottom of the page, or in a list of references at the end of the review, the dissertation or thesis.

In this system the first reference to a **book** would appear as:

P. Rowe, *The Craft of the Sub-editor* (Basingstoke: Macmillan, 1997), p. 37.

The place of publication is followed by a colon, after which appear the publisher, a comma and then the date of publication. Later references to the same book can be abbreviated by shortening the title, if this can be done without losing details that mark out its distinctiveness, and by omitting the author's initials and the publication details:

Rowe, *The Craft*, pp. 102–3.

A reference to a **journal article** would appear as:

Brian T. Trainor, 'The State, Marriage and Divorce', *Journal of Social Work*, vol. 9, no. 2 (1992), p. 145.

The title of the article appears between quotation marks. The name of the journal is given in full and, like the book title, is italicised. Then come the volume number, issue number and date. A later reference to the same article could be abbreviated by omitting the author's initials and shortening the title. The journal name can be abbreviated or, indeed, omitted.

Trainor, 'The State', *JSW*, pp. 138–9.

Where there are several authors, full details of all their names and initials must appear in the first reference, but not in subsequent references. Where there are two authors you can give just their last names, but, if there are several, give the first author's name followed by the abbreviation *et al.* meaning 'and others'. When this is used in the actual reference, it is not usually italicised as it is here.

The Harvard system – the Author-Date system

Like all parenthetical systems this inserts into the actual text, enclosed in brackets, the author's name and the details of the publication. In the Harvard system this includes the year of publication and the page numbers of the reference. These refer to the end of the review, dissertation or thesis, where readers can find a comprehensive list – a bibliography – of all the sources cited and used with the full details of the texts to which these abbreviations refer.

Using your sources

There are different ways of using your sources, depending on what you think is most important in that sentence or paragraph: your own ideas or your author's.

1 Imposing your ideas before and after the extracts

Previously we pointed out that frequent use of direct quotations, particularly when this involves large blocks, suggests that you haven't made the ideas your own by thoroughly processing them. It might be assumed that instead of presenting the arguments in your own words you are merely hiding behind the author's.

However, this depends on how well you show that you do understand it by using the ideas persuasively before and after the quotation. The key is to show that you have fully processed the material into your own thinking. Whenever the text does not express an idea in a unique and telling way that cannot be reproduced in any other way, acknowledge the source and put it into your own words. In this way, you impose yourself on your sources and let your own voice come through, instead of appearing to be just a neutral translator without your own ideas and interpretations.

Moral Thinking   EXAMPLE

In this extract of his thesis, the author is discussing R.M. Hare's criticisms of moral intuitions. He lays the groundwork for Hare's argument and then, after the quotation, makes clear in his own words the implications of this.

> However, the unquestioning way in which we hold these intuitions tempts us to assume that they amount to objective characteristics of the external world, and all that is necessary to defend or evaluate our decisions is to resort to the descriptivist strategy of appraising each decision we make to see how well they match up to our descriptive account of these supposedly objective characteristics. This results in what Hare describes as the 'descriptive fallacy',
>
> > What more natural...than...to assume that actions, people, etc., do have certain properties which, according to the rules for the use of the moral words, entitle one to apply the various moral words to them? So, for example, it will be natural to suppose that there are properties which, when an action has them, entitle us to call the action wrong.[1]
>
> In effect, we believe our moral judgements are logically grounded in descriptions of fact. As Hare describes it, descriptivism is the belief that the meaning of statements determines their truth-conditions. The result is that we struggle to get beyond our intuitions, many of which might amount to baseless opinion and mere prejudice.

2 Integral and non-integral references

This, too, is an effective way of positioning yourself prominently in the argument you are developing, so that you signal this is *your* argument, rather than the author's. A non-integral reference places the author's name in brackets outside the structure of your sentence, so that it has no grammatical function in it. In this way, your own voice is more prominent as you take control of the text.

Non-integral reference	**EXAMPLE**

Perhaps artists need to feel politically motivated against oppressive regimes in order to etch their identity clearly against a social and political reality they deplore. After all, 'In a dark time, the eye begins to see' (Roethke, 1966, p. 239).

The alternative is an integral reference, where the author's name appears in the actual text itself with only the page numbers, or the year of publication and the page numbers, in brackets. In the first of these below, using the phrase 'As Roethke points out' or 'In the same way Roethke argues' is a signal that through your implied agreement you are sharing the responsibility of the argument, whereas in the second you give the responsibility entirely to the author.

Integral references	**EXAMPLE**

As Roethke (1966) points out, perhaps artists need to feel politically motivated against oppressive regimes in order to etch their identity clearly against a social and political reality they deplore. After all, 'In a dark time, the eye begins to see' (p. 239).

Roethke argues that artists need to feel politically motivated against oppressive regimes in order to etch their identity clearly against a social and political reality they deplore: 'In a dark time, the eye begins to see' (1966, p. 239).

As you can see, the non-integral reference is useful for two reasons:

1 it allows you to lay emphasis on the idea rather than the person who is the source of it;
2 and it allows you to assert your control over the ideas you cite: you can use your sources to support your own argument and, therefore, reduce the risk of your review being dominated by your authors.

3 Paraphrasing

Of course, an obvious way of showing that you are in control of the references you are using is to put the extracts into your own words. In this, too, you can use either non-integral or integral referencing as you can see in the examples below. However, unlike the examples above, when you paraphrase an author's words, only the author and the year need to be included.

> **Paraphrasing**   EXAMPLE
>
> Certain diets that reduce the levels of serotonin in the brain appear to produce higher levels of aggression. Historically, periods of famine, and carbohydrate and protein malnutrition have been associated with significant increases in crime and violence (Valzelli, 1981).
>
> Valzelli (1981) argues that those diets responsible for reducing the levels of serotonin in the brain appear to produce higher levels of aggression. Historically, periods of famine, and carbohydrate and protein malnutrition have been associated with significant increases in crime and violence.

Synthesising sources

In previous chapters, we have emphasised the importance of synthesising your sources to create new patterns of ideas that will lay the foundation for a different way of approaching a problem. Citing several sources at once within the same citation is the best way of demonstrating that this is what you have done.

1 **Your pattern of ideas may reflect the thinking of more than one author, so you will need to cite more than one source at the same time.**
   In this case, arrange the authors in alphabetical order, separated by semi-colons.

   > If a child does not receive love from its parents in the early years, it will neither integrate their standards within its behaviour, nor develop any sense of moral conscience (Berkowitz, 1962; Farrington, 1978; Rutter, 1981; Storr, 1972).

2 **A source may have more than one author.**
   When it has two or three authors, give all the surnames, separated by commas, with the last one separated by the word 'and'.

   > Recent evidence has shown that cinema attendance in the 1950s declined less as a result of the impact of television, than through increasing affluence and mobility (Brown, Rowe and Woodward, 1996).

   > Computer analysis has shown that the hundred most used words in the English language are all of Anglo-Saxon origin, even the first words spoken when man set foot on the moon in 1969 (Lacey and Danziger, 1999).

   If there are more than three, cite them all the first time – for example: (Brown, Kirby, Rowe and Woodward, 1991) – but, when you cite them again, use just the first name followed by *et al.* – for example: (Brown et al., 1991).

3 **There may be many studies that have reported a similar finding – too many to include references to them all.**
   In this case put 'e.g.' at the beginning of your citation to indicate that this is just a selection of sources, rather than a complete list.

   > There is a substantial amount of literature that echoes Saul A. Kripke's assessment of Wittgenstein's development of the private language argument (e.g. Blackburn, 1975; Grandy, 1985; Hacker, 1986; Moore, 2003; Robinson, 1992).

4 **You may have synthesised more than one source by the same author.**
   In this case, arrange your sources chronologically, separated by a comma.

> Homelessness was shown to have increased as a result of the change in legislation and with the tighter monetary policy that doubled interest rates over a period of two years (Williams, 1991, 1994).

If the author has published more than one work in a single year, cite them using a lower-case letter after the year of publication.

> Williams (1994a, 1994b) has shown that higher interest rates, while doing little to arrest the decline in value of the currency, have seriously damaged companies engaged in exports and increased the levels of home repossessions.

5 **An author may cite another author.**
   In this case, if you want to use the comments of the cited author, then you acknowledge both authors, but only the author of the text in which you found the comments is listed in the reference list.

> In describing recent studies that tended to show that men become dangerous when their personal aggressiveness is unnaturally contained, Masters (1997, p. 37) cites a comment by Anthony Storr, who says, 'Aggression is liable to turn into dangerous violence when it is repressed or disowned.'

> Anthony Storr (cited in Masters, 1997, p. 37) argues that, 'The man who is able to assert himself in a socially acceptable fashion is seldom vicious; it is the weak who are most likely to stab one in the back.'

Bibliographies

All of these works that you've quoted or referred to are listed in a bibliography, along with everything you've consulted but may not have used. In contrast, a reference list contains just those works you have quoted or referred to. Although a bibliography is essential for parenthetical systems, like Harvard, it's not with the footnote system. Even so, it's useful to include one: it makes it easier to check what you've read without having to work through your footnotes.

Listing the sources – the formats

If you've been systematic from the start, the bibliography is quite easy to compile, particularly if you've adopted the habit of recording the details of your sources at the top of the page before you take notes, or, better still, used a computer database or a card-index with a separate card for each source listing its details.

There are different conventions governing the way you list the texts, but as long as you are consistent there should be no problem. In both of the following systems, where there is more than one entry by the same author arrange them chronologically under the author's name. Where a book or article has been written by two or more authors, enter it into the alphabetical list according to the last name of the first author, but make sure you give full details of all the others.

1　Modern bibliographical format

This is used with the Harvard referencing system. It's slightly clearer than the alternative, because it's easier to see the alphabetical progression of the sources with the author's last name coming first, so it's probably wise to use it with the footnote system too.

For books and other free-standing publications

Author's last name, first name and/or initials, year of publication (in brackets), full title of the work (italicised), place of publication and publisher (in brackets).

For articles

Author's last name, first name and/or initials, year of publication (in brackets), full title of the article (in quotation marks), title of the journal (italicised), volume number (if published in volumes), issue number and page numbers.

> Author, N. (year of publication) *Title of Book* (place of publication: publisher).

> Author, N. (year of publication) 'Title of Article', *Title of Journal,* vol. 2, no. 1, pp. ••–••.

EXAMPLE

1　Alexander, Leo (1949) 'Medical Science under Dictatorship', *New England Journal of Medicine*, vol. 241, pp. 39–47.
2　Ford, John C. (1944) 'The Morality of Obliteration Bombing', *Theological Studies*; reprinted in Wasserstrom, Richard A. (ed.), (1970) *War and Morality* (Oxford: Oxford University Press), pp. 1–18.
3　Robinson R. E. and Gallagher, J. (1962) *Africa and the Victorians: The Official Mind of British Imperialism* (London: Macmillan).
4　Singer, Peter (1979) *Practical Ethics* (Cambridge: Cambridge University Press).

2　Footnote system

For books and other free-standing publications

Author's first name and/or initials, author's last name, full title of the work (italicised), place of publication, name of the publisher, and date (in brackets).

For articles:

Author's first name and/or initials, author's last name, full title of the article (in quotation marks), title of the journal (italicised), volume number (if published in volumes), issue number, year of publication (in brackets), and page numbers.

> N. Author, *Title of Book* (place of publication: publisher, date).

> N. Author, 'Title of Article', *Title of Periodical,* vol. 2, no. 1 (date), pp. ••–••.

EXAMPLE

1   Leo Alexander, 'Medical Science under Dictatorship', *New England Journal of Medicine*, vol. 241 (1949), pp. 39–47.
2   John C. Ford, 'The Morality of Obliteration Bombing', *Theological Studies* (1944); reprinted in Richard A. Wasserstrom (ed.), *War and Morality* (Oxford: Oxford University Press, 1970), pp. 1–18.
3   R. E. Robinson and J. Gallagher, *Africa and the Victorians: The Official Mind of British Imperialism* (London: Macmillan, 1962).
4   Peter Singer, *Practical Ethics* (Cambridge: Cambridge University Press, 1979).

Electronic references

In contrast, for electronic references there are different methods of citing, so it's worth consulting your supervisor for your department's preference. The best general advice is to make sure you list enough accurate information for your readers to locate the source, including the date you last accessed it to cover yourself in case it has been taken down in the meantime.

The information you provide should include, the author, initials, the year of publication, the title of the article, blog, etc., the URL address and the date you last accessed it.

> Baird J, Lucas P, Kleijnen J, Fisher D, Roberts H, Law C. (2005). *Defining optimal infant growth for lifetime health: a systematic review of lay and scientific literature.* http://www.mrc.soton.ac.uk. Last accessed 24.4.2019.
>
> Keen, S. (2007). *Strategies for disseminating qualitative research findings: Three exemplars.* http://www.qualitativeresearch.net. Last accessed 13.7.2019.

Software

Finally, you may find that software packages, like *Procite*, *Endnote* or *Citation*, can make compiling your bibliography much easier. These will help you create and position footnotes or endnotes as well as automatically compile a bibliography in the style you need to use and amending it as you make changes to the text.

You can download copies of exercises relevant to this chapter from the companion website (www.macmillanihe.com/greetham-literature-review).

Summary

1   Make sure that whatever reference system you choose is clear, accurate and consistent.
2   To impose yourself on your sources and let your own voice come through, use the ideas persuasively before and after the quotations.
3   To position yourself, rather than the author, prominently in an argument use non-integral references.
4   Cite your sources so that you show you have synthesised them into a new pattern of ideas to lay the foundations for a new way of approaching a problem.
5   A bibliography contains all those sources you have used, including those you have consulted without referring to.

What next?

Now that you have acknowledged all your sources, you can begin to revise your review. In the next chapter, we will revise the organisation and thinking in the review represented by its structure.

Note

R.M. Hare, *Moral Thinking: Its Levels, Methods and Point*, (Oxford: Oxford University Press, 1981), pp. 67–8.

PART 8

Editing

Chapter 27

Revision 1: Structure

In this chapter, you will learn…

> - how to revise with your reader in mind;
> - how to shift your focus from the writer to the editor;
> - the steps you need to work through to revise the structure;
> - how to check you have developed your arguments consistently and signposted them clearly;
> - how to revise the connections between your paragraphs and the structure within them.

It comes as some surprise to some students to learn that more marks are gained through each successive revision than in many of the stages that preceded them.

It is in the revision stage that the quality of your work really begins to shine through. So don't waste much of your valuable work by settling for the first thing you can write. Revise your work again and again to produce the quality it deserves.

Revising for your reader

It's difficult to see something from someone else's perspective, but that is what we need to do, if we are to communicate effectively with others and convince them of our ideas. So far you have been writing for you: you've been writing as you think, clarifying and developing your ideas. But now your second and subsequent drafts are for your reader. Your aim is to make sure that your ideas come through so clearly that someone who knows nothing about your subject can understand it and feel the impact of your ideas as you do.

- The first draft is for you.
- The second and subsequent drafts are for your readers.

Shifting our focus from the writer to the editor

To do this successfully, we have to learn to shift our focus from the writer to the editor: from the creative activity of converting our ideas into language to the more self-conscious focus on the way we use words, phrases, sentences and structures. The editor inside of us should be demanding an answer to questions like:

- How does it sound?
- Is it fluent?
- Does it move logically from one stage in the argument to another?
- Are there sections that need more development or more evidence?

The one guiding principle that runs throughout this is to approach your work as you think your readers will. In other words, experience the same confusion they might experience with certain passages without papering over the cracks by making allowances for what you've written. If it's not clear, rearrange it and rewrite it. But at the same time, don't allow your changes to obscure the rich insights you saw when you first generated and developed your ideas. These first engaged your interest and will more than likely engage your readers' too.

Approach your work as you think your readers will.

Remind yourself that no-one should have to read one of your sentences twice to figure out what it means. The clear and simple writing you're aiming to achieve only comes through a process of repeatedly revising your work until it is the best you can get it. The effortless feel of talk in print that flows across the page in light, elegant prose only comes from a cumulative process of repeated revisions that edges you closer with each revision to the clearest expression of your ideas.

Revise with a purpose

Although this sounds a long, confusing and complicated process, it's not if you organise it well. The problem is that there are so many things to look for. So simplify it by revising a number of times with a clear purpose as you look for different things each time. The easiest way is to revise first a number of times for structure and then a number of times for content. And, as a safeguard, save each draft in a different file. That way, if you lose the latest draft, you won't have to start all over again.

Structure

When we talk about the structure of a piece of writing, we're talking about the thinking that went into it:

- whether it is organised logically;
- whether the connections between our ideas are consistently developed;
- and, of course, whether we have signposted these connections so our readers can see them clearly.

This underlines the importance of the planning stage. If you've not done this carefully enough, you're likely to find that your review comes across as a loose collection of ideas, which makes it difficult to understand the overall shape and direction of your arguments. If this is the case, work through the following exercise.

Read through your review highlighting with a coloured pen the topic sentences, headings, subheadings and other structural features of each paragraph and section. Then, write in the margin brief descriptions of the content, the key ideas and the sort of processing you are doing, whether this is description, critical evaluation, analysis or synthesis, so you can put down on a sheet of paper a simple statement that sums up the content of each paragraph and the type of processing you're doing in each one.

Once you've done this, read it through as if you have never read it before to see if it will make logical sense to someone reading it for the first time. If it doesn't, reorganise and edit it until it does.

At times you will no doubt find this difficult. We can all become too attached to what we've written. But you need to be ruthless, deleting paragraphs or whole sections if they are digressions, and reorganising the order of ideas if it makes no consistent, logical sense.

The steps

To check the structure and logical clarity of your review, work through the following simple steps.

1 Consistent arguments

First, check that your review develops from one argument to another in a consistent way. As you move from one to another make sure the connections between them are clear, not just to you who know them well, but to someone reading your review for the first time. Are any connections missing or obscured? Are there any irrelevant digressions that could come out to make the remaining flow of arguments crystal clear? Make sure all your arguments are relevant to the analysis of the key issues that you mapped out in your introduction for your readers to follow. Have you picked up all the issues raised in the introduction?

- Does your review develop consistently?
- Are the connections between your arguments clear to anyone reading your review for the first time?
- Are any connections missing or obscured?
- Are there any irrelevant digressions that could come out?
- Are all your arguments relevant to your analysis in the introduction?
- Have you picked up and discussed all the issues you mapped out in the introduction?

2 Signposting

After you have taken out all those sections that are irrelevant, check that each connection is clearly signposted, so your readers know what you are doing at each point and they are in no danger of getting lost.

- Are the connections clearly signposted?
- Is there a clear indication of how a paragraph connects with the previous one?
- Do you indicate clearly how you will be developing the argument in the paragraph?

3 Introduction and conclusion

Throughout your review, you need to ensure that you pick up all the issues raised in the introduction. Likewise in the conclusion, you need to ensure that you have delivered on all your promises: that you have overlooked none of the issues you raised in the introduction. Like all good conclusions, it must take us back to where we started and fulfil our promises. By the same token, make sure you have evaluated and explained in the conclusion the significance of your findings. They won't speak for themselves.

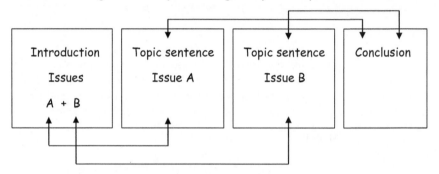

Equally important, make sure that you have moved from the general to the specific throughout your review. If yours is a stand-alone review, you need to ensure that you arrive at the point where you are able to draw all the main issues together and reveal a new synthesis. If yours is a review for a dissertation or thesis, you will want to lay the foundations for your research by arriving at the problem you want to research and the gap you want to fill.

- Have you delivered on all your promises: have you overlooked any important issues?
- Have you evaluated and explained the significance of your findings?
- Have you moved from the general to the specific throughout your review?

4 Paragraphs

Now move on to the level of paragraphing. Here we are concerned about two things that will affect the coherence and consistency of our review:

- the connections between our paragraphs;
- the structure within them.

The connections between our paragraphs

The first thing we need to check is whether our paragraphs follow each other fluently and that we have made our reader fully aware of the logical connections between them. If there are no obvious connections or just abrupt changes of course, check that the paragraph is in the right place.

If it is, look at the transition to see if there is a better one that would indicate more clearly the direction you want to take the argument. Alternatively, move it to a more prominent position in the topic sentence. If a paragraph starts abruptly without a clear indication of how it connects with the previous paragraph and without giving any idea as to how you will develop the argument in this one, go back to Chapter 24 and choose a clearer transition.

If you find paragraphs are floating without any clear rationale, make sure wherever possible that your topic sentence ties it in with the map of the review that you laid out in the introduction. When it appears you're drifting like this, think about introducing a short reminder paragraph where you remind the reader of the central issues you outlined in the introduction, recap briefly what you have done so far and then outline what is still left to be done.

- Have you picked up the map of the review that you laid out in the introduction?
- Do your paragraphs follow each other logically and fluently?
- Are they in the right place?
- Do your paragraphs start abruptly?
- Is there a better transition that would indicate more clearly the direction you want to take the argument?
- Can it be moved to a more prominent position in the topic sentence?
- Are any paragraphs floating without a clear rationale?

The structure within paragraphs

Within each paragraph, ask yourself whether the logical structure of the argument is consistent and clear from sentence to sentence. Some sentences you will have to move to a position in which the logic is clearer. Others you will have to delete. In what remains the argument will now be much clearer. With some sentences, you will just need to choose another logical indicator to make the development of your argument clearer, or move it to a more prominent position, usually to the beginning.

- Is the logical structure of the argument consistent and clear from sentence to sentence?
- Can I delete some sentences that add nothing or make the argument confusing?
- Can I move the logical indicator or choose another to make the development of the argument clearer?

5 Relevance

As you work through the literature, your thinking will change, you will come across sources that fill you with a wealth of new ideas and, almost inevitably, after you've been turned around in this way a number of times, you will wonder where exactly you are. This is not unusual. If your ideas are developing in response to what you read and you're not just reproducing them in a loose, descriptive list, you will at times lose sight of the central issues you started out with that form the focus of your review.

When this happens, you will have to take stock and remind yourself of the most important issues that you now need to focus on. From there, you can check that all the sources you have included are relevant. As you do this, check that you have actually used your sources and not just described and listed them. You should have in front of you a coherent structure that ties all your sources together with your introduction, which outlines exactly what is to come, and then with your conclusion, which ties together everything you have found in your sources.

- Are all the sources you have included relevant to the issues that are the focus of your work?
- Have you actually used your sources and not just reproduced them in a loose, descriptive list?
- Is there a coherent structure that ties all your sources together?

The final check

Before you finish with the structure, it's worth just doing a final check. Similar to the exercise above, read the topic sentence of each paragraph one after the other. The first thing you are doing here is looking for the type of processing you're doing in each paragraph: describing a point of view, analysing the implications of an argument, critically evaluating it or synthesising ideas. Together they should represent a series of clear, logically developed arguments and analyses from beginning to end that will form a coherent review.

To make this clearer, look at what it should not be. If you were to find a series of paragraphs begin with an author's name, this might indicate that, instead of critically evaluating, analysing and synthesising your sources, you were merely describing what an author had done or had reported. If this occurs, it is likely that you have lost sight of the central issues that are your focus and, instead, you have allowed an important source to take centre stage. In contrast, you can see the obvious markers of deep-level processing that you should be looking for in the transitions we've discussed in previous chapters, words like 'moreover', 'nevertheless', 'conversely' and so on.

Taking stock   **EXERCISE**

After that, do a final stocktake by asking yourself 10 simple questions to assess your work. This will allow you to assess it from a distance and take overall stock of it:

1 Have I overlooked anything significant to my review?
2 Have I explained clearly and comprehensively each part or are there sections that the reader will find confusing?
3 Have I made clear the relevance of the sources I have chosen?
4 Have I included sources just because they are interesting and not because they are strictly relevant to the review?
5 Have I presented my arguments in the most logical order?
6 Have I linked my paragraphs in a fluent manner to produce a cohesive review?
7 Have I got the balance right between description and deep-level processing: critical evaluation, analysis and synthesis?
8 Have I developed my arguments clearly and consistently?
9 Have I supported my arguments with enough evidence drawn from my sources?
10 Can I make the language I use clearer?

Once you have finished revising the structure of your review, you will see how much sharper and clearer are the connections between your arguments. The transition from one paragraph to the next should now be fluent and easy to read. Someone reading it for the first time should be able to see how each part fits into a structure that is clear, consistent and cohesive.

 You can download copies of the lists in this chapter from the companion website (www.macmillanihe.com/greetham-literature-review).

Summary

1 No-one should have to read one of your sentences twice to figure out what it means.
2 Revising the structure means revising the thinking that went into the review.
3 Your arguments must be consistent and the connections clear to anyone reading them for the first time.
4 You need to ensure that in the conclusion you deliver on all the promises you made in the introduction.
5 Wherever possible, tie your topic sentences in with the map of the review you laid out in the introduction.

What next?

Now that we have sharpened up the structure of our review and made clear the connections between our paragraphs, in the next chapter we will turn our attention to the content: the words, phrases and sentences we use to express and develop our ideas.

Chapter 28

Revision 2: Content

In this chapter, you will learn…

- how to identify all the spelling mistakes that a spellchecker fails to pick up;
- the most common grammar mistakes that you need to check;
- how to revise your words and sentences to make your meaning clearer;
- how to give your sentences real impact by de-cluttering your work;
- the different ways of reducing your word count.

Now that we've revised the structural features of our review, we've made it easier for the reader to follow our thinking from one paragraph and section to the next. Nevertheless, our thinking can still be highjacked by the words we use, which can lead the reader off in a direction we hadn't intended.

As we discovered in previous chapters, there is a tension between our thinking and our writing. The flexibility of language, the capacity of words to hold many shades of meaning, even different meanings altogether, is at odds with the logical consistency we need for clear thinking, which calls for sharp, clear and constant meanings. Consequently, as we turn our attention to revise the content of our review we must ask ourselves questions like:

- Do our words and sentences develop our arguments in the direction we want them to go, or have we been pushed in a direction simply because we've chosen the wrong phrase?
- Do they convey our ideas succinctly and clearly?
- Are there different words that would convey our ideas more accurately?

The steps

As we did in the last chapter, in this one we will work through a simple series of routine steps to revise our work until it represents the clearest expression of our ideas.

1 Spelling

The obvious place to start, of course, is with your spelling. However, this is not a simple exercise of using a spellchecker. As we all know, there are some mistakes that this will simply not pick up.

An obvious example is homonyms, words that have the same sound, but a different spelling and meaning. Those that appear most often include:

   their and there
   you're and your
   two, too and to
   find and fined
   passed and past
   dessert and desert
   weather and whether
   site, sight and cite
   compliment and complement
   stationery and stationary

Confusions

Other mistakes a spellchecker may not pick up result from our confusion about whether to use 'c' or 's' in the spelling of words like:

   advice and advise
   practice and practise
   licence and license

The simple rule is that the noun is spelt with a 'c' and the verb with an 's'. Then there is a group of words that don't exactly sound similar but are frequently confused just the same; words like 'accept' and 'except', 'loose' and 'lose', and 'then' and 'than'.

Mistakes

A spellchecker will pick up none of these, nor will it pick up simple mistakes that we all make, like typos that form actual words. We might type 'adverse' when we mean 'averse', or 'effected' when we mean 'affected'. We might simply miss words out as we get our ideas down fast: prepositions and conjunctions, like 'and', 'or', and 'the'.

When we read through our work, these are difficult to identify. As we know what we're trying to say, we automatically fill in the spaces and correct the spelling in our minds without consciously recognising the error. Similarly, dates, names and figures might be spelt correctly at one point in the review, but then in our haste we get them wrong at another. And unless we make a deliberate effort to search for these types of error, we are likely to miss them.

Getting it right

The problem is that many of us are inclined to believe that spelling is not that important as long as we can be understood. But getting these small details right can be critical, if for no other reason than what it says about you. Your readers may infer from your mistakes that if you haven't paid enough attention to this sort of detail, you may not have paid enough attention to other more substantive detail, like representing your sources accurately.

- Have you identified all the homonyms?
- Have you corrected all the confusions over whether to use 'c' or 's' in some words?
- Have you found all the typos, the missing words and the inconsistencies in spelling dates, names and figures?

2 Grammar

The same can be said for your grammar. If you break the rules, make sure that it is deliberate, that you know what you are doing and you're doing it for reasons of style, to produce an effect, and not as the result of a lack of knowledge. Whether you keep to the rules or decide to break them, the key is clarity: it must be the best way of making your meaning clear.

However, spotting unintentional grammar mistakes can be much more difficult than spotting spelling mistakes. Like spelling, the closer you are to it the more details escape your attention. You may not see things that would be obvious to someone else who is not as close to your work. So perhaps ask a friend to read it through and return the favour when he or she has work to proofread. However, if you're forced to do it all yourself, look out for the following common mistakes.

Common mistakes   **EXAMPLE**

Among the most common mistakes found in students' work are the following:

Tenses – check that you have used the right tense or not changed the tense in the middle of a sentence from, say, the past to the present.

Plural and singular verb forms – it's not unusual to find someone changing from the singular to the plural verb form in the middle of a sentence. You might refer to 'a team' in one part of the sentence and then change the verb for a plural subject: 'them' or 'they'.

Punctuation – among the many punctuation problems is the use of the apostrophe. Make a point of checking that you have not missed any or used them incorrectly to indicate possession and contraction.

Apostrophes   **EXERCISE**

Punctuate the following statements with apostrophes.

1 Im going to the students common room for a break.
2 Its appearance suggests its far too complicated.
3 They arent coming to dinner, so were going out.
4 Ive filed the companys accounts.
5 Peoples appearances change with age.
6 Consultants reports tend to be very complex.
7 Heres my thesis. Wheres yours?
8 Whose cars parked over the other side of the road?
9 Is that Toms suitcase or is it theirs?
10 This is someones diary. Whose is it?

Answers:

1 I'm going to the students' common room for a break.
2 Its appearance suggests it's far too complicated.
3 They aren't coming to dinner, so we're going out.
4 I've filed the company's accounts.
5 People's appearances change with age.
6 Consultants' reports tend to be very complex.
7 Here's my thesis. Where's yours?
8 Whose car's parked over the other side of the road?
9 Is that Tom's suitcase or is it theirs?
10 This is someone's diary. Whose is it?

- Have you checked that you have consistently used tenses?
- Have you used the right verb forms consistently for plural and singular?
- Have you checked your punctuation?

3 Words and sentences

If spelling and grammar are problems that we have to get right, so too are long sentences. If you leave sentences long and complex for your readers to negotiate, you run the risk of losing them and, therefore, losing the valuable marks your work deserves. So, wherever possible cut them up and reduce them to two or more simple sentences.

The same applies to long words, although they have a different effect on our writing. They may not confuse readers quite as much, but they can leave them wondering whether that's what you really meant to say. Your meaning will be clearer, more direct and your writing more effective if, wherever possible, you replace long obscure words with short and simple ones.

- Have I cut up all long sentences into shorter ones?
- Have I replaced long, obscure words with short and simple ones?

4 De-cluttering

For the same reason, we need to look at particular types of words to measure the effect they have on the clarity of our writing. In Chapter 24, we warned of the effect of too many adjectives and adverbs shoring up weak nouns and verbs, respectively. Quite simply, they can drown the clarity of our ideas, not only making it difficult to understand them, but robbing them of the impact they first had on us and which they should have, in turn, on those who read them.

Strong nouns and verbs

Rather than drowning them in this way, make sure you choose strong nouns and verbs that use a minimum of modifiers. Constantly remind yourself that the fewer verbs you have to modify with adverbs and nouns with adjectives the better will be your writing. It will make it more direct, concise and economical.

Strong nouns and verbs   EXAMPLE

In the following sentence, by substituting stronger, more specific nouns and verbs you can see how the sentence gains in clarity and directness.

> Theatre promoters are likely to comb through unfavourable reviews *looking carefully* for any isolated expression of a *favourable comment* that can be used to promote their plays.

> Theatre promoters are likely to comb through unfavourable reviews in *search* of any isolated expression of *approval* that can be used to promote their plays.

The active voice

To achieve the same end, use the active voice wherever it's relevant. In Chapter 22, we saw the impact this can have on your writing. It will help you present your ideas more clearly by making them more direct and concise. So, wherever possible make the 'doer' the subject of the sentence. Nevertheless, this won't always be the best policy: in some circumstances it is 'what is done' or the 'receiver of the action' that is more important.

The active and passive voice   EXAMPLE

In the following example, it is what was done that is more important than by whom. Consequently, re-writing the sentence in the passive form makes the point more effectively:

> Professor Jenkins and Doctor Taylor of University College, London, last month achieved the most significant breakthrough yet in the treatment of colon cancer.

> The most significant breakthrough yet in the treatment of colon cancer was achieved last month by Professor Jenkins and Doctor Taylor of University College, London.

- Have I de-cluttered paragraphs by removing all unnecessary words and sentences?
- Have I removed all unnecessary modifiers in favour of strong nouns and verbs?
- Have I written in the active voice?
- Have I only used the passive voice when what is done or the receiver of the action is more important than the doer?

5 Reading it out aloud

Now that you have revised your review in each of these ways, it's time to read it through to see how it sounds. If you can, the best way of doing this is to get someone else to read it through to you, so you can listen to the flow and rhythm of it. And, of course, while you listen you are also free to note when it is difficult to understand what you've written.

In this way, you are better able to identify those points where the fluency breaks down, all the clumsy sentences and the passages where the logical order of your arguments is unclear. You'll be able to see more clearly grammatical errors, where you need punctuation marks to signal pauses and breaks in sentences, and unclear sentences that need to be re-written. It should read like talk in print, with the prose flowing across the page with a light, easy rhythm that holds the reader's attention.

Changing the pace

It's also worth considering whether you may want to change the pace at certain moments to make your points more effectively. In Chapter 23, we considered the impact of short as opposed to long sentences. Long sentences are best suited to the development of the core elements of an argument, while short sentences are effective in grabbing the reader's attention with a vivid piece of detail or with an insight you feel is a key point to get across. As you listen to someone reading your review aloud, you will be able to decide when you need to rescue a vivid insight from drowning in the sea of words around it.

- Does it have an easy flow and rhythm that will hold the reader's attention?
- Are there any clumsy sentences and passages where the logic breaks down?
- Would it be better to use short sentences to get across a key point more effectively?

The final checks

This should now have brought you to the point where you are confident that your review reads well and the logic of your arguments is consistent and clear. The final checks are all about whether you have missed anything and whether you've cited everything clearly.

Loose ends

First, check the notes you've written yourself to see if you have missed anything. Are you still happy with your assumptions; is there anything you would like to change? Go over your reasoning again and look for inconsistencies and loose ends. If you come across any leads you want to follow up, make sure it will be profitable to do so. You don't want to be diverted down side tracks.

Up-to-date literature

Second, check the literature to see if you've missed anything. Go over the latest articles and texts, particularly the latest editions of journals you've found most useful. One purpose of a literature review is to show that your work is based on all the latest findings in the most recent studies. This is more important in the natural sciences and in some social sciences than in the humanities; nevertheless, it is still worth checking even in the humanities.

Citations and plagiarism

Next, make sure all your citations are correct and your bibliography and reference list are accurate. Go over your review one more time to see if you can identify any passages in which you may have accidentally plagiarised a source. You might have failed to give a citation, or you might find a passage in which you have adopted the same wording as your source. Remember, if there is anything distinctive about your source, cite it.

Word count

Finally, check your word count, if you have been set a limit or you have set yourself a limit within your dissertation or thesis. If you've exceeded this, look at the following things:

- **Repetition** – there may be sections that say the same things, but in different ways. Can you safely cross-reference them, rather than describe the same points again?
- **Less relevant sections** – as you have written your review your ideas will have taken much clearer shape. As a result, you might now see that certain sections are no longer quite so relevant.
- **Unnecessary material** – as you look to economise on words, you may realise that you've described material, which, instead, you could have presented in a table and drawn your inferences from there.
- **Long quotations** – in a previous chapter, we discussed the tendency for readers to infer from long quotations that the writer hasn't processed the ideas sufficiently and is merely hiding behind the words of the author. To avoid this and to save words, think about editing them. They will probably still do the job you want them to do.

 You can download copies of the lists in this chapter from the companion website (www.macmillanihe.com/greetham-literature-review).

Summary

1 If you fail to get your spelling right, readers may assume that you have paid insufficient attention to other, more substantive detail.
2 If you break the rules of grammar, make sure it is clear that this is deliberate and not the result of a lack of knowledge.
3 If you leave sentences long and complex, you run the risk of losing your reader and valuable marks.
4 The fewer adjectives and adverbs you use to modify nouns and verbs, respectively, the more direct, concise and economical will be your writing.
5 Check the notes you've written yourself to see if there's anything you've missed or would like to change.

To conclude

Now that you have finished your revision of the different aspects of the structure and content, you should have in front of you a review that is quite different from the one you started with. It should now be a more cohesive work, in which each part together develops your thinking clearly and consistently. Equally important, with a simpler, more direct and economical use of words, your ideas should now be clearer and more concise. The result is likely to be an effective piece of writing that will have a sharper and more lasting impression on your readers.

Conclusion

I began this book by making the point that a literature review presents an exciting challenge to carve out of the literature an opportunity to do something truly original. Now that you have read this book and completed your review, whether it's a stand-alone review or it lays the foundations for your own research, you will know how exciting this challenge can be.

You will probably also be aware of how creative you can be in response to it – how innovative your ideas can be. You have learnt to generate your own original ideas, analyse and synthesise the literature to create your own novel approach to a problem and then write your review using your own voice to produce a work that is clearly and lucidly written, interesting to read and full of insights.

Thinking for yourself

When you began this project, you might have been full of doubt as to whether you could achieve so much. Like most students, you have probably spent years in education learning how to recycle your authorities, describing their arguments to show how much you understand. Given this, while you would have no doubt been confident that you could produce a descriptive synopsis of the relevant literature, critically evaluating your sources and analysing and synthesising ideas to create a new way of approaching the problem will have seemed an altogether more difficult challenge.

However, as I said at the start, if this project seemed a daunting challenge when you began, it was so only because it was something new, something you hadn't done before. Now you know that you have the abilities to do it successfully. As a result, I hope this has given you the confidence, like many before you, to think for yourself.

The significance of the review

In this lies the lasting significance of your review. For those doing a stand-alone review, this challenge will have revealed that you do, indeed, have many of the important professional skills you need to be a success in your profession. But more than that, whether it's a stand-alone review or one that lays the foundations for your own research, its overwhelming importance lies in what it reveals about your abilities to think.

As I said in earlier chapters, so much of our education systems seem designed to develop and assess our lower cognitive abilities to describe, memorise and recall what we have read; to show *what* we know and *what* we think, rather than *how* we think. In this project, the focus has been on *how* we think. We have learnt how to be good thinkers, thinking about our thinking while we think.

Good thinkers think about their thinking while they think.

If there is one thing above all of real value in your achievements, it is this: that you now know how to use your higher cognitive abilities, that you are capable of deep-level processing. You have learnt not just how to critically evaluate your sources, but how to analyse concepts and arguments, and then synthesise your ideas into new innovative ways of approaching a problem.

A passion for ideas

This not only equips you to tackle the most challenging problems you might face in your personal and professional lives, but, perhaps more important, it generates a passion for ideas in all of us who do a review, an irresistible drive to get to the bottom of things.

It is this that has driven those like Albert Einstein, Immanuel Kant and Charles Darwin, who have made the most remarkable breakthroughs in science, philosophy, technology and literature. Along with the courage to think unconventional thoughts, they have been willing to disregard the cultural conventions that ruled their professional lives and think differently.

- An irresistible drive to get to the bottom of things.
- The courage to think differently.

It is that temperament, that habit of mind, which means we are no longer willing just to accept what we are told: the customary, unexamined expectations of our professional lives, the social conventions that hem us in as we take our place in the adult world and the political wisdom of an older generation that we are expected to embrace with awe and reverence. Revolutions of all kinds, both large and small, are born of this.

Bibliography

Andrew Booth, Anthea Sutton and Diana Papaioannou, *Systematic Approaches to a Successful Literature Review* (London: Sage, 2016).

Arthur J. Cropley, *Creativity in education and learning* (London: Kogan Page, 2001).

Denise D. Cummins, *Good Thinking* (Cambridge: Cambridge University Press, 2012).

Adrian Desmond and James Moore, *Darwin* (London: Michael Joseph, 1991).

Patrick Dunleavy, *Studying for a Degree in the Humanities and Social Sciences* (London: Red Globe Press, 1986).

Helena Echlin, 'Critical Mass' in *The Sydney Morning Herald*, 10 February 2001; for the complete article see *Areté*, www.aretemagazine.com.

Albert Einstein, *Ideas and Opinions* (London: Souvenir Press, 1973).

Rudolf Flesch, *The Art of Clear Thinking* (New York: Harper & Row, 1951).

Antony Flew, *Thinking about Thinking* (London: Fontana, 1975).

O.R. Frisch, *What Little I Remember* (Cambridge: CUP, 1979).

L. Gick and K.J. Holyoak, 'Analogical problem solving', *Cognitive Psychology*, 12 (1980), pp. 306–55.

Bryan Greetham, *Smart Thinking* (London: Red Globe Press, 2016).

Bryan Greetham, *How to Write Your Undergraduate Dissertation* (London: Red Globe Press, 2018).

Stephen W. Hawking, *A Brief History of Time* (London: Bantam Press, 1988).

D. Hofstadter, 'Analogy as the core of cognition', in D. Gentner, K. Holyoak and B. Kokinov (eds), *The Analogical mind: Perspectives from cognitive science* (Cambridge, MA: MIT Press, 2009), pp. 499–538.

K.J. Holyoak and K. Koh, 'Surface and structural similarity in analogical transfer', *Memory & Cognition*, 15 (1987), pp. 332–40.

Daniel Kahneman, *Thinking, Fast and Slow* (London: Penguin, 2012).

Thomas S. Kuhn, *The Structure of Scientific Revolutions* (Chicago: University of Chicago Press, 1971).

H. Margolis, *Patterns, thinking, and cognition* (Chicago: Chicago University Press, 1987).

P.B. Medawar, *Induction and Intuition in Scientific Thought* (London: Methuen, 1969).

Sylvia Nasar, *A Beautiful Mind* (London: Faber and Faber, 2001).

Chitu Okoli, 'A Guide to Conducting a Standalone Systematic Literature Review,' *Communications of the Association for Information Systems*, 37 (2015), Article 43.

Bertrand Russell, *The Problems of Philosophy*, 1912 (Oxford: Oxford University Press, 1986).

Michael Scriven, *Reasoning* (New York: McGraw-Hill, 1976).

S. Toulmin, *Human understanding: The collective use and evolution of concepts* (Princeton: Princeton University Press, 1972).

John Wilson, *Thinking with Concepts* (Cambridge: Cambridge University Press, 1976).

William Zinsser, *Writing to Learn* (New York: Harper & Rowe, 1988).

Index

References to illustrations are printed in **bold**.